NEMESIS

OSPREY PUBLISHING

Nemesis

Medieval England's Greatest Enemy

Catherine Hanley

OSPREY PUBLISHING
Bloomsbury Publishing Plc
Kemp House, Chawley Park, Cumnor Hill, Oxford OX2 9PH, UK
Bloomsbury Publishing Ireland Limited,
29 Earlsfort Terrace, Dublin 2, D02 AY28, Ireland
1385 Broadway, 5th Floor, New York, NY 10018, USA
E-mail: info@ospreypublishing.com
www.ospreypublishing.com

OSPREY is a trademark of Osprey Publishing Ltd

First published in Great Britain in 2025

© Catherine Hanley, 2025

A catalogue record for this book is available from the British Library

ISBN: HB 9781472867445; PB 9781472867483; eBook 9781472867490;
ePDF 9781472867476; XML 9781472867452

25 26 27 28 29   10 9 8 7 6 5 4 3 2 1

Maps by www.bounford.com
Diagrams by Tina Ross
Family Trees by Stewart Larking
Index by Alan Rutter

Typeset by Deanta Global Publishing Services, Chennai, India
Printed and bound in Great Britain by CPI (Group) UK Ltd, Croydon CR0 4YY

To find out more about our authors and books visit www.ospreypublishing.com. Here you
will find extracts, author interviews, details of forthcoming events and the option to sign up
for our newsletter.

For product safety related questions contact productsafety@bloomsbury.com

For James

A much better husband and father
than a certain French king of my acquaintance

Contents

List of Illustrations, Maps and Family Trees

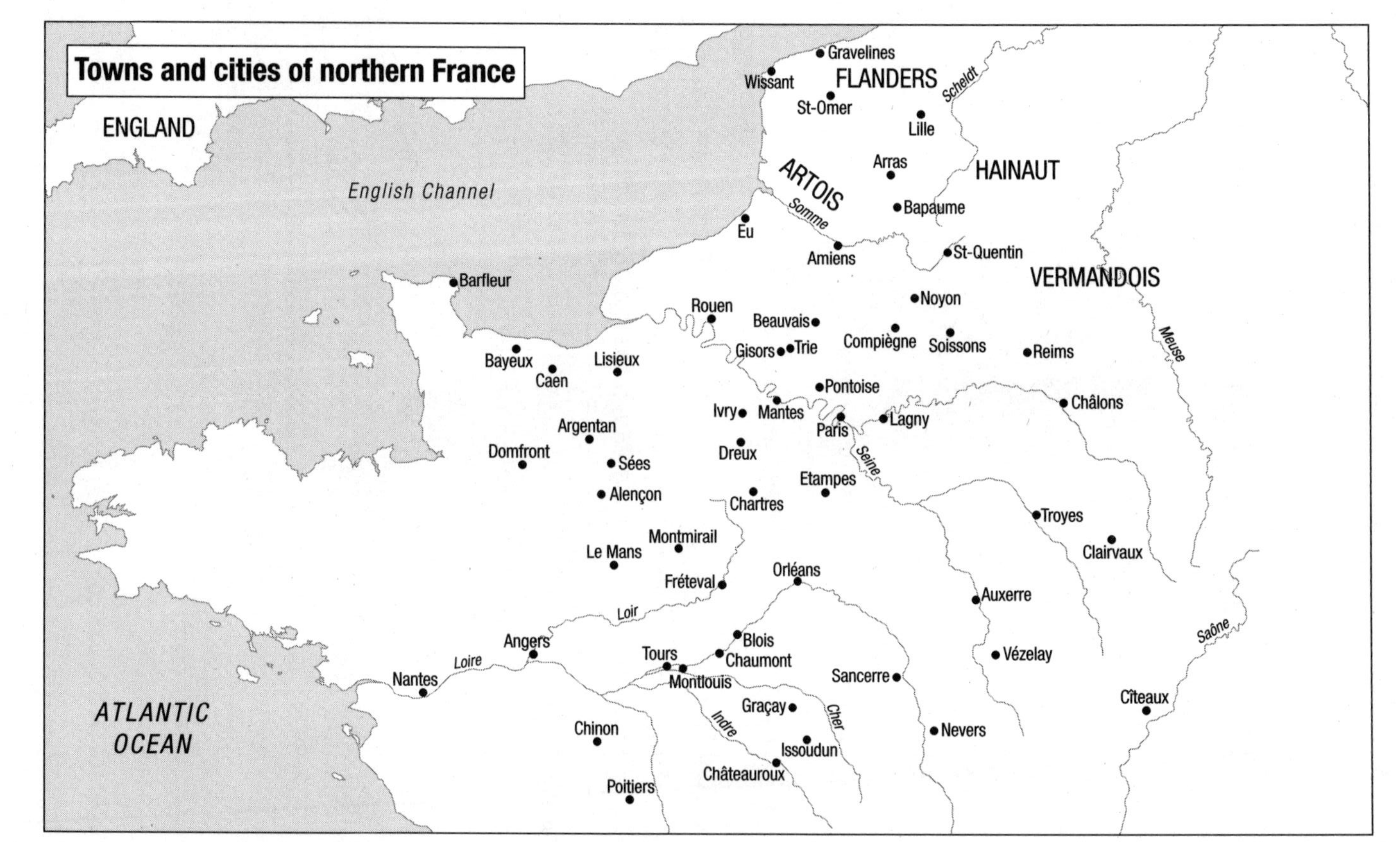

Towns and cities of northern France
ENGLAND
English Channel
ATLANTIC OCEAN
FLANDERS
ARTOIS
HAINAUT
VERMANDOIS
Scheldt
Somme
Meuse
Seine
Loir
Loire
Cher
Indre
Saône
Gravelines
Wissant
St-Omer
Lille
Arras
Bapaume
St-Quentin
Eu
Amiens
Barfleur
Rouen
Noyon
Beauvais
Gisors
Trie
Compiègne
Soissons
Reims
Bayeux
Caen
Lisieux
Pontoise
Châlons
Ivry
Mantes
Paris
Lagny
Argentan
Domfront
Sées
Dreux
Etampes
Troyes
Alençon
Chartres
Clairvaux
Le Mans
Montmirail
Orléans
Fréteval
Auxerre
Angers
Blois
Chaumont
Vézelay
Nantes
Tours
Montlouis
Sancerre
Cîteaux
Graçay
Chinon
Issoudun
Nevers
Châteauroux
Poitiers

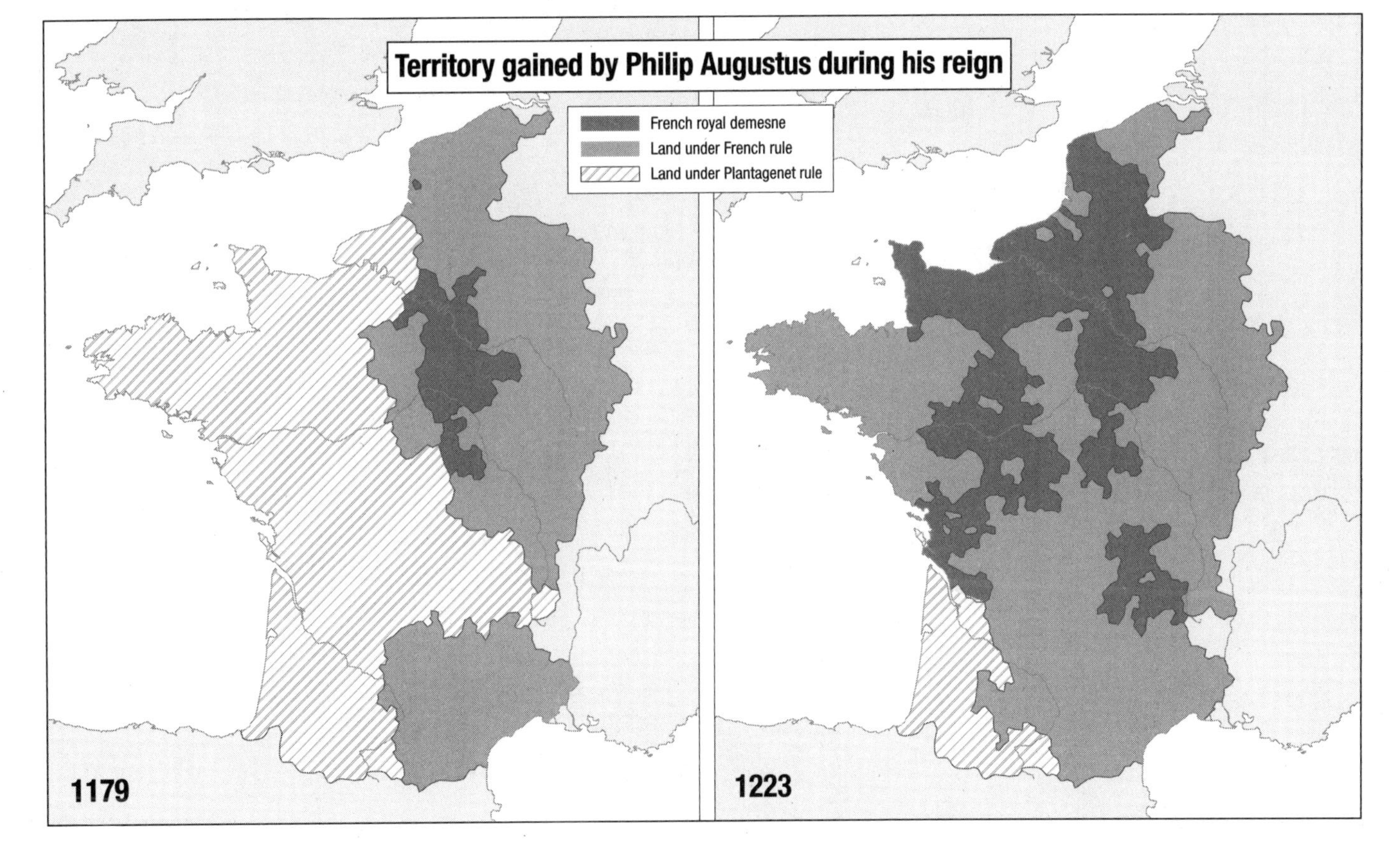

Territory gained by Philip Augustus during his reign
French royal demesne
Land under French rule
Land under Plantagenet rule
1179
1223

Family Trees

Key to family tree abbreviations:

abp = archbishop of
bp = bishop of
ct = count of
ctss = countess in her own right of
d = duke of
dss = duchess in her own right of
k = king of
ld = lord of
m = married
mq = marquis of

Family Tree 1

Louis VII and his descendants

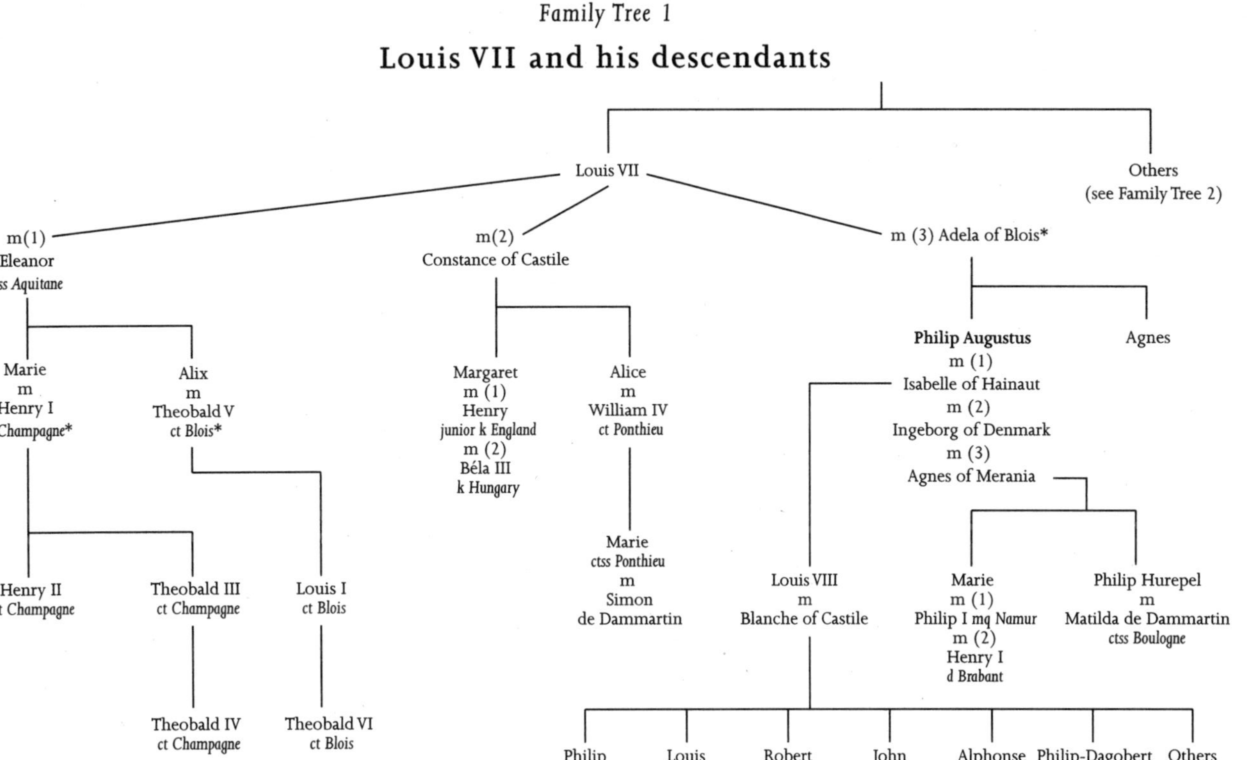

* Adela of Blois, Henry I of Champagne and Theobald V of Blois were siblings

Family Tree 2
The Capetian cadet branches

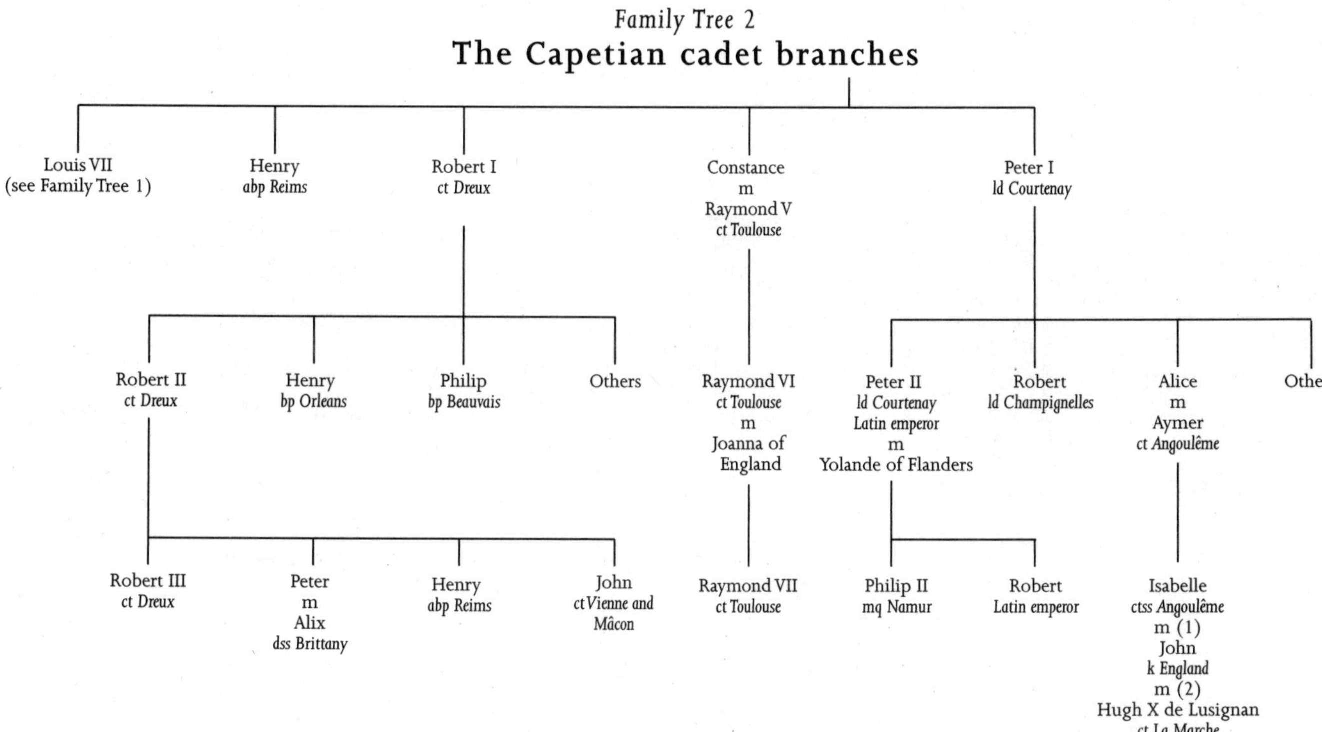

Family Tree 3

The houses of Boulogne, Flanders and Hainaut

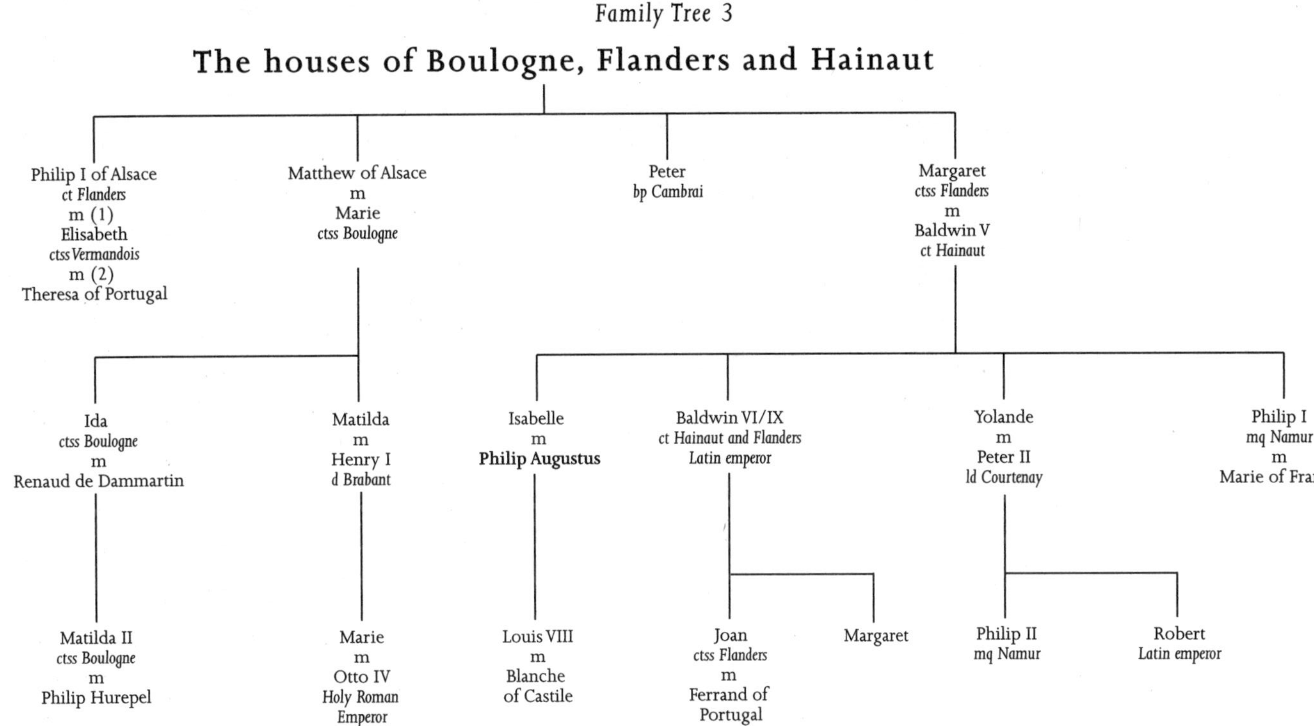

Acknowledgements

As ever, the production of this book has been a team effort, and I'm glad to be able to acknowledge the many people who helped along the way.

Firstly, I'd like to express my gratitude to the Department of Archaeology and History at the University of Exeter for the Honorary Senior Research Fellowship I hold there, which has enabled me to benefit not only from access to research resources, but also from the wonderful collegiality of fellow medievalists at seminars and in correspondence. Further access to research resources was enabled by Karen Collings at Wiveliscombe Community Library in Somerset, who seems actively to *enjoy* tracking down the ever more obscure texts I am continually requesting. There will be more on the way soon …

Many thanks are due to my editor at Osprey, Kate Moore, and my agent, Kate Hordern: they listened to my (possibly over-) enthusiastic proposals about Philip Augustus and saw the potential inherent in them, including the fact that the narrative is told from the opposite point of view from your average Anglophone history book, and therefore contains a different picture of Henry II and his boys from the one that readers might be used to.

As the production process went forward it was a delight once again to work with managing editor Gemma White, and I benefited enormously from the expertise of copy-editor Julie Frederick, proofreader Anne Halliday and indexer Alan Rutter. The maps drawn by Denise Bee at Bounford.com and the line drawings by archaeological illustrator Tina Ross are fantastic, and Stewart Larking made sense of some insanely complicated family trees.

None of my acknowledgement sections would be complete without a reference to my great friend and fellow medievalist Dr Sean McGlynn, an expert on the politics and warfare of this historical period, and I'm glad to be able to continue that tradition here with thanks for our discussions on Philip, even though we differ markedly in our opinions of him and his achievements. It's all part of the research process! Dr Andrew Buck and Professor John D. Hosler were once again kind enough to point me in the direction of the latest scholarship on the Third Crusade, which has made that chapter much better than it otherwise would have been. In thanking them I would like to note that any new, unorthodox or unpopular interpretations of related material contained in this book are mine, not theirs.

My family continues to offer unstinting support, appreciated even more than usual this time as I contrasted our lives with those of certain medieval families that were the very definition of 'dysfunctional'. Our now teenage and twenty-something children have had book dedications of their own in recent years, so this one is for James, my husband for more than a quarter of a century. As noted on a recent anniversary card: 10/10, would marry again.

A certain monk, lying in his bed, was thinking a great deal about the sons of King Henry, three such outstanding knights and the fourth and younger likewise, and how there was no ruler on earth who enjoyed such offspring, and what would be their future. Eventually he slept, and it seemed to him that he saw on the bank of a river four birds sitting, namely males of the ducks who the common people call mallards. And although those birds are by nature very beautiful, a voice said to him: 'Do you see those birds? They are the sons of King Henry, whom you were thinking about. And do you want to see their future? Look up for a moment.'

When he did this, he saw the bird called the falcon above in the sky flying on swift wings, and immediately those four birds, one after the other, suddenly submerged themselves in the water of the river as if in fear of that bird, and afterwards appeared no more. And at once the voice added: 'Do you wish to know who is that bird flying overhead? Assuredly, it is Philip, son of the king of France.'

GERALD OF WALES[1]

Introduction

The God-Given

It was something of a miracle that Philip Augustus ever sat on the throne of France at all.

None of the kings of the Capetian line to which Philip belonged had ever failed to pass the crown on to a son, but by 1160 it looked like the sequence might finally break: Louis VII was forty, recently widowed and the father of four daughters. He took the only option open to him and married again, mere weeks after the death of his second wife, in high hopes that the teenaged Adela of Blois would give him the male heir he craved. But another five agonisingly long years passed with no pregnancy.

Louis began to despair, while all of France wondered fearfully what would happen if he were to die without leaving a son. The principles of female succession or succession through the female line had never yet been tested in the realm, because there had been no need, but now everyone was forced to confront uncomfortable questions.* In such a situation, would the crown pass to one of Louis's daughters and thus to their ambitious husbands? Or via one of those daughters to any son she might have in the future? Or was the royal succession strictly male-only, in which case Louis's

---

*Female succession and succession through the female line were not the same thing. The former meant that a title could actually pass to a woman; the latter held that an heir had to be male himself, but that his title could pass to him via a female relative, normally his mother.

younger brothers would be next in line? Would anyone who lost out decide to make a formal challenge? And, most importantly, would competing claimants to the throne start a war that would bring death and destruction to the innocent?

All of these worries were stopped in their tracks in the spring of 1165 when it became clear that Queen Adela was pregnant. The pressure on her was immense and unfair, given that neither the sex of her baby nor its safe delivery was under her control; she, Louis and the whole realm could do nothing but hold their collective breath until 21 August, when she went into labour. Adela was in luck: she gave birth to a healthy and surviving boy. He was christened Philip, a family name used in each of the last few generations, and such was the seeming miracle of his arrival – the answer to Louis's prayers – that he was immediately given the epithet *Dieudonné*, 'the God-Given'. Later in his life Philip would gain another soubriquet, bestowed by the French monk and chronicler Rigord in honour of the emperors of old, whose conquering deeds he emulated, and this is the name by which he is universally known to this day: Philip Augustus.[1]

The twelfth-century chronicler Gerald of Wales, who was present in Paris at the time of Philip's birth, studying at the university there, later recalled the immense joy and the jubilant celebrations in the city as bells were rung, candles were lit and people danced in the streets. He also heard an ominous prophecy:

The author of this work, a young man in the city and at that time completing his twentieth year, more or less, woken from the bed where he had already laid down to sleep, leapt at once to the window, and, looking out, he saw in the street two old women [...] When he had asked them the cause for all this noise and rejoicing, one of them looked at him and answered, saying: 'We now have a king given to us by God and a powerful heir to the kingdom by God's gift, through whom shame and loss, punishment and deep disgrace, full of confusion and disaster, will accrue to your king.' [...] For the woman knew that he and his companions came from the kingdom of England.[2]

The celebrations were a mark of joy, but also of relief. The king had a son, which meant that a war of succession would be avoided. But it also meant that a huge weight of responsibility settled on the tiny shoulders before the baby was even out of his cradle, because the future of France rested on him, and him alone.

The Capetian line represented stability, having occupied the French throne in direct father–son succession since the year 987, a record many other kingdoms envied. One of the particular strengths of Capetian monarchs was that they did not merely designate a successor, but actually had him crowned during the lifetime of his father; in this way, the junior king could learn from the senior, and there was no frantic scramble for the throne when the incumbent died, as there was a ready-made and crowned successor already in place. They enjoyed family loyalty to a degree almost unknown in other realms; it was expected that sons would be on good terms with their fathers and that younger brothers would support their elders, and this was genuinely the case most of the time. A Capetian king was also considered to be *rex christianissimus*, 'the most Christian king', working with and supported by the Church, the moral leader of his people as well as their secular ruler. The majority of them took this responsibility seriously in both their public and private lives, adhering to Church doctrine and rarely taking mistresses, and they could reasonably be looked up to as exemplars by their nobles and people.*

This was all in stark contrast to the situation across the Channel, where the Anglo-Norman and Plantagenet kings and their families engaged in constant squabbles, and there was

---

* The fifteen Capetian kings who reigned from 987 to 1328 fathered fewer illegitimate children between them than Henry I of England did on his own, to say nothing of the dozens produced by his successors.

a contest for the throne every time an incumbent died.* Not content with this internal strife, the English ruling dynasty had additionally been at loggerheads with the Capetians for the best part of a century: Henry I had warred with Louis VI from the early 1100s to the 1120s; Louis VI and Louis VII had both fanned the flames of the conflict in England between King Stephen and Empress Matilda in the 1130s and 1140s; and Louis VII's relationship with Henry II had been going rapidly downhill since the 1150s, particularly following Henry's marriage, without Louis's permission, to Eleanor of Aquitaine, the wife Louis had recently divorced. The fact that Eleanor fell pregnant immediately after her second wedding and then bore Henry son after son, having given Louis only two daughters in fifteen years of marriage, probably did nothing to improve the French king's mood.

The two kings had patched things up for a while, the reconciliation marked by the betrothal in 1158 of Henry's son Young Henry to Louis's daughter Margaret. But when Henry II actually had the children formally married, again without Louis's permission, in 1160, any pretence of cordiality disappeared entirely.† Henceforward the kings of France and England would be antagonists, the situation not helped by the fact that, due to his Angevin and Norman ancestry and his wife's inheritance of Aquitaine, Henry ruled more of France than Louis did.

This was the situation into which Philip was born, and throughout the 1170s, as he left the nursery and began his education and royal training, he was well aware of the danger. Technically, Henry II was the vassal of the French king for the

---

*The name 'Plantagenet' originates with Geoffrey of Anjou, the husband of Empress Matilda and the father of Henry II; he was known by this nickname due to his habit of wearing a sprig of broom, *planta genista*, in his hat. He did not pass this on to his children as a hereditary surname, but it is a generally accepted shorthand for the English ruling house, so we will use it throughout this book to refer to that family. The other option for a dynastic name is 'Angevin', but to avoid any potential confusion we will use this term only to refer to matters relating to the county of Anjou.

† Margaret was Louis's daughter by his second wife, so she and Young Henry were not closely related by blood, but the spiritual and step-relationship between bride and groom was still enough to make the whole enterprise very dodgy indeed.

lands that he held in France, but his power posed a significant threat and he was not to be trusted.

This book is not a biography of Philip in the traditional sense, although it does run chronologically from his accession to his death.[3] Rather, it is the story of his relationship with the Plantagenet family – Henry II, his sons and grandsons – so it will focus on his activities in that area and will have less to say about other aspects of his reign. In telling this tale, we are fortunate in the survival of a large number of relevant documents: Philip ran a very effective administration and his charters and acts were carefully archived, which means that we can still read his own words and the actual text of a number of the peace treaties and agreements he made. His was also a great age for the writing of narrative chronicles, both in England and in France, and these writers provide us not only with factual information, but also with their own (sometimes conflicting) opinions of people and events. Let's meet them now, so we know who they are and something of their priorities when we encounter them later in the book.

In France the three most important primary works for Philip's reign were written by two monks of the abbey of Saint-Denis, just outside Paris. The earlier of the two was Rigord, who composed his *Deeds of Philip Augustus* during the first half of the king's reign, before it was brought to a halt by his own death in 1208. Rigord is generally positive about Philip, though he does become a little more critical as the work, and the years, pass. His narrative baton was taken up by William the Breton, whose *Life of Philip Augustus* initially covers some of the same ground as Rigord and then continues in greater detail after 1208 and for the rest of the reign. William eventually left the cloister and took up a post as chaplain in Philip's own household, so he was an eye-witness to many of the events he describes, which makes his text all the more valuable.

William also wrote a second work, the Latin epic *Philippidos* (given in French as the *Philippide* and in English either with the same title or occasionally as the *Philippiad*, in the manner of Homer's *Iliad*). This was completely different in style to the monastic chronicles and was intended to present Philip Augustus in the mould of the ancient epic heroes. Both the *Philippide* and William's *Life* have to be taken with the occasional pinch of salt, as he always adheres closely to the official royal line and seeks to portray Philip in the best light, whatever the circumstances.

The works of some later French chroniclers are also very useful to us, as, writing after Philip's death, they were able to look at the events of his reign in the context of hindsight. Among these are the quasi-official *Great Chronicles of France*, which is in effect a synthesis of the works of the many consecutive chroniclers of Saint-Denis, but which does sometimes depart a little from them to offer an updated view of events.

One very interesting later character (and, I have to admit, probably my personal favourite) is the writer known only as the Minstrel of Reims. In contrast to others, he was in no way writing for the court or the high nobility, or for posterity, but rather for an audience of commoners in the towns and on the street corners. His *Tales of a Minstrel of Reims* is unpolished, attention-grabbing, decidedly biased and sometimes earthy, but nevertheless enormously entertaining. The Minstrel might not be the most accurate source for the facts of what was happening at any given time, but he can certainly tell us what the gossip was.

There were also a number of accomplished chroniclers at work in England during the reigns of Henry II and his sons, and they give us an important opposing point of view of Philip Augustus and his actions. The two on whom we will rely to the greatest extent are Roger of Howden and Roger of Wendover, both churchmen, with the former contemporary to the first half of Philip's reign and the latter writing during the second half and continuing after Philip's death. Perhaps unsurprisingly, both Rogers present the Plantagenets in a favourable light and tend to be critical of Philip.

For the section of this book which takes place on crusade we rely on Roger of Howden again, because he was part of Richard the Lionheart's host, as well as three other works. Two of these are eye-witness accounts written by men who were great fans of Richard and therefore dismissive of Philip: the anonymous *Chronicle of the Third Crusade*, and the *History of the Holy War*, by an Anglo-Norman writer called Ambroise. Philip Augustus, unfortunately for his later reputation, did not think to bring a gaggle of tame chroniclers with him to amplify his every deed, so the only French viewpoint is the text known as *Eracles*, which dates from several decades after the crusade.

Finally, there are a couple of works that give us more varied perspectives than the rather black-and-white offerings of the other French and English chroniclers. Gerald of Wales hailed from the British side of the Channel, but he was no friend to Henry II and thus his *Instruction for a Ruler* tends to lavish praise on the Capetians rather than the Plantagenets, even as he writes from England. The *History of William Marshal*, dating from the 1220s, is the earliest surviving biography of a secular, non-royal individual, and (given how long its protagonist lived) it covers a number of decades. William Marshal served Henry II, three of his four sons and one of his grandsons in turn. He also held extensive lands in France, and the text is based on his own personal recollections, so it contains plenty of insight unavailable elsewhere. However, it is another work that needs to be used with caution: its author's entire purpose was to praise Marshal in everything that he did, so the various kings and princes on both sides of the Channel are portrayed positively or negatively depending on their relationship with him at any given time.

While we're on the subject of caution, it might be useful to say a few words about medieval names and naming conventions. These are a perennial problem for anyone reading and writing about this era, because a large number of people made use of a small number of forenames, with certain families using the same one or two over and over again.[*] Fortunately, we should be able to

---

[*] For example, every French king from 1060 to 1316 was called either Philip or Louis, and during the course of this book we will meet three individuals all called Count Robert of Dreux.

circumvent this issue, via the use of surnames or nicknames where they exist, or with titles or regnal numbers, so each individual is clearly distinguished. For simplicity I have Anglicised all names that have an English equivalent, so we will encounter (among others) Philip and William rather than Philippe and Guillaume; Henry and Frederick rather than Heinrich and Friedrich.

None of this, alas, helps us with the other persistent issue in chronicles of the period, which is the tendency of the (generally male and clerical) writers not to bother recording women's names properly. Sometimes they fail to note one at all, instead giving the name of a male relative, such as 'the daughter of King Alfonso', or similar; at other times they just assign a female name almost at random. Even the highest-ranking women were apparently not of sufficient importance for chroniclers to take the trouble to individu- alise them, as evidenced by all three of Philip Augustus's wives: the first is referred to in different texts as both Isabelle and Elisabeth, the second as Ingeborg and Botilda, and the third as Agnes and Marie.

All of this brings us back to Philip himself. Infant mortality was rife in the twelfth century, but he was fortunate enough to survive the dangers of early childhood, and Louis VII began to plan the traditional Capetian ceremony of having his heir crowned as junior king. This was to take place on the Feast of the Assumption (15 August) 1179, shortly before Philip's fourteenth birthday, but as preparations were in train, disaster struck.

The royals and nobles of France had assembled at Compiègne, about halfway between Paris and the traditional coronation venue of Reims. Along with some others, the young prince was allowed to go hunting in the nearby forest, but upon sighting a boar Philip rode after it and became separated from the rest of the party. Lost, he and his horse wandered alone in the extensive woodland for a day and a night, until he came across a charcoal burner who was able to help him find the correct route back to Compiègne. Philip fell ill as a result of this experience, and his condition worsened to such an extent that his life was despaired of.[4] This threw the realm, and Louis VII, right back into the uncertain situation that had prevailed before Philip's birth, and the desperate king took desperate measures: he travelled to England to pray at the shrine of St Thomas Becket. No reigning French king had ever set foot on English soil before, but Louis's efforts proved successful and Philip made a full recovery. This came at a cost, though: the stress and the exertion took its toll on the now ageing king, and he suffered a stroke while he was on his way back to Paris.

Philip's coronation – now all the more important due to his father's infirmity – was rescheduled, and would take place at Reims cathedral on the Feast of All Saints (1 November) 1179. This time he got there without a hitch, and found himself outside the imposing building. The situation, and the weight of the responsibility that was about to descend upon him, could have been overwhelming, but he was not intimidated; in fact, he already had plenty of ideas and plans lined up.

And then, it was time. The procession formed up and began to move. Philip Augustus would enter Reims cathedral a boy, and emerge a king.

PART I

Henry II

1179–89

I

A Nest of Vipers

The new king might have been young, but he was not stupid. Neither was he unprepared to face the task ahead: he had been the heir to the French throne since the day of his birth, he had spent his entire life learning at a rapid pace, and he was already in possession of a great deal of political acumen. As Philip processed into Reims cathedral on 1 November 1179, as he was solemnly anointed with the holy oil, as he had the crown placed on his head and as he received the loud acclamation of all those present, he was fully aware of the nests of vipers that surrounded him.

There were no fewer than four significant rival factions at the French court. The first – and, perhaps surprisingly, the quietest – were Philip's paternal relatives, the other Capetians, of whom there were many. Louis VII might have experienced a great deal of trouble in fathering a son, but he had been one of seven brothers, of whom two were still alive: Robert I, count of Dreux, and Peter I, lord of Courtenay.* They were vigorous men in their fifties with large families (the fathers of twelve and eleven children, respectively), and Robert had a decent claim to be the next male-line

---

* The other four brothers in Louis VII's family had been Philip, the eldest son and original king-designate, whose death at the age of fifteen had left the second-born Louis as the heir to the throne; Henry, the previous archbishop of Reims, who had died in 1175; Hugh, who had died as a child; and another Philip (born after the death of his eldest brother), archdeacon of Paris, who had died in 1160. There was also one sister in the family, Constance of France; she was still alive in 1179, but after separating from her husband, Count Raymond V of Toulouse, she had departed on a pilgrimage to Jerusalem and we will not meet her in person.

heir to the throne until King Philip had sons of his own, but both were content to mind their own business. Peter was at this time in the Holy Land, but Robert attended the coronation to support his nephew, along with several of his adult sons.

The second group, one which had held sway in France for many years, was the Blois–Champagne faction, comprising King Philip's mother, Queen Adela, and her four brothers: Henry I, count of Champagne; Theobald V, count of Blois; Stephen I, count of Sancerre; and William Whitehands, the archbishop of Reims, who was presiding over the coronation ceremony and who actually placed the crown on his nephew's head. Three more sisters were married to the duke of Burgundy, the count of Bar and the count of Perche, so the family network was extensive. The Blois–Champagne clan had long been staunch allies of Louis VII, and they were united to the royal family by several marriage ties: in a rather headache-inducing arrangement, Louis had wed Adela while giving his two eldest daughters as wives to her brothers Henry and Theobald.* Count Henry of Champagne, therefore, might also stake a claim to being the next heir to the throne via his marriage to King Philip's eldest sister.

However, after a long run this faction was beginning to wane in influence, with Archbishop William the only member present at the coronation. Count Henry was away on crusade, and Queen Adela could get away with the excuse that she needed to stay by the side of her ailing husband, but Theobald and Stephen had both absented themselves in protest at the prominence given in the ceremony to their great rivals.

These rivals were members of the up-and-coming party of the Flanders–Hainaut alliance, headed by Philip of Alsace, the powerful and ambitious count of Flanders, who was given the honour of carrying the king's sword in the coronation procession.

---

* Louis's two eldest daughters were Marie and Alix, born to his first wife, Eleanor of Aquitaine. The unorthodox marital arrangements meant that Henry of Champagne (who married Marie) and Theobald of Blois (who married Alix) were Louis's sons-in-law as well as his brothers-in-law, and that they were Philip's brothers-in-law as well as his uncles.

Count Philip had no children, and both his younger brothers had pre-deceased him, so his heir was his sister Margaret, who was married to Baldwin V, the count of Hainaut. Margaret and Baldwin had several children, including a son, another Baldwin,* who was in line to become count of both Flanders and Hainaut in due course, and a daughter, Isabelle, who Count Philip was intending should be married to the new King Philip.

All of these groups, though, were dwarfed by the power and influence of the last: the Plantagenet family. Henry II, king of England, was also the ruler of vast expanses of France, being duke of Normandy and count of Anjou, Maine and Touraine in his own right and also duke of Aquitaine via his marriage to Eleanor, who was the duchess there in her own right.[1] Henry actually exercised direct control over more of France than Philip did, although he perforce acknowledged the French king as overlord for those lands. He was not at Philip's coronation himself, though his three eldest sons were.

Henry and Eleanor had seven children, some of whom Philip already knew well. The eldest was the twenty-four-year-old Henry, known as the Young King because he had been crowned during the lifetime of his father.†[2] He was Philip's brother-in-law, married to Margaret, Louis VII's third daughter (the elder of two by his second wife), and he had spent a good proportion of his time at the French court while Philip was a boy. It was intended that he would inherit all his father's titles in England and France, so the friendly relationship that he and Philip enjoyed would be advantageous. So high was the Young King's profile that he carried the

---

* French comital houses tended to use the same first names over and over again: Baldwin V's father, grandfather, great-grandfather and great-great-grandfather had all been called Baldwin, a run bettered only by the thirteen consecutive Hughs who were lords of Lusignan from the tenth century to the thirteenth. This sort of continuity emphasised a house's dynastic power, but it does sometimes make life confusing for modern writers and readers of medieval history. The younger Baldwin would later be Baldwin VI of Hainaut, Baldwin IX of Flanders and Baldwin I of the Latin empire of Constantinople, all at the same time.

† This was an occurrence unique in English history, modelled on the Capetian custom, but it ended up being so disastrous for all concerned that the experiment was never repeated.

crown in the coronation procession and supported Philip's head when the crown was placed upon it.

The second son was Richard, aged twenty-two, who was to inherit Aquitaine after the death of his mother, and who already ruled it because she had ceded the duchy to him — not an unusual situation when the female holder of a title had grown sons.[3] He was generally known as the count of Poitou, one of the duchy's subsidiary titles, as his father remained the titular duke of Aquitaine. Richard was also slated to become Philip's brother-in-law, as he was betrothed to Alice, the fourth of Philip's half-sisters.*

There would be no family lands for the third son, twenty-one-year-old Geoffrey, to inherit, but he was to be provided for by marriage: he was betrothed to Constance, duchess of Brittany in her own right, and he would rule there in due course. A fourth son, John, who was not present at the coronation, was rather younger than the others — in November 1179 he was twelve and had as yet played no role on the political stage. Henry II's three daughters, Matilda, Eleanor and Joanna, had all been sent abroad for their marriages and were respectively the duchess of Saxony and Bavaria, the queen of Castile and the queen of Sicily.[4]

As the newly crowned King Philip looked at the faces surrounding him in Reims cathedral, he had all of these people and their relationships firmly mapped in his head. The major question facing him, as he left the ceremony to begin his reign, was: what was he going to do about them all? He was young and inexperienced, and they were many and powerful, but did that mean that pure survival was his only goal? Was he content to be merely the first among a group of squabbling lords, or was he going to attempt to impose a genuine royal authority on France? If so, how?

* Alice was the second of Louis VII's daughters by his second marriage, and was thus a full sister to Margaret, the Young King's wife. Philip's sibling group was completed by his one full sister, Agnes, who was at this time nine years old and already in Constantinople preparing for her wedding to Alexios, the heir to the imperial Byzantine throne. She and Philip would never meet again and she does not play a role in our story here.

At the age of just fourteen, Philip unhesitatingly decided that the best form of defence was attack.

Officially, Philip had been crowned as the 'junior' king, because the ceremony had taken place during the lifetime of his father. So far, so Capetian. But the stroke that had afflicted Louis VII following his return from England meant that Philip had to take the reins of power into his own hands straight away, and he officially dated his reign from 1 November 1179, the day of his coronation.[5]

Perhaps surprisingly, there seems to have been no question of a regent being appointed. The nobility of France, the counts and dukes, were only considered to come of age when they reached twenty-one, and if any of them inherited their estates as a minor it was normal for a regent, usually their mother, to act for them until that time. But Philip did not want any of his authority to be ceded to another, particularly with the factionalism and favouritism that this would entail. He was aided in this by the precedent that his father had ruled without a regent despite acceding to the throne while underage – although Louis VII had been seventeen, not fourteen – and he was sufficiently forceful to sweep the question aside. No protest was made, and a contemporary noted that the new king was 'a boy in age' but 'mature in mind and deliberation'.[6]

Philip therefore took immediate personal possession of the royal seal, the all-important mark of authority that confirmed that documents issued by the crown were authentic – much to the chagrin of his maternal uncles, who had been hoping that their sister, as queen mother, would be appointed regent and that they would enjoy vicarious authority. To start with, Philip issued documents in both his own and his father's names (referring to the latter with great fondness), but he later moved on to using his own name only.[7]

One of the first things that Philip did to establish himself was to play the different factions off against each other. To this end he agreed to marry Isabelle of Hainaut, the daughter of Baldwin V and the niece of Philip of Flanders; the wedding took place on 28 April 1180, and the new ten-year-old queen was subsequently crowned. This was, of course, something of a coup for Count Philip, who had been pushing for the match, but it was also a major insult to the Blois–Champagne faction, because Isabelle had been betrothed for years to Henry (later Count Henry II of Champagne), the elder son of King Philip's sister Marie.

Accepting the match was a carefully calculated gamble on Philip's part, in that he knew he would be causing a great deal of displeasure, but it was worth it for the gains. The prosperous county of Artois came as Isabelle's dowry,* and would therefore be under the king's control, meaning that his direct authority would spread into territory that had hitherto been part of Flanders. Less tangibly, but an important symbolic point, was that the new queen could trace her descent from Charlemagne, so in uniting her line with his own Capetian one, Philip was enhancing the prestige of the royal dynasty.

The king had not been afraid to upset his sister, and next he demonstrated that he was not above offending his mother, either. Queen Adela was already put out at not being asked to act as Philip's regent, and his marriage to Isabelle of Hainaut caused her real alarm at the sudden increase in the fortunes of Count Philip of Flanders. She began, pre-emptively, to fortify her own dower lands against the possibility of attack, but this was an action that required the king's permission, which she had not sought. Rather than letting her get away with it, Philip showed no compunction

---

* Artois was a county in Flanders (which was then part of northern France, the kingdoms of Belgium and Netherlands not yet being in existence). A dowry was the payment, in the form of lands, goods or money, that came with a bride to her wedding, and was then controlled by her husband. It formed a permanent part of the joint wealth of the couple and could be passed down to their children. This was distinct from a dower, which was the lands or other incomes that a husband set aside for his wife for her use if he pre-deceased her. These were hers only conditionally, to support her during her own lifetime, and she could not bequeath them to anyone else; they would be returned to her late husband's family after her death.

in confiscating his mother's estates, and she fled to the court of her brother Theobald in Chartres rather than remaining in Paris.

Henry II of England was taken aback by the speed at which the new young king in France was shaking things up, and he was particularly worried at the threat to his own interests posed by the increasingly powerful Count Philip of Flanders. This led him to do something quite unusual, in the context of his recent family history: he put aside his differences with his eldest son, and the two of them agreed to work together to counter Flemish influence.

Young Henry, a familiar face at the French court, was on good personal terms with Philip, so he was able to oil the wheels while Henry II assumed the role of experienced and benevolent elder statesman. He arranged a personal summit with Philip in June 1180, which seems to have been the first time the two kings ever met face to face. It took place at the traditional site for meetings of the kings of France and England: in the shade of a large elm tree, situated between Gisors and Trie, which marked the border with Normandy. There, 'partly by gentle words and partly by threats', Henry 'prevailed upon the king of France, in spite of the advice of the earl [sic] of Flanders, to banish from his mind all the displeasure and indignation which he had felt towards his mother and his uncles'.[8] In order to sweeten the deal, Henry renewed at the same time the Treaty of Ivry, a peace agreement he had made with Louis VII back in 1177. The text of the new agreement oozed friendship and bonhomie:

I, Philip, by the grace of God, king of the Franks, and I, Henry, by the same grace, king of the English, do will that it shall come to the notice of all, both present as well as to come, that we have renewed the treaty and friendship, by word and oath, which my liege lord, Louis, king of the Franks, and I, Henry, concluded between ourselves before Ivry [...] to the effect, that we now are, and wish henceforth to be, friends, and that each will protect the other in life and limb, and will defend his worldly possessions to the utmost of his ability against all men.[9]

At this point Henry appeared to be genuine in his wish for peace with France, although this was probably more to do with anxiety over his own interests rather than any particular personal concern for Philip. Henry had recently become involved in a dispute with the Holy Roman Emperor, Frederick Barbarossa – the only man in Europe whose secular power was greater than his own – so he could certainly do with minimising any potential trouble in France.* However, this benevolence towards Philip was a rare misstep by the English king, who was normally very good at seeing the long-term implications of his actions, but whose foresight seems temporarily to have failed him. He had achieved short-term peace and stability, but in helping Philip to find his feet he had created a rod for his own back which was to return to beat him in the years to come.

Louis VII died on 18 September 1180, having never recovered from his stroke and having played no part in government since his son's coronation. Such epitaphs of him as we have are positive, referring to him as 'the most pious king of the Franks' and noting that at the site of his tomb, Barbeau Abbey,† 'saintly and religious men celebrate the divine office day and night for his soul, for that of all his predecessors, and for the state of the kingdom of the Franks'.[10] But the memorials were few and muted, Louis already having faded from the public eye and public

---

* Frederick Barbarossa was in conflict with his powerful vassal Henry the Lion, duke of Saxony and Bavaria, who was Henry II's son-in-law (as the husband of the king's daughter Matilda), and the marriage alliance meant that Henry II was being drawn in. He would later give asylum to Matilda and Duke Henry when they were temporarily banished from the Empire.

† All the previous Capetian kings had been interred at Saint-Denis, but Louis had chosen to be buried at the Cistercian abbey of Barbeau, which he himself had founded, situated on the banks of the Seine about 30 miles south-east of Paris. As it later transpired, this means that his remains escaped the desecration that occurred during the French Revolution in the eighteenth century, when the royal tombs at Saint-Denis were broken open and the bodies and bones tossed into a ditch.

consciousness while his son's star rose. Philip was already the real king, not his sick father.

At the time of Louis's death Philip had not long turned fifteen, still so young that 'his cheeks were only just covered in a fine down'. But this was deceptive, and those great men of the kingdom who 'thought only of his lack of years, and not of the strength of his will' were in for a shock, as 'he showed himself to be a king in war, an old man in head and a young man in action, a mature man by the strength of his mind'.[11]

Blois–Champagne and Flanders–Hainaut notwithstanding, Philip was shrewd enough to know that his principal and most dangerous opponents were the Plantagenets. The key here was never to let them all unite against him, for, as contemporaries realised, if they ever did manage to act as a team, the consequences would have been significant. Gerald of Wales was aware of this:

O good gods! If such brothers had observed fraternal agreement among themselves and filial affection as sons of their father [...] how great and beyond estimation, how illustrious and unsurpassed in the ages would have been the father's glory and the sons' victory! [...] For what strength could resist their force, what kings these kings, what kingdoms such war leaders?[12]

It was thus very much in Philip's best interests to keep all the Plantagenets in disagreement with each other, and he started as he meant to go on by exploiting the fractious relationship between the English king and his heir. In 1182 Henry the Young King was twenty-seven years old and had seen his brothers come into their inheritances in Aquitaine and Brittany, while he was merely the holder of an empty title. He was, of course, the heir not only to the English crown but also to vast estates in France, but with Henry II still only in his late forties they were a distant future prospect, and Young Henry felt short-changed, denied the settled status of his younger brothers. Philip now stirred things up by encouraging Young Henry to demand the immediate transfer of the duchy of Normandy to his control, which, as Roger of Howden noted, caused Henry II headaches on several levels:

> Henry, king of England, the father, crossed over from England to Normandy, in consequence of the annoyances and vexations which his son king Henry was causing him. For, having gone with his wife to Philip, king of France, he was devising all the evils he possibly could to the detriment of the king, his father, contrary to good faith and the oaths of fealty which he had often taken to him; demanding of him, in conformity with the advice of Philip, king of France, his wife's brother, the whole of Normandy, or else some other part of his territories, in which he and his wife might take up their abode, and from which he might pay his knights and servants for their services.[13]

Philip did not quite manage to cause a complete breach at this point, because the Young King allowed himself to be bought off with the offer of a generous cash allowance from his father – money and prestige being more attractive than the irksome responsibilities of governance – but he had sowed some useful seeds.

These seeds germinated not long afterwards when it became clear that Richard was growing increasingly unpopular with the barons of Aquitaine, thanks to his harsh rule and uncompromising personality. Philip's whispers in the ear of Young Henry prompted him to get involved, supported by Geoffrey, and the two brothers launched an invasion of Richard's lands. As the royal overlord of Aquitaine, Philip could have intervened – and indeed his previous acceptance of Richard's homage for the duchy meant that he should have supported his vassal – but in fact he deliberately sat back to let events take their course. Henry II therefore felt obliged to step in himself, in order to stop his sons from killing each other, and such was his energy and authority that he did succeed in making them all swear peace early in 1183. However, it was only weeks before the fragile veneer of harmony collapsed and they were all at each other's throats again, much to Philip's delight. He remained in Paris, along with his sister Margaret (who had been left there by the Young King for safe-keeping, so she could not be captured and taken as a hostage by either Henry II or Richard)* and sat back to watch the fireworks.

Henry the Young King, unfortunately for him, was no match whatsoever for Richard in military terms. He had spent years enjoying the glamour and mock-war of the tournament circuit in northern France, becoming very popular as a result, but Richard had spent those same years engaged in real war against tough, rebellious opponents. Henry II also took Richard's part on this occasion, meaning that Young Henry and Geoffrey were in danger of being crushed. This did not suit Philip, who wanted the conflict to go on as long as possible. He therefore took practical action by sending a troop of mercenaries to Young Henry, to bolster his flagging cause and inflict as much damage as possible on the resources of Henry II and Richard.

This did help prolong the conflict for a little while, but in May 1183 the Young King fell desperately ill with dysentery — a common illness, and particularly prevalent among those on military campaigns. On 11 June, he died. A chronicler who was personally acquainted with the family wrote:

> His death was the occasion to us of the deepest grief, not only because he was the son of our most dearly beloved lord, king Henry the second, the most excellent king of the English, but also because he was of the most handsome countenance, of the most pleasing manners, and the most free-handed in his liberality of all the individuals with whom we have ever been acquainted.[14]

Despite the differences between them, Henry II was deeply upset by the loss of his son, both on a personal level and because it

---

* This was not an idle fear of Young Henry's; when he had rebelled against his father ten years previously, Henry II had taken Margaret – despite her status as his daughter-in-law, the wife of one king and the daughter of another – into his custody and imprisoned her as a hostage for his son's good behaviour.

meant that all his long-held plans for the distribution of his lands and titles after his death now lay in tatters.

The Young King's death was also a disaster for Philip, although for very different reasons. There might have been some element of personal sorrow and regret, for he had known and liked Henry for most of his life, but the main basis for Philip's dismay was that the Young King was supposed to have been his long-term peer and adversary on the English throne, and he was by far the easiest to deal with, and to dominate, of any member of the Plantagenet family. Contemporaries praised Young Henry for his affability, courtesy and generosity (not to mention his good looks), but they tended to gloss over the inconvenient facts that he was also feckless, irresponsible, vain and not particularly intelligent. For a king of Philip's shrewdness and political intelligence, dealing with Young Henry would have been about as challenging as netting a dead fish, but now he faced the prospect of the bellicose Richard succeeding in due course to the English throne. He would need to regroup.

One immediate political consequence of the Young King's death was a dispute between Philip and Henry II over the Vexin, a strategically important and much-disputed area that straddled the Franco-Norman border. Back in 1158, when the match between Young Henry and Margaret had originally been arranged, Louis VII had agreed that the Norman Vexin would be Margaret's dowry, but that he would retain control of it until the actual wedding took place.* As Margaret was only six months old at the time, Louis looked forward to a decade or more of undisputed control of the region. Unfortunately for him, he had made the mistake of handing over the baby into Henry II's keeping as a mark of good faith, and could therefore do nothing when Henry II found some compliant churchmen and held the wedding in 1160.

---

* The Norman Vexin, as the name implies, had traditionally been part of Normandy. However, Louis VII's father, Louis VI, had wrested control of it from the English king Henry I earlier in the twelfth century, and then Geoffrey Plantagenet (Henry II's father) had officially ceded it to Louis VII in the 1140s in return for the French king's recognition of Geoffrey as duke of Normandy.

This sounds almost unbelievable, but it is nevertheless true: Margaret of France was just two years old when she married Young Henry, who was only five himself. Neither of them could possibly have understood the promises they were making (or, more probably, that were made by others on their behalf). Henry II was roundly criticised, but the ceremony was deemed legal and could not be undone, and he had demonstrated that he was unapologetically willing to perform actions that others might deem unpalatable in order to further the cause of his own kingship. He was the big winner in the situation, as the binding marriage contract meant that the Vexin belonged to the infant couple, which in turn meant that Henry controlled it in their names until they came of age. He immediately appointed his own governors and castellans throughout the region, and indeed continued to rule it himself even after Young Henry reached his majority.

Technically, though, the Vexin did belong to Young Henry, as it was he who was married to Margaret, who had brought the lands as her dowry. If they had produced any children, the lands could have been passed on, but this was not the case, and was the principal reason why the Vexin became the subject of dispute.* Philip's position was that, as a childless widow, Margaret's ties to the Plantagenet family could be considered severed, and she should be returned to him. She was still only twenty-five, and thus retained her value on the marriage market, so she could remain in Philip's care until he could make another match for her. He argued that the Vexin should return with her; Henry II disagreed.

These discussions dragged on until a compromise agreement was reached, whereby Margaret herself returned to France but Philip transferred the dowry of the Vexin to his next sister, Alice, who had long been betrothed to Henry II's second son, Richard.† Given that they were both by now in their mid-twenties, and that

---

* Margaret had given birth to a son, prematurely, in 1177, but the baby lived only three days and she never fell pregnant again.

† Margaret remained in Paris for a couple of years, and then moved to Hungary in 1186 to become its queen as the second wife of Béla III. She would be widowed again in 1196, still with no children; at that point she embarked on a pilgrimage to the Holy Land, where she died of illness in 1197.

Alice had been in the English king's custody since she was eight, it was both strange and somewhat insulting that no wedding had taken place, so perhaps Philip hoped that this concession would motivate the Plantagenets to get a move on.

He also made a more immediate gain: as part of the agreement, Henry II promised to pay personal homage to Philip for all his lands in France, something he had previously refused to do. This was important from a symbolic point of view, as the rendering of homage was a personal, physical act involving the vassal kneeling before his overlord. Thus, although the Henry who performed the ceremony was the duke of Normandy and the count of Anjou, Maine and Touraine – titles which he held separately and in addition to the crown of England, not as part of it – all the onlookers were still treated to the sight of the king of England kneeling before the king of France.

This was gratifying, but what Philip really needed to do was to rearrange his long-term strategy with regard to the Plantagenets. There was still plenty of scope to exploit filial and fraternal conflict, and Philip chose to court not the new heir, Richard, but the known troublemaker and loose cannon, Geoffrey. Henry II's third son had a deserved reputation for deceit and double-dealing, agreed on even by contemporaries who would not normally see eye to eye: Roger of Howden called him a 'son of iniquity', while Gerald of Wales accused him of 'pouring out words smoother than oil [...] able to unknit whatever has been joined together and with a tongue powerful enough to ruin two kingdoms [...] an unreliable hypocrite and dissembler in all things'.[15] Even within his own family, Geoffrey's loyalties were fluid: his alliance with Young Henry against Richard had been prompted more by the desire to stir things up than by love and respect for his eldest brother. He resented Henry II, who had betrothed him to Constance of Brittany at a young age but then delayed the actual wedding as long as possible so that he could retain control of the duchy himself.*

---

* By the time Geoffrey and Constance were actually married (that is, when he could assume control of Brittany in her name) he was twenty-three and she was twenty. That seems young now, but it was unusually late for a royal marriage in the twelfth century.

And he had never been on good terms with Richard, who was a mere twelve months older than himself but had gained Aquitaine as a result of that seniority.

Geoffrey had not continued the fight in Aquitaine after Young Henry's death, but his relations with Richard remained hostile, so he was a good horse for Philip to back in his quest to sow even further discord in the Plantagenet family. Before the French king could concentrate fully on that aim, however, he had an over-mighty domestic vassal who needed to be cut down to size.

By early 1184 Count Philip of Flanders was becoming a problem. He was in dispute with the king over the county of Vermandois, and this was threatening to spill over into armed conflict, which needed to be dealt with promptly.* It was time to break the Flanders–Hainaut coalition and bring it into proper submission to the crown, just as the king had earlier done with the Blois–Champagne faction.

Count Philip's trump card was his niece, Queen Isabelle, who gave him a marriage connection to the royal family and a great deal of influence at court. King Philip therefore decided that the best way to snub the older man was to announce, in March 1184, that he wished to divorce his wife. In so doing, he demonstrated an unpleasant tendency – albeit one that was very common among powerful men at the time – to treat the women in his life as mere pawns to be moved around at his will, rather than fellow humans with lives and emotions of their own.

Divorcing a wife (or, to be more precise, having a marriage annulled) was not quite as straightforward as simply making

---

* The background to this is complex, but in short: Count Philip's first wife, Elisabeth, had been countess of Vermandois in her own right, which meant that he had controlled it for many years in her name. She had recently died and he was now claiming that Vermandois should be his, although the legal heir was Elisabeth's surviving sister, Eleanor. The king chose to support Eleanor, ostensibly to uphold traditional rights of inheritance but probably also because he was looking for an excuse to pick a fight with Count Philip.

an announcement, and nor could Philip make a case for it on purely political grounds. Marriage was a religious institution and the Church held that it was for life, with a few exceptions, so Philip would need to find a suitable loophole. One of the allowable grounds for separation was infertility – the procreation of legitimate offspring being a cornerstone of matrimony – but that was hardly a viable option here: although the couple had been married for four years, Philip was only eighteen and Isabelle a mere fourteen, and it is probable that they had not yet even begun to co-habit as man and wife.[*]

The other obvious route was to claim consanguinity. At this time the Church had very strict rules about the allowable degree of blood relationship between those seeking to marry each other, and it was prohibited up to the seventh degree: that is, those who were sixth cousins or closer could not marry. Given how intertwined most of the noble families of France were, it was often possible to unearth a distant connection, previously unknown,[†] which rendered an inconvenient marriage dissolvable. Philip therefore set his clerks to work on researching his and Isabelle's genealogy, and summoned a council to discuss the matter.

The fullest account of this episode is that of a contemporary writer named Gilbert of Mons. He was the chancellor of Hainaut and an advisor to Baldwin V, Isabelle's father, and therefore in possession of good information, although naturally his sympathies lay with Isabelle and her family rather than with the king. He was adamant that Philip's motive in seeking the divorce was related to the Flanders–Hainaut alliance, and that the innocent Isabelle was treated 'unjustly', with 'evil plans' being discussed by 'a council of

---

[*] There is a possibility that the marriage had been consummated, as otherwise Philip's easiest path to annulment would have been non-consummation and he would simply have declared this. However, if the couple had slept together this was likely to have been (for now) a one-off event simply to validate the marriage. The dangers of extremely early pregnancy and childbirth were well known and therefore avoided where possible.

[†] Or not: it was not unheard of for a man to marry a wife whom he knew was within the prohibited degree of kinship, on the basis that it gave him the opportunity to play the consanguinity card later on if he wanted to dissolve the marriage for any reason.

ill-intentioned men'. She was not even informed of this council, Gilbert noted, 'with not even her father the count of Hainaut and the count of Flanders knowing about it'.[16] If this was indeed the set-up that Gilbert thought it was, matters looked bleak for the young queen.

However, in concentrating on the political relationship between himself and the count of Flanders, King Philip had overlooked and underestimated his wife, who now took matters into her own hands:

> The queen, putting aside her precious clothing and assuming humble garments, walked barefoot through the churches of the city, begging most high God to deliver her from the counsels of malicious men being conducted against her most severely. The lepers and all the paupers, perceiving that evil was being done to her, crowded before the queen's palace with loud voices. The king and his men heard them, begging God to confound the queen's adversaries and deliver her from their evil power.[17]

This was clever. Isabelle could not hope to be taken seriously in any personal appeal to the all-male council, but twelfth-century queens had a great deal of what we might now call 'soft' political power, and she used that to her advantage. The sympathy she engendered in the population of Paris caused a change of heart in some of those on the king's council, and led to a rare intervention in state matters from Count Robert I of Dreux, Philip's Capetian uncle. He was present at the deliberations along with his three eldest sons – Robert, his heir (later Count Robert II), Henry, the bishop of Orleans, and Philip, the bishop of Beauvais* – and they

---

* Given that royal and comital families were often large, and that not every child could be provided for, it was common for younger sons and daughters to be 'donated' to the Church at a young age. They would take holy orders in the expectation of being appointed to high-ranking positions as bishops or abbesses, which would make them socially equal to their secular brothers and sisters and enable them to offer religious and political aid to their families. The problem was that such donations were made on the basis of birth order rather than inclination or aptitude, so some appointments were wildly unsuitable. In the case of the Dreux brothers, Henry appears to have been

all advised against the divorce. The king seems to have changed his mind suspiciously easily and quickly, and declared that he no longer had plans to divorce Isabelle. She almost immediately went to her father, telling him that she was upset that there should be conflict between him and King Philip.

> Completely overcome with tears [she] begged her father and his household knights to pity her, and to help her lord the king (whom he [Baldwin] had offended for a long time on account of the count of Flanders) against the cunning of the count of Flanders, so that she would be more dear to the lord her king and the French people.[18]

Baldwin then switched his allegiance from the count to the king.

So the end results of the entire 'divorce' controversy were that Philip kept his wife, who had revealed herself to be both clever and loyal; that the long-standing Flanders–Hainaut alliance was broken; and that a humbled Philip of Flanders, deprived of his main ally and facing a king who had numerous other vassals backing him, submitted to the crown without further bloodshed. And Philip Augustus had demonstrated that a shrewd and foresighted king did not necessarily have to draw his sword in order to achieve his political aims.

With Blois–Champagne and Flanders–Hainaut now under firmer control, Philip was in a much stronger position to press his advantage against the Plantagenets. To this end he continued to court Geoffrey, and he additionally benefitted from yet another new rift between Henry II and Richard. This had been occasioned by the former's reorganisation of his plans for the inheritance of his

a conventional sort of bishop, while Philip (who had been appointed to the see of Beauvais while still in his teens) certainly wasn't. He enjoyed a long career in the service of his cousin the king, and we will meet him again later.

titles following the death of Young Henry. Richard, as the eldest surviving son, was now to step into his elder brother's place as the heir to England, Normandy, Anjou, Maine and Touraine. This was uncontroversial and no more than expected, but Henry II saw this as *replacing* Richard's title in Aquitaine rather than adding to it. To Henry, this was a good opportunity to provide for his youngest and hitherto landless son, John, and he summoned Richard to Normandy to tell him that he was expected to hand over the duchy in return for John's homage and his own promotion to the position of heir to the other estates.

Richard was furious, and refused. Aquitaine was his, had always been his. He had shed blood and sweat for the duchy, and had been ruling it and fighting against rebellious barons there for eight years. He was in no mind, therefore, to wrap it in a ribbon and hand it over to the untried sixteen-year-old John. We might also wonder whether Geoffrey was disgruntled by this new plan of his father's, even on top of his general jealousy of Richard. His rule of Brittany was not affected by these new inheritance plans, as he was duke there in right of his wife, but now that there were apparently family lands and titles going spare, he might have expected Aquitaine to fall to him rather than to the younger John. In any case, the whole question was moot: Richard slipped away from his father's court, headed for Poitou and sent a defiant message saying he would never surrender Aquitaine as long as he lived. Henry was, in turn, enraged.[19]

Naturally Philip exploited the family divisions, inviting Geoffrey to Paris, making much of him and apparently also appointing him seneschal of France, or at least considering doing so.[*] Some contemporaries put this down to Geoffrey wheedling himself into Philip's good books ('Count Geoffrey had by now so won over the minds of King Philip and of all the great men of France [...]

---

[*] *Seneschal* can have different meanings in different contexts; in France in the twelfth century the royal seneschal was the most senior of the officers of the crown, heading up the royal household and responsible for raising and organising troops when necessary. The position was not hereditary, and could be awarded or rescinded at the king's pleasure.

he had stirred up the king of the French and the whole of France against his father with persuasive words'), but it does seem more likely, from the evidence and from what we know of the parties, that it was Philip using Geoffrey for his own ends, rather than the other way round.[20] The question of the seneschalty of France is a particularly interesting one, as the position was traditionally held by the count of Anjou. It is possible, therefore, that Philip was putting an idea into Geoffrey's head about asking his father for Anjou (which bordered Brittany) so that he would hold the ancient family title in his own right, in addition to his *jure uxoris* control of Brittany.* Philip had tried a similar tactic before, of course, when he persuaded the Young King to demand the rule of Normandy, and this had caused Henry II 'annoyances and vexations'.[21] Philip might also have given Geoffrey a few tactful reminders that he was next in line for the main prize, with only the unmarried, childless Richard ahead of him in the queue for the English crown.

That must remain hypothetical for now. In the meantime the most fertile ground for dispute was Aquitaine, and the fight between the brothers. In the summer of 1184 Henry II returned to England, which he had not visited for two years, and immediately Geoffrey and John invaded Poitou, the northern part of Aquitaine. John had no army so the troops were from Brittany, brought by Geoffrey and not terribly enthusiastic at being dragged into a fight that was no concern of theirs. They had very little hope of taking the duchy, or of persuading the barons there to defect to them en masse, so it was really no more than raiding, but it was annoying enough to goad Richard into retaliation and he launched raids of his own into Brittany.

Philip needed to be careful. He did want the Plantagenets at each other's throats, but on the other hand he did not want large parts of France going up in flames, nor to give the impression

---

* *Jure uxoris* was a legal term, meaning 'by marriage' or 'in right of his wife'. In this case it meant that Geoffrey was duke of Brittany only because he was married to Constance; if he died, she would remain duchess in her own right, and any subsequent husband would then be duke *jure uxoris*. Transmission of the title would be to her children, regardless of who their father was.

that he did not have overall control of his kingdom and his vassals. Thus, when Henry II summoned all three sons to England in the autumn of 1184 to make peace, Philip let them get on with it. He must have suspected that it would not last, however, and was not taken by surprise when hostilities resumed in the spring of 1185 as soon as Richard and Geoffrey got back to France.

It was at this point that Henry II played a different card, by temporarily releasing his wife, Eleanor of Aquitaine, from the captivity in which he had held her since the rebellion of their sons back in 1173–4. He took her to France and demanded that Richard surrender Aquitaine to her, as she was its rightful duchess. Richard had no choice but to comply – and, indeed, he was probably happy to do so, as the occasion meant that he could show public respect for his beloved mother. He could also be confident that she would always take his part against Henry, if she were required to choose. Unfortunately for them, though, it turned out that this was not an opportunity for Eleanor to return to public life: Henry only wanted Richard's submission, and then she was returned to England and to imprisonment, although she was not so closely confined as before.

Philip still had Geoffrey in his pocket, with all the potential for trouble that involved, and young John was looking promising as another option. However, the French king was dealt a severe blow in August 1186 when Geoffrey, then staying with him in Paris, suddenly died. Accounts vary as to whether he was trampled by a horse during a tournament or whether he succumbed to illness, although it is entirely possible that both were involved – injuries sustained during a tournament could easily lead to infection and fever. Rather than having his body sent back to Brittany or any of his family's lands, Philip had Geoffrey buried in the cathedral of Notre Dame in Paris. He grieved very publicly and somewhat performatively: Gerald of Wales claims that due to 'the violence of his grief, he [Philip] would have been ready to throw himself with him [Geoffrey] into the gaping tomb, had not his men pulled him back by force'.[22] This seems rather an overreaction, in a 'methinks he doth protest too much' kind of a way, but there was never any suggestion of foul play, and Geoffrey's loss was certainly a setback for Philip rather than being in any way convenient.

Geoffrey was twenty-seven at the time of his death, and he left a widow and either one or two small daughters (the younger of the two died at around the same time, though it is unclear whether this occurred before or after Geoffrey's demise). The duchy of Brittany, the inheritance of Brittany, and the future of the duchess of Brittany and her heirs would all prove to be fertile grounds of Capetian–Plantagenet conflict in future years,[*] but for now Philip was obliged to reorganise his political priorities once again.

The major antagonism within the Plantagenet family was, for the foreseeable future, going to be between Henry II and Richard. The natural option for Philip, therefore, was to befriend Richard and encourage him in any disputes with his father. This was a much trickier prospect than using either the shallow Young Henry or the willing troublemaker Geoffrey, but it was a challenge Philip relished. He had served his apprenticeship: he was twenty-one years old and seven years into his reign, and he had already seen off a number of powerful threats to his rule. He was ready for the next phase of the game.

[*] We will return to this point in Chapters 5 and 6.

2

From the Devil He Came

The speed and alacrity with which Philip was capable of switching his alliances between the Plantagenet sons should probably have given Richard some kind of warning. In hindsight — and perhaps this was also evident to the more astute among the contemporary observers — the French king was clearly acting in his own political interest, but Richard did not seem to think it odd that the man who had only recently sided with his brothers in a war against him was now making overtures of friendship. Of course, Richard could benefit from being on good terms with Philip, who was his overlord for Aquitaine (particularly if Richard might need to defend the duchy against an armed incursion from Henry II and John), but he could and probably should have acted with a little more caution. Instead, he enthusiastically welcomed Philip's advances, seeing them only as a way to get back at his father.

In light of the new situation, Philip reorganised his overarching campaign against Henry II on several fronts, one of which involved a custody battle over the heirs to Brittany. The duchy had not changed hands at Geoffrey's death, because Constance was duchess in her own right, but she was an isolated, widowed young mother who ruled a territory trapped (both politically and geographically) between France, Normandy and England. She was therefore in need of the 'protection' of one king or the other, or so they believed. As the duke of Normandy, Henry was the overlord of Brittany; but as king of France, Philip was the overlord of Normandy. Both were extremely keen to have control of the marriage rights of Constance (who was still only twenty-five) and of her surviving daughter and heiress, the three-year-old Eleanor of Brittany, because this gave Philip or Henry the valuable opportunity to reward a loyal man of their choice with marriage to an heiress and, through him, to influence the future political direction of Brittany. Moreover, it soon became apparent that Constance had been in the early stages of pregnancy when Geoffrey died. If the child she carried was an all-important male heir, then the situation would change again – and if he happened to be born in French or Anglo-Norman territory, so much the better for the king concerned.

Constance was much more strong-minded than either Philip or Henry gave her credit for.[1] Resisting any pressure to move to their courts, she remained in Brittany and gave birth in Nantes on Easter Sunday (29 March) 1187. The baby was a boy and, as a signal of her intent to remain independent, she avoided giving him a name from her late husband's family: he was christened Arthur, a name of traditional Breton significance. Constance was well aware that her son would soon be pushed and pulled between the competing powers, for he was not only her heir to the duchy of Brittany, but also a potential contender for the crown of England: he was Henry II's only grandson in the male line, and Richard and John were both unmarried and childless.*

In addition to their squabbling over Brittany, Philip also reminded Henry – again – that he had not yet arranged for the marriage of Richard and Alice to take place. The poor woman was by now in her late twenties and had been in Henry's keeping for the best part of two decades, her life permanently on hold as she watched her youth and prime childbearing years pass her by. True to form,

---

* Henry II did have eight other grandchildren already. Four of them were girls: Arthur's sister Eleanor of Brittany, Richenza of Saxony, and Berengaria and Urraca of Castile. The four boys were all sons of Henry's eldest daughter Matilda and her husband Henry the Lion of Saxony: Henry, Lothar, Otto and William, who were at this point aged around fourteen, thirteen, twelve and three. In the absence of other contenders, they were considered potential heirs to England, as they were male themselves even though descended through a female line, but the son of a son was always preferable so they were bumped down the hereditary queue by Arthur's arrival.

Philip's concern does not seem to have been for her personally but rather for the political insult to himself and his family, and the future of the Vexin.

In the summer of 1187 Philip took a more practical approach to his disputes with Henry, invading the county of Berry, which lay at the north-eastern edge of Aquitaine, bordering Touraine and Blois. He took Issoudun (about 80 miles north-east of Poitiers) and Fréteval with ease, and then moved on to besiege the fortified town of Châteauroux.

Sieges were a significant part of warfare, occurring much more frequently than pitched battles, and they were important because control of a castle or other fortified position meant that the holder could dominate an area for miles around. By capturing Châteauroux as well as Issoudun and Fréteval, therefore, Philip would be able to take some quite sizeable bites out of the edge of Aquitaine.

Sieges were so common that contemporaries often recorded them only very briefly, but in this case we have quite a full narrative of the event, written by the French chronicler William the Breton.[2] William tells us that Philip was keen to engage, 'hardly able to bear the necessary delay in making ready the siege machinery', and he goes on to give his readers a classic depiction of the situation and of the wide range of techniques available to a besieger. Châteauroux was 'defended by towers and high curtain walls as well as deep ditches', seemingly 'secure against any enemy and truly impregnable', and defended not only by its own citizens but also troops sent by Henry II. Nonetheless, Philip was undaunted. He set miners to work under cover of a 'tortoise' (*testudo*), while a petrary (*petraria*) launched stones, and a tall belfry (*belfragia*) was moved close to the walls.* Meanwhile, archers and crossbowmen

---

* A *tortoise*, sometimes also called a *sow* or a *cat*, was a covered roof on wheels that sheltered men who were beginning to dig mines (before they got deep underground), or who were working on the surface to attack the base of a wall with picks, from missiles launched by those inside the castle. A *petrary* was a small stone-throwing machine that worked by balance and traction, men pulling down on ropes on one side of a pivoted beam in order to fling the other arm in the air and release a missile. A *belfry* was a temporary moveable siege tower made of wood or wattle which enabled the attackers to reach the same height as the defenders on their wall. They could then loose arrows or

loosed arrows and quarrels. Ladders were set against the walls. Some of the men climbing them were pushed away, and fell, but others were able to engage in hand-to-hand combat, which William describes in a heightened literary style: 'One man is struck on the head by a spear or a mace; another has his brains knocked out by a besague;* but neither the besague, nor the spear, nor the axe, nor the glaive, produced a decisive result.'

As it happens, William's description of the siege of Châteauroux is actually so 'textbook' that he is probably employing a great deal of poetic licence. He was later a royal chaplain who travelled with the king and wrote narratives based to a great extent on what he had witnessed personally, but he had not yet taken up this post and was thus writing his account of the siege in hindsight and based on second-hand information. However, his depiction does give us a good idea of what many sieges looked like in the late twelfth century; William saw plenty of others in his time, and he was writing for an intended audience made up of military experts who would not take kindly to wild inaccuracies.

Philip did not capture the town, because on 23 June Henry II approached with a relieving army, and Philip – despite the fervour ascribed to him by William the Breton – was sensible enough to realise that he did not want to get trapped in between two hostile forces. Another peace treaty was agreed, the negotiations mediated by a papal legate on behalf of a Church that would much rather have Philip Augustus and Henry II on good terms with one another than at each other's throats.†

---

crossbow quarrels across or down (which was more effective than shooting upwards), or they could cross straight over to the battlements without needing to climb ladders.

* A besague (in Latin bisacuta) was a type of double-headed axe, one with blades in opposite alignments (a vertical blade on one side of the shaft, like a standard axe, and a horizontal blade or pick on the other side, like a mattock). The same term might be used for an implement being used as a tool or as a weapon, but this makes little difference to the narrative: when a stronghold was being besieged the defenders were liable to pick up anything that came to hand.

† This legate is not named by William the Breton, but he appears to have been Cardinal Octavian di Paoli. Octavian had recently been sent to England to oversee the coronation of Henry II's son John as king of Ireland, but had offended the archbishop of Canterbury to such an extent that the

One final point to note about this siege is what it reveals about Philip's character and martial expertise. Traditionally he has been portrayed by historians as a Machiavellian schemer who avoided combat, preferring instead to lurk in the shadows rubbing his hands together while hatching clever plans – which, to be fair, is not altogether inaccurate, in that Philip was intelligent and did often achieve his aims via politics rather than war. However, the flip side of this is that his military prowess has been vastly under-rated. As will become apparent in later chapters, Philip was not afraid to instigate practical military action, and nor was he loath to lead and engage in it himself. He would develop into a particu-larly noted breaker and taker of castles, which makes sense when we think about it: capturing castles via sieges was as much an intellectual exercise as a martial one, and he was well suited to such a task.[3]

Philip's new peace agreement with Henry II did not stop him from pursuing his aims by other means, and when he returned to Paris he was accompanied by Richard. The French king was extremely attentive to his guest, as Roger of Howden observed: 'Every day they ate at the same table and from the same dish, and at night had not separate chambers.'[4] This quote is regularly misinterpreted as meaning that the two men were in some kind of romantic or sexual relationship, but this is not the case – the idea of it was to get across the degree of political and personal trust between them. In a world where many rulers and great men were rightly suspicious of each other, and food might be poisoned, eating from the same dish was a demonstration of confidence. Similarly, in an environment where everyone carried a knife, shar-ing a bedroom or even a bed indicated that you trusted the other man not to stab you to death in your sleep. Indeed, this appears to be a standard form of wording representing alliance or recon-ciliation, as another chronicler used it in precisely the same way

coronation did not take place. To what degree this affected Henry II's attitude to Octavian's role in the present negotiations with Philip must remain a matter for conjecture.

about Henry II and his son Henry the Young King, who can hardly be accused of a romantic relationship.[5]

Philip therefore demonstrated his own faith and gained Richard's, and this gave him ample opportunity to whisper insinuations into the Plantagenet's ear. *Your father hasn't had you crowned, as he did for your elder brother. He hasn't even made an official announcement that you're his heir. He's already said he wants you to hand Aquitaine over to John — what if he intends to disinherit you completely and leave everything to your little brother? Trust me, not him.*

The author of the *History of William Marshal*, writing in (somewhat bitter) hindsight in the 1220s, is clear that it was Philip who instigated the extreme distrust between Richard and Henry II at this time, and that it had dire long-term consequences:

> The King of France embark[ed] on a base course of action which subsequently proved injurious to all the realm of England [...] the King of France made it known to the count of Poitiers that, if he became his good friend and crossed to his side, he would give him for his own Touraine, Anjou and Maine, and fully confirm the gift. To his misfortune, Richard believed him.[*] He came to him in secret and paid him homage for the gift. But the King never kept his word on this, and in the same way he often behaved towards all the brothers, one after the other, causing them all mischief [...] one by one, they were all tricked and deceived.[6]

Philip's plans were coming along very nicely indeed.

———

As 1187 progressed, there was further good news for Philip: he was to be a father. Queen Isabelle, now seventeen, had fallen pregnant early in the year, and by the summer her condition was obvious to

---

[*] 'To his misfortune, Henry/Richard/Geoffrey/John believed him' more or less summarises the entire relationship between Philip and the sons of Henry II.

all observers. She was confined in Paris, and on 5 September she gave birth to a son, who was named Louis.* Philip, naturally, was delighted, and so were his subjects:

> Upon his birth the city of Paris, where he was born, was filled with such joy that every night for seven days, by the light of flaming torches, the people of the whole city ceaselessly offered due praise to their Creator and led choruses in song. At the very hour of his birth, messengers were dispatched through all the provinces announcing to the far corners of the kingdom the joys of such a king. They were overflowing with joy, praising and blessing God.[7]

The joy of the people was genuine. The birth of a male heir was hugely significant not just for Philip but for the whole of France, because it meant stability: there would be none of the uncertainty over the succession that had dogged Louis VII's reign for over thirty years, none of the worry about whether war would break out if the king died without leaving a son. Instead the continuity of the Capetian line would be maintained, with the additional bonus that the new prince was descended not only from Hugh Capet on his father's side, but also from Charlemagne on his mother's. Philip's decision of three years earlier not to proceed with the planned divorce had paid off: Isabelle of Hainaut was an asset to him, not only because of her now-proven fertility and her royal descent, but also because she was dutiful and popular, a helpmeet and a support to the king as well as the mother of his child. And, given the youth of the couple, they could expect a string of additions to the royal nursery over the next couple of decades, strengthening the succession beyond any doubt. Philip could now begin to make

---

* Much to the dismay of modern historians and indexers, every French king from 1060 to 1316 was called either Philip or Louis. They alternated the names for the eldest son in each generation, so where we find two instances of the same regnal name in a row (Louis VI and VII; Louis VIII and IX; Philip III and IV) it is a sure sign that an eldest son of the other name pre-deceased his father.

dynastic plans of his own, though he would take care not to make the same mistakes that Henry II had in dealing with his offspring.

This significant event in Philip's life is perhaps an appropriate point to step back from our narrative for a moment to consider him as a person rather than just as a king. We have heard of his actions since he came to the throne, but what can we discover about his personality? His looks? His beliefs, likes and dislikes? In an era when so much power was invested in one individual, and the personal was thus very much the political, the character of a king had an impact that was felt far beyond his own circle of family and friends.

We do know something of Philip's appearance, and we can extrapolate a little more. We can assume, for example, that he was of around average height, on the basis that no observer of the period makes any particular mention of him being otherwise, as they did for others. Richard the Lionheart was pronounced by a number of chroniclers to be tall, as was his and Philip's slightly younger contemporary Sancho VII the Strong of Navarre, while Tancred of Sicily was routinely described as being short.* In a similar vein, the lack of any comments about Philip being spectacularly handsome (or otherwise) suggests that there was nothing unusual or startling in his looks, and the bizarre suggestion in several modern works that he had only one eye is a complete myth, not supported by any contemporary evidence. In terms of build he was sturdy and robust, barrel-chested as many of the Capetians were, and at this stage he had a mop of unruly brown hair. In later life we know he had a taste for good food and fine wine, which meant that he tended towards the corpulent, but in 1187, when he was only twenty-two, this was still in the future, and an active life of riding and hunting would have kept him in trim.[8]

---

* Neither of these last two descriptions is particularly surprising: when Sancho's remains were exhumed and examined in the twentieth century, it was discovered that he had stood at a mighty 7ft 3in, and Tancred was so short that some modern commentators speculate that he may have been a person with dwarfism. What the descriptions do show is that contemporaries were likely to remark upon anything out of the ordinary, so their lack of comment on Philip's height is, in itself, indicative. We will meet both Tancred and Sancho in later chapters.

Philip's character is a little more difficult to make out, and there are several apparent contradictions. He could certainly play the cheerful *bon viveur*, but he was also sometimes anxious, with a particular fear for his own life. Perhaps this latter was the result of the experiences of his childhood: as the long-awaited, much-desired and – crucially – *only* male heir, he was fussed over, and his health would always have been a cause for concern. We certainly know that his father was frantic with worry when Philip was lost in the forest shortly before the initial planned date of his coronation in the summer of 1179.

There is no doubt that Philip had some traits that would now be considered unpleasant. His lack of care for, and sometimes ill-treatment of, the women in his life had already been demonstrated by this time and would later become a recurring theme. He was also violently anti-Semitic, and had, as one of the earliest acts of his reign, expelled the entire Jewish population from France.[9] In this he was influenced by the contemporary Christian Church, which taught that Jews were evil, along with Muslims, heretics and various others. Philip had a reputation to maintain as *rex christianissimus*, and persecuting members of other religions was deemed wholly acceptable and even laudable – but even so, his actions with regard to the Jews in France were disproportionate and cruel.

Philip appears to have been severely practical, having little interest in the great flowering of courtly literature and poetry that took place during the second half of the twelfth century, and never being noted as a particular patron of the arts, as some other royals were. We may imagine that his education had been accelerated and compressed (Louis VII being aware that Philip was likely to accede as a minor, given his own age) and therefore geared very much towards his future as a king and a political and military leader, with little time for wider or more well-rounded study. He had a basic level of literacy, but seems not to have had any great expertise in the Latin that was the *lingua franca* of the Church and of European politics, needing to work through clerks who could translate for him.[10] Again, this can be attributed to his academic education being cut short as soon as he was crowned at the age of fourteen and immediately took on the responsibilities of governance.

Two things remained constant throughout Philip's life and reign. One was his almost uncanny ability to read his political opponents and to know exactly how best to provoke a reaction from them. And the other was his single-minded, often ruthless, determination to do what was best for France in every circumstance. He wanted to protect his realm, strengthen and enlarge it, and increase its power and influence on the wider international stage. He had apparently been demonstrating this resolve since he was a boy, with Gerald of Wales claiming that as a small child Philip addressed Henry II (who was meeting with Louis VII in Paris) directly with the words:

'I entreat you, O king, on behalf of my father, asking that you love him more than usual, be loyal to him, and cease henceforth from troubling him. For all will learn for certain that whoever presumes to disturb him in this his old age, will constitute me, through God's grace, his most severe avenger, when the place is right and the time comes.'[11]

This was written in hindsight and in the knowledge of Philip's later triumphs, so its seemingly prophetic nature should be taken with a healthy dose of scepticism, but the French king's determination certainly was evident from the moment of his coronation as a teenager. This drive to empower France was the underlying foundation of Philip's lifelong struggle against the Plantagenet dynasty, although the rivalry would change in nature over the years. At this time, 1187, the antagonism was still generally political, with Philip showing some give-and-take about truces and treaties as he sought to move his pieces round the board in quest of the most advantageous position. But later, as we shall see, his hostility towards the ruling family of England turned into a violent personal antipathy.

To be fair to him, it was not only in terms of international prestige that Philip wanted to improve France; there is plenty of evidence that he also thought about effective domestic governance and the well-being of his people. Over the course of his reign he would make significant reforms to royal organisation and financial management, and would take the then-unusual step of recognising and promoting talent even when it was manifested by men of non-noble birth – much of his administration was run by these 'new men' to great effect.

Philip undertook construction work that was to the benefit of others besides himself, including those much lower down the social scale. It was 'in response to the entreaties of many people' that he moved some of the major open-air Paris markets and erected dedicated buildings for them, 'so that when it rained the merchants could sell their wares good and dry, and at night they could keep them safe from attack by robbers'. He also constructed a wall around Paris and ordered the paving of all its streets ('a very difficult but quite necessary project, one which none of his predecessors had dared undertake because of the excessive effort and expense of the endeavor') so that the capital's inhabitants, visitors and traders did not have to traipse through mud.[12]

It was towards the end of 1187 that news of disaster in the Holy Land reached France. The Latin states there, established following the First Crusade of almost 200 years earlier, had been under pressure for some time, but catastrophe had struck on 4 July when Muslim forces led by the Ayyubid sultan, Saladin, had defeated the crusader army at the battle of Hattin, almost wiping it out. Some 200 captured Templar and Hospitaller knights had been executed, other knights and men who survived the battle had been enslaved, Guy of Lusignan, the king of Jerusalem, was imprisoned, and the holy relic of the True Cross had been lost and was now in Muslim hands. Saladin then marched on Jerusalem, and the Holy City – defended by Queen Sybil, Patriarch Heraclius and a mere handful of knights and squires – had fallen to him on 2 October.*

The news was so shocking that Richard took the cross immediately upon hearing it, in November 1187. As crowned kings with greater responsibilities, Philip and Henry had to be a little more circumspect, and in January 1188 they met to discuss the issue at the traditional venue of the elm tree between Gisors and Trie. Few observers expected anything tangible to come of the meeting, but 'contrary to everyone's expectations, through the miraculous agency of the Lord', they both agreed to take the cross.[13]

There are several possible reasons why Philip might have made this somewhat uncharacteristic move, and the true answer is probably a combination of all of them. Firstly, as Capetian king of France he was *rex christianissimus*, 'the most Christian', and refusing to help the Church when it was in such dire need would damage that reputation, to say nothing of the additional loss of face if Henry II were to volunteer while Philip did not. Philip's primary concern was always France, but it would be good for his kingdom's position on the wider international stage if he were to go on crusade; there was a huge swell of public opinion throughout western Europe in favour of the campaign. Plus, of course, he was as conventionally pious as most other kings, brought up firmly within the Roman Christian tradition, so he might well have felt a genuine inclination to do his bit. We must also take into consideration that Philip and Henry II distrusted each other to such an extent that neither of them was willing to commit to being away from his kingdom for a long period of time unless the other went as well. The agreement was reached, therefore, but it is noticeable that both kings took the cross without announcing any immediate plans to travel abroad.

---

* Guy, a knight of Poitou and a younger son of Hugh VIII of Lusignan, was king of Jerusalem by right of marriage to its heiress, Sybil of Jerusalem. She was queen in her own right as she was the daughter of Amalric I and the sister of Baldwin IV ('the leper king'), who had died unmarried and childless. 'Patriarch of Jerusalem' was the highest ecclesiastical position in the Latin states in the Holy Land; Heraclius was a French cleric who had been in the East since the 1160s and had held various positions before being chosen for his present appointment.

It was a promise that would be fulfilled at some unspecified point in the future, although they did set to raising funds straight away.

In the meantime all the familiar squabbles continued, with Philip now appearing to lose ground. Henry had still not arranged the wedding of Richard and Alice, and as Philip could not actually force him to do so, he could only continue to complain about it. Then, in February 1188, he suffered a setback on the question of Brittany when Henry obliged Duchess Constance to marry Ranulf de Blundeville, the earl of Chester and the holder of extensive lands in Normandy, who was a loyal man of his own.* Philip's hold on Richard also began to slip when the latter – his own crusading vow notwithstanding – decided to cause trouble by making another of his family's sporadic attempts to claim the county of Toulouse.† This led the count of Toulouse, Raymond V, to appeal to Philip for aid, as the king was overlord both to him and to Richard. Philip made an attempt to draw Henry II into the conversation, in the hope of causing further familial disagreement, but Henry washed his hands of the whole matter, saying that Richard had acted without his advice or approval and that it was nothing to do with him.[14] Given that Henry therefore appeared to be distancing himself from Richard even further, Philip headed for the county of Berry and the stronghold of Châteauroux once again, confident that this time Henry would not come running with a relief army. He was right: Châteauroux fell to him easily, and the inhabitants of most of Berry indicated that they were prepared to submit to

---

* We might find it understandable that the lady was not too keen on this arrangement, as was all too common, but in this particular case Ranulf did not seem very willing either. The marriage lasted ten years, during which time they hardly saw each other, Constance issued charters in her own name with no reference to Ranulf, and Ranulf stayed away from Brittany and made no real attempt to style himself as duke. The age gap probably didn't help: at the time of the wedding Constance was twenty-six or twenty-seven while Ranulf was only seventeen or eighteen.

† The background to this is complicated and not really part of our story, but it boils down to Raymond V of Toulouse (the current count) and Eleanor of Aquitaine (Richard's mother, through whom he derived his claim) being descended from rival claimants to the county of a century previously. Louis VII and Henry II, when they were Eleanor's husbands, had both raised claims on her behalf, but these had been somewhat half-hearted and probably no more than a useful distraction from other events.

the French king's direct authority rather than being the subject of further armed conflict.

Another meeting between the two kings to discuss this and other matters was scheduled for August 1188 at the elm tree between Gisors and Trie. Philip made his way there with a number of his lords, and it is of note that he now had his domestic situation under such tight control that this group included both the count of Flanders (still Philip of Alsace) and the count of Champagne (now Philip's cousin/nephew Count Henry II, who had succeeded his father upon the latter's death). Philip's proposal was that they should either leave the situation as it now stood – that is, he would retain his recent gains in Berry in return for Richard being able to keep what he had seized of the borderlands of Toulouse – or that they should swap them back. Either of these outcomes would involve Henry II making a concession, so this would be a test of how far Philip had progressed in the last few years. Unfortunately, he was to find that Henry had lost none of his famed cunning.

The elm tree itself was huge and ancient, its trunk so wide that four men with their arms outstretched could scarcely encircle it, and it cast shade over a wide area. By the time Philip arrived, he found that Henry had got there first and that he and his sizeable entourage had taken up their position in the shade, leaving Philip and the French to stand for three consecutive days in the hot sun. Petty, perhaps, but effective: the attempts at negotiation were bad-tempered in the extreme, and ended with Henry declaring that he would not cede anything whatsoever. To emphasise his point, he indicated the enormous elm: 'Just as this tree cannot be split or uprooted, so the French cannot take anything from me. When I have lost this tree, then I will lose my lands.' The talks were over. Henry left and, in a gesture of frustration that showed he had not yet mastered the maturity and ability to conquer his emotions that would be his future hallmark, Philip had the tree cut down.[15]

This failed attempt at negotiation was a setback for the French king, but he had his standard tactic to fall back on, so he reminded Richard once more that Henry II had still not clarified his succession plans. He encouraged Richard to demand that his father name him publicly as heir before he or any of them set off on crusade, no doubt pointing out that without such a declaration there remained a possibility that Henry would bypass Richard and favour John.

This worked. At yet another meeting in November 1188 (this time at Bonsmoulins in south-eastern Normandy), Henry was irritated by Richard and Philip arriving together, and things went downhill from there. Richard demanded that Henry confirm him as his heir in public, and Henry declined to do so. And it was at this point that Philip was rewarded for all his months of patient persuasion and pressure, as Rigord tells us: 'For this reason, Richard, count of Poitou, clearly angered, turned away from his father and went over to the most Christian king of the Franks. And in the presence of his father, he rendered homage to King Philip and confirmed the treaty by oath.' This gesture from Richard was both provocative and insulting to his father, who could do nothing but look on. The significance of the act was emphasised by the fact that chroniclers from both sides of the Channel agreed on the precise nature of what happened: Rigord's account is supported by Gerald of Wales, who agrees that Richard did homage to Philip 'there before his father's eyes', and Roger of Wendover, who notes that Richard's homage was offered 'before them all'.[16]

This time Philip seemed to have caused a definitive split in the Plantagenet family, and he was ready to take action to knock his first king off the board.

The moves towards the final checkmate began in early 1189, when Philip and Richard launched raids on some of Henry's border-lands. Henry was by this time ill, and he sought negotiations rather than springing into armed action as he normally would. Philip and Richard believed this was merely a ruse, and they continued their campaigning. This did not meet with the approval of the Church, which was worried about the crusade that all three men had promised to go on — as allies — and which now looked further away than ever. Emperor Frederick Barbarossa, who had also taken the cross, had already set off, but there was no chance of the kings of France and England doing the same while they were still at odds over what the Church considered a secondary concern.

Four archbishops were sent to mediate, two from each side: Baldwin of Forde, the archbishop of Canterbury, and Walter de Coutances, the archbishop of Rouen, representing England and Normandy; and Philip's uncle William Whitehands, the archbishop of Reims, and Henry de Sully, the archbishop of Bourges (in Berry), for France. They were all present at some discussions that took place at Whitsun in 1189. Philip's demands were still the same – the marriage of Richard to Alice, Richard to be publicly declared his father's heir – but he and Richard now added a new one, a requirement that John should also go on crusade. Neither of them trusted John enough to be left to his own devices while the rest of them were away. If Henry agreed to all this, then Philip would restore the lands he had taken in Berry. However, Henry did not, and he still stubbornly refused to be drawn into a public acknowledgement of Richard as his heir.

All this merely played into Philip's hands. The French king almost certainly did not believe that Henry would really disinherit Richard in favour of John: Henry did not get on with his elder remaining son very well, but when it came down to it he would not be able to bring himself to overrule proper hereditary succession. After all, a long campaign on exactly this point of principle was the only reason he was on the English throne himself.[*] Philip was astute enough to realise that Henry was just burying his head in the sand, unwilling to recognise the truth of what must eventually

---

* Henry II's mother, Empress Matilda, had been the only surviving legitimate child of Henry I, and his publicly designated heir. Following her father's death, Matilda was usurped by her cousin Stephen of Blois (the son of Henry I's sister), who became king and who intended to pass the crown to his own son. Matilda – and, when he was old enough, her son Henry – had fought a nineteen-year war to reclaim the throne on the basis that they were Henry I's true hereditary heirs. Henry II was thus not likely to overturn a lifetime's devotion to the principle of hereditary succession even if he preferred one son to another.

happen – and he was also well aware that Henry had not made any public declaration in favour of John, either.

There was only one winner in this situation, and it was Philip. He had so effectively disseminated the rumour about John, and persuaded Richard of the truth of it, that the only way Henry could deny it was to make a public declaration in favour of Richard. This he was determined at all costs not to do – having learned the lesson of crowning his eldest son too soon, and also because he hoped to keep Richard under control by prolonging the suspense – so the rumours ran unchecked, and Philip could watch as Henry mired himself more and more deeply in trouble of his own making.

After this unsuccessful conference broke up, Henry retired to Le Mans, the city where he had been born, for a rest in an attempt to overcome the illness that he probably already knew would be his last. Philip and Richard would allow him no respite, though, attacking and capturing La Ferté, about 25 miles to the north-east; then, on 12 June, they turned on Le Mans itself.

Henry could see them coming, and he ordered his men to set fire to the city suburbs to slow the French army down while he gathered his knights and his energy to retreat in the opposite direction. But the wind changed, and in the heat of summer the fire was blown very quickly into the main city, which was soon ablaze. Henry had to beat a very hasty retreat and had cause to regret his actions:

> When the king had fled about two miles from the city, pursued by the French and by his son, turning around on a certain hill from the top of which he was able to see the burning city, he uttered these apostate words: 'O God, since today, to heap up my confusion and increase my disgrace, you have so vilely taken from me the city that I have loved most on earth, namely, the one in which I was born and raised, where my father lies buried.'[17]

Whether or not Henry had any sympathy for those whose homes were burning – either inadvertently because of the wind or due to his direct order – does not seem to have been of any particular interest, although we might spare them a thought.

Henry did not attempt to rally and fight; instead he headed south to Chinon, his ancestral home in Anjou. By the time he got there he was so ill that he was bedridden for a fortnight. He was only fifty-six but had spent almost his entire life in the saddle and on the move, traversing and re-traversing his vast domains in an attempt to keep control of them all at once, and this had taken its toll on his health. Kings, and especially kings with numerous rebellious vassals, tended not to live very long, and mid-fifties was actually about par for the course.* Henry, in particular, was famed for 'torment[ing] his body with excessive hardship [...] he allowed himself no peace or rest [...] passing his days restlessly [...] he accelerated the other complaints of his body, if no other then certainly the mother and minister of many evils, old age'.[18]

While Henry was indisposed, Philip overran much of the rest of Maine, helped by the fact that many of Henry II's men there could see the way the tide was turning and knew that Richard would soon be their lord and king. Then the two allies moved into Touraine, and Tours itself fell to them on 3 July. This finally forced Henry out of bed, and there was a meeting the next day. We do not know exactly what was afflicting him, but it involved a high fever, and the various descriptions of him having an ulcer, and of pain spreading through his feet and legs, which were first red and then black, indicate that he might have been suffering from dry gangrene, which was incurable.

Richard had no sympathy for his father: 'Count Richard had no pity whatever for him, indeed he told the King of France that he was feigning.'[19] However, when the kings met face to face Philip was shocked at Henry's appearance:

---

* Of the four previous kings of England since the Conquest, Henry I had made it into his late sixties, but he was an outlier: the others (William the Conqueror, William Rufus and Stephen) had all died in their forties or fifties. It was a similar story in France, where Louis VII had made it to sixty but his three immediate predecessors had all died in their early to mid-fifties.

All the high-ranking men present there could well see that King Henry [...] had been suffering from a very serious illness. The King of France fully realised this, for he could not help but do so, and he said: 'My lord, we well know that there is no question whatsoever of your standing.' He therefore ordered a cloak to be brought, but Henry countermanded the order and said that he had no wish to be seated, that what he wanted was to hear and see what they intended to ask of him.[20]

This personal sympathy for Henry's physical condition did not prevent Philip from pressing full advantage: 'The king of the French, seeing that God and good fortune had now delivered his enemy into his hands, was unwilling to hear a word of peace until the king of the English had placed himself in all things completely in his mercy.'[21] To a modern eye it might seem somewhat tasteless of Philip to take advantage of a dying man in this way, but medieval kings had to be ruthless, or they did not last long. Any failure by Philip to do so would have been interpreted as unacceptable weakness.

Philip reiterated all his previous demands, and this time the weakened Henry had no choice but to agree. He would perform homage to Philip for all his continental lands, name Richard as his sole heir, arrange the wedding of Richard and Alice, and would pay Philip an indemnity of 20,000 marks against the expenses he had incurred during the military campaigns that had brought them to this point.*[22] 'The king of England places himself wholly under the counsel of the king of France,' ran the agreement, 'so that whatsoever the latter shall think proper to be done, the king of England will fulfil without gainsaying.'[23]

Henry was taken back to Chinon in a litter, only to discover that his beloved and trusted John had also conspired against him, which was the final straw. He died on 6 July 1189, just two days

---

* A mark was a unit of accounting (not an actual coin) worth two-thirds of a pound sterling or 13s 4d. Henry's promise of 20,000 marks therefore equated to £13,333 6s 8d, roughly half the average annual income of the English crown at that point.

after his last meeting with Philip. Henry's last words were apparently 'Shame, shame on a conquered king!', but there was also another story about him in circulation:

> When Henry II, as a boy, had been brought to the court of Louis, king of France, and Bernard, abbot of Clairvaux, of good memory, happened to be there at that time, the king asked the abbot what he thought of the boy, who was expecting to inherit such a great breadth of lands and kingdoms. The holy man looked at the boy, who happened to have glanced around and was fixing the gaze of his eyes on the ground at that point, and answered as if by a prophetic spirit: 'From the devil he came and to the devil he will go.'[24]

Abbot Bernard's choice of words was based on an old tale about the counts of Anjou, Henry's paternal family, being descended from the devil. The Plantagenets had been happy for this legend to remain in the public consciousness while Henry seemed all-powerful, but now it came back to kick him as he lay in agony and lapsed in and out of consciousness. There was no question that his death, when it came, was due to illness, but his condition had been exacerbated by the actions of those around him, including Philip. William the Breton noted that Henry had been 'defeated and pushed towards his death by his own children', but Rigord, closer to events at this stage, was clear that he had 'ruled successfully in every respect up until the time of Philip, king of the Franks'.[25]

Philip had crushed his most powerful vassal, and sent Henry back to the devil. But he had little time or leisure to celebrate: in ridding himself of one adversary he had merely created another, and the new king of England was going to be an entirely different prospect.

PART II

Richard I

1189–99

3

Crusading Kings and Rivals

Philip might already have been planning his next move, but the formalities still needed to be observed: on 20 July 1189 Richard was invested as duke of Normandy, and two days later Philip accepted his homage for the duchy. At the same time the two men renewed the terms of the final agreement that had been made between Philip and Henry II before the latter's death, with the exception of the now-unnecessary clause about Henry naming Richard his heir.

Richard then travelled to England to be crowned. This relieved Philip from the tedium of his company for a while, but the French king kept a careful eye on Richard's initial acts in his new role in order to guard his own interests. Two things were of immediate interest, both concerning Plantagenet family relationships. The first was that Richard released his mother from her captivity, which meant that there was now a new (or, at least, new to Philip) player on the scene. Eleanor of Aquitaine had been in captivity for sixteen years, since Philip was a small boy, so he knew of her only through hearsay – but even this was enough for him to realise that he would need to be on his toes when dealing with her. She might now be in her late sixties, but she was at least as clever as he was and had a great deal more international political experience. Pertinent to Philip's interest was the fact that he had no chance of ever turning Eleanor and Richard against each other, as he had done with other members of the family, so he would have to find another way to deal with them.

The most promising option for creating further conflict between the Plantagenets was, of course, John, and Philip paid close attention to the way in which the brothers interacted at this early stage of Richard's reign. On the surface, the initial indications were not promising for him: Richard confirmed John as count of Mortain (a subsidiary Norman title, generally kept within the incumbent duke's immediate family), and loaded him down with honours in England. John received the counties of Derby, Nottingham, Cornwall, Devon, Somerset and Dorset as well as other individual castles, and was married to a rich heiress. But appearances could be deceiving, and there was useful intelligence for Philip in all of this. John's new gains did not form a coherent enough bloc to give him much real power. They were all in England, well away from Richard's continental lands, and there was nothing for John in France besides the confirmation of the minor Mortain title his father had always meant him to have – no Aquitaine or Anjou, as might have been the case. Finally, there was no declaration that John was Richard's designated heir, either to the English throne or to any of his other lands.

The heiress John married was Isabelle of Gloucester, to whom he had been betrothed since he was nine years old. She was countess of Gloucester in her own right, and had for a long time been the means by which Henry II intended to provide for his landless youngest son. However, John had never been keen to go through with the wedding, as he was holding out for something better; in obliging him to marry, therefore, Richard was actually *curtailing* John's ambitions, not widening them – John would henceforward have no chance of making a prestigious international match. He would, it was true, now have control of the vast Gloucester estates, but again this was very much a domestic position, not an international one. Moreover, John and Isabelle would not have much time to produce heirs, as she was already around thirty years of age, some six or seven years older than her new husband.[1] This all suited Richard very well, and he pushed the wedding through on 29 August despite the objections of Baldwin of Forde, the archbishop of Canterbury, who said that the couple were too closely related – as indeed they were, according to Church law.* Philip stored all this information up for future use, adding to his existing knowledge that John was perennially dissatisfied, had been in conflict with Richard before, and had not been above betraying his father when he thought he might benefit.

Richard was crowned king of England on 3 September 1189. But his new realm was not at the top of his current list of priorities, and he would not stay there long. Indeed, his immediate reaction was little more than seeing England as a cash cow to finance his crusade, and he marshalled the full resources of the crown for the project as well as raising more money by slightly dubious means. He sold off lands and offices, and seized the wealth of those who had died intestate: 'The king most obligingly unburdened all those whose money was a burden to them […] joking one day with his companions who were standing by, he made this jest: "If I could have found a buyer I would have sold London itself."'[2]

All of this meant that Richard was now able to expedite his crusade plans, and so was Philip. The spirit of alliance and goodwill which they had previously enjoyed, however, was already waning now that Richard was a king, and therefore Philip's peer and principal antagonist rather than merely a tool to be used against Henry II. They met at Nonancourt on the Norman–French border on 30 December 1189, and the agreement they reached, while ostensibly friendly, already carried overtones of mutual suspicion:

> I, Philip, king of the French, will keep good faith with Richard king of the English, as my friend and ally for life, for limb, and worldly honour; and I, Richard, king of the English, promise to keep the same good faith with the king of the French as my lord

* Marriages were prohibited up to the seventh degree of affinity, and sometimes such distant relationships involved tracing a tangled skein of connections, but in this particular case the consanguinity was close, obvious and a matter of public knowledge. John and Isabelle were second cousins, because their fathers had been first cousins; John's paternal grandmother (Empress Matilda) and Isabelle's paternal grandfather (Earl Robert of Gloucester) had been half-siblings.

and friend, for life, and for limb. We also agree to lend aid each
of us, if necessary, in defending the territories of the other as
zealously as if they were his own possessions.[3]

The territories of Richard's that Philip promised to defend if
necessary were extensive: Henry II's original planned division
between his sons had never come about, and in the end Richard
had inherited the lot, a span of 900 miles from northern England
down to southern Aquitaine, and everything in between. It did not
escape Philip's notice that it would be an extremely difficult task
for Richard to control it all, even if he spent his entire time riding
from one part of his domains to another, as Henry had done, to
the detriment of his health. And exerting such control would be
almost impossible if Richard were not in his domains at all, as was
now going to be the case, so Philip had various opportunities in
front of him.

In contrast to Richard's unmarried and childless state,
Philip's family situation was looking positive at this point, and
in a world of dynastic politics this was a significant advantage
the French king had over his rival. Queen Isabelle, now aged
nineteen, was pregnant again, and an addition to the nursery to
keep the two-year-old Louis company would be very welcome.
But, tragically, this was not to be, as Philip was to find out
in mid-March 1190 even as he sat in a meeting with Richard
discussing crusading plans: 'While the kings were speaking,
planning the journey, there came a messenger, in great haste.
With his head bowed he came before the king of France and
said that the Queen had died.'[4]

Isabelle had gone into what seems to have been a premature
labour, and had died in childbirth. Moreover, in the worst of all
possible worlds, she had been delivered of twin boys who had
both also perished. At this time childbirth was incredibly dangerous – a mother in labour had a greater chance of dying than a
knight in battle, and there was no armour she could don to protect
herself – and labouring with twins was particularly risky, given
the added complications and the fact that the births were often

premature and the babies small.* Isabelle had been young, healthy and well nourished, and had already survived one confinement, but all of this counted for nothing, and she had not lived to see her twentieth birthday.

This was a wrenching personal and political blow for Philip, but despite the fact that he was said by one observer to be 'so completely devastated that he was on the verge of deciding to abandon his plans for the pilgrimage', his position meant that he could not.[5] Instead he made elaborate arrangements for Isabelle's funeral, for the construction of her tomb and for priests to say perpetual Masses for her soul, and carried on with his crusading plans.

Somewhere along the way, the idea that John would have to travel to the Holy Land with Richard and Philip had been dropped. The most likely reason for this is that the realisation was finally dawning on Richard that it might be better for him if John were not allowed to spend too much time in Philip's company. Leaving him in England, therefore, was the better option, even allowing for the trouble he might cause there. At least their mother would be able to keep an eye on him, as she was to be Richard's regent in his absence. Philip and Richard would therefore travel without John, and once they were in the Holy Land they would join up with the existing forces of the crusader states, and also with Emperor Frederick Barbarossa, who had already been en route for some while, taking the slow overland journey.

On 24 June 1190 – the Feast of St John the Baptist and therefore an auspicious date – Philip received his pilgrim's scrip and staff from Archbishop William Whitehands at Saint-Denis, as well as the *oriflamme*, the sacred war banner of the kingdom of France. Philip clearly did not need either a staff to aid walking or a scrip (a type

---

* There are no recorded instances of twins in the Capetian dynasty before 1190, but they occur relatively frequently afterwards, so perhaps it was Isabelle who introduced some kind of genetic predisposition. Sadly, being a twin continued to be extremely hazardous, and most of them died at or shortly after birth. It was not until the fifteenth century that any of those born into the French royal family even survived their first year, and only in the eighteenth century that any (in this case the twin eldest daughters of Louis XV, who were born in 1727) reached adulthood.

of satchel) to carry his belongings, but they were the universally recognised symbols of pilgrimage, so taking them up marked the official start of his crusade.

In planning to leave his kingdom for an uncertain length of time, Philip did not forget to organise governance arrangements, and he drew up a very detailed testament, because 'it is the duty of kings to plan for the well-being of their subjects in all ways, and to place public good before their own'.[6] France was to be left in the hands of his mother, Queen Adela, and her brother Archbishop William; the two of them would also take guardianship of Louis, who was far too young to accompany Philip abroad. The testament contained comprehensive instructions on how they were to dispense justice, and noted specifically that 'the queen and the archbishop will report to us three times each year concerning the state and affairs of our kingdom'.

Philip's son Louis was formally designated his heir, to be guarded and guided in the event of Philip's death 'until he reaches the age when he can, with God's counsel, govern his realm'. But Philip did not specify any further line of succession; and, given the complications that would have arisen if anything had happened to him *and* to Louis, this is perhaps surprising. Philip had no brothers – the next most obvious solution in the event of a king leaving no son – and also no daughters, so the question of whether a man could become king by right of marriage to an heiress (as was the case in Jerusalem at this very time) was moot. Philip did have other near relations, though, so it is likely that the question of inheritance through the female line would raise its head in some form. The two principal candidates would be Count Henry II of Champagne (the king's senior nephew, as the elder son of Philip's eldest sister), and Count Robert II of Dreux (Philip's first cousin, as the eldest son of the late Robert I, who had been Louis VII's brother), with the former more closely related to Philip but the latter being able to claim descent through an exclusively male Capetian line.

It is puzzling that Philip should have made no pronouncement on the subject of the extended succession, given his general care for the well-being of France, and we can only speculate on his reasoning. Perhaps he genuinely cared for the future only in terms of himself and his son, and would leave France to take its chances if they were both gone? Given what we know of his rule so far, and the meticulous provisions in his testament, this seems an unlikely scenario. Or perhaps Philip simply could not bring himself to believe that he would die abroad – his father, after all, had returned safely from his crusade, as had many other French lords, some of them more than once. But we do know that he was often fearful for his life, so he might not have considered himself invincible despite his youth and good health. The most probable reason, therefore, is caution: that Philip was reluctant to name a secondary heir in case it gave that man ideas and he attempted to supplant Louis while Philip was abroad. Death by 'ambitious adult male relative' was not unknown for small royal children, after all.

As it happens, both Henry II of Champagne and Robert II of Dreux were joining the crusade (indeed, they had already departed), so Philip would be able to keep a firm eye on any potential threat to his heir. In fact, virtually every adult male of high rank in France was joining the campaign, which had the advantage that he could keep them close, but might also have been very dangerous – if matters went awry it was not beyond the realms of possibility that almost every county in France would soon have a minor or inexperienced ruler.

Philip and Richard met up at Vézelay (in Burgundy, about 120 miles south-east of Paris), and there they 'concluded a treaty of mutual security: that each would keep faith with the other, and that they would share equally everything they acquired by right of war'.[7] One of the contemporary crusading chronicles gives a description of the scene outside the town that was evocative and – to start with – optimistic:

The endless throng seemed beyond numbering. The mountains and valleys were filled with pitched pavilions, and all around far and wide the face of the earth was covered with tents. The camp covered the cultivated fields of the plain so that from a distance it looked like a new city, with the most impressive variety of pavilions in different styles and shapes, divided into different colours.

There you would have seen a martial band of youth: assembled from various regions, fit and ready for war. It seemed that they would easily master the whole breadth of the globe,[*] overcome the countries of every nation [...] You would have reckoned that no rough terrain, no fierce enemy could defeat them, and that they would never give way.

But the same writer ends his description on an ominous note, and one that would prove to be prescient, because all his hoped-for success would only happen 'as long as they supported each other in one mind with united strength and mutual assistance':

For although an army may glory in its great numbers, be protected by its weapons and burning with passion, if disputes arise within it or friends fall out it is routed and destroyed [...] when the common bond is broken it is completely overwhelmed, torn to pieces by its own members.[8]

From Vézelay the two kings travelled together as far as Lyon, publicly emphasising their amicable relationship: 'They frequently paid their respects to each other with great munificence, showing each other mutual honour and esteem [...] They completed their daily stages with eagerness and joy.'[9] They did not intend to remain together on the whole journey, however: the unwieldy size of the joint host meant that it was more practical to take different routes and to embark from different ports. Richard headed for Marseille to meet his ships, while Philip, who did not have a fleet of his own, crossed the border into the Empire to make his way to Genoa, where he had arranged to hire transport vessels.

It was at some point on this landward part of his journey that Philip received some momentous and unwelcome news: Emperor

---

* Yes: despite the enduringly irritating modern myth, medieval people were perfectly well aware that the world was round.

Frederick was dead. He had set out with his army as long ago as May 1189, and had been making solid, if slow, progress overland, but on 10 June 1190 he had drowned while crossing a river in Cilicia (in modern-day Anatolia, in Turkey). This was not a catastrophe for the Empire itself – Barbarossa was in his late sixties and had five adult sons, the eldest of whom, Henry of Hohenstaufen, was already crowned king of the Romans* and acting as regent while the Emperor was on crusade – but it would have a profound effect on both the progress and the prestige of the crusade. For now the imperial army was continuing on its way under the command of Barbarossa's second son, Frederick, the duke of Swabia.[10]

This turn of events gave Philip something to think about as he arrived in Genoa, paid 5,850 marks of silver for his passage and that of his army, and took ship.†[11] His destination was Messina on the island of Sicily, where he had arranged to rendezvous with Richard.

The kingdom of Sicily (which, at this time, comprised the southern half of mainland Italy as well as the island itself) had been the scene of much upheaval during the past year. King William II had died in November 1189, aged only thirty-five and leaving no children; and as he also had no siblings, nieces or nephews, his designated heir had been his paternal aunt, Constance of Hauteville.‡ Her

---

* 'King of the Romans', sometimes also referred to as 'king of Germany', was a subsidiary title of the Holy Roman Empire, and normally conferred on the current Emperor's designated heir. Henry of Hohenstaufen (who would become Emperor Henry VI when he was crowned by the pope) was twenty-four, the same age as Philip Augustus, and had been king of the Romans for twenty years, so there was no doubt about the imperial succession.

† As we noted earlier, a mark was worth two-thirds of a pound sterling or 13s 4d. Philip's payment of 5,850 marks was therefore equal to 3,900 pounds sterling, or slightly more in Parisian pounds, as the two currencies did not quite match. This was a substantial proportion of his annual crown income, but he had raised additional money in recent years from his confiscation of property from France's Jewish population and via a crusade tax known as the 'Saladin tithe'.

‡ William's paternal grandfather, Roger II of Sicily, had married three times and fathered a large number of children over a period of more than thirty-five years. Constance was his youngest and

claim was not universally supported by the nobility, because she happened to be married to Henry of Hohenstaufen, king of the Romans and now the Emperor-designate, and the lords feared that the kingdom of Sicily would be subsumed into the Empire, ceasing to exist in its own right.

Amid this uncertainty, a nobleman named Tancred of Lecce had staked a claim. He was William II's first cousin, the son of the late king's paternal uncle, and thus a member of the royal Hauteville house in the male line, but he was illegitimate and therefore would not normally be an acceptable candidate for the throne. He was, however, a military commander of great experience who enjoyed the support of many of the nobles, and he was on the spot in Sicily while his rivals were hundreds of miles away in Germany and unable to leave it while the crusade was in progress. Tancred had seized the throne and been crowned king of Sicily early in 1190.

This might not have caused too many problems for the French and English crusaders, who were merely intending to stop off in Sicily on their way to the Holy Land, but there was an additional complicating factor. William II's widow had vocally supported Constance's claim to the throne, and had then been deprived of her dower lands and incomes by Tancred before being thrown into prison ... and she was Joanna, the youngest daughter of Henry II of England, and Richard the Lionheart's sister.[12]

Philip was well aware of the delicate situation as he docked in Messina, the island's second city, on 16 September 1190, and the best thing he could do for now was to keep his head down. He accepted Tancred's offer of accommodation in the palace there and settled in, because he and Richard had sworn that whoever arrived first would wait for the other rather than setting off for the Holy Land on his own.

Richard arrived a week later. Philip proposed that they should leave straight away, but Richard's family pride was having none of it. He demanded Joanna's release and the return of her dower, added a few additional and extravagant financial demands of his own, and

only surviving child, and although she was William II's aunt, she was actually younger than he was.

then, as a warning to Tancred (who was in his capital of Palermo, 120 miles westwards), he let his troops run riot through Messina in an orgy of violence, murder, rape and looting. Fortunately for his alliance with Philip and for the crusade, he made sure the carnage stopped short of 'the quarters of the French around their king's lodging, which he spared out of respect for his lord the king'.[13]

Tancred released Joanna almost straight away and then, after some wrangling, made Richard a large cash offer in lieu of Joanna's lands, which Richard accepted and pocketed for his crusade expenses without reference to his sister, who was thereby left penniless and dependent on him. As part of the deal Richard formally recognised Tancred as king of Sicily, and consented to the marriage of one of Tancred's daughters to Arthur of Brittany, to whom he referred, according to Roger of Howden, as 'our nephew, and, if we shall chance to die without issue, our heir'.[14] Philip had nothing to do with these negotiations or their outcomes, and he was far too astute to recognise Tancred officially when this might antagonise the much more powerful new Emperor, whose lands shared a long border with France. He therefore declined the offer of another of Tancred's daughters as a wife for Louis and stayed out of the agreement. As it transpired, he was right to do so, and both of these arrangements of Richard's (recognising Tancred as king of Sicily, and Arthur as his heir to England) were to be beneficial for Philip later on.

In the meantime, Joanna arrived in Messina, and Richard immediately offered her as a bride to Philip. In theory this might have been a suitable match — the widowed king and the widowed queen, almost exactly the same age and from families who were in alliance with each other — but nothing came of the idea. Possibly this was because Philip was not personally inclined to marry again so soon after losing Isabelle, but more probably because there was not much political advantage in him becoming Richard's brother-in-law via marriage to Joanna when he was already scheduled to become so via Richard's marriage to Alice. Philip would be better served by waiting until his crusade was over and then seeking out a different international match that would widen his diplomatic circle of alliances.

By now it was November and the seas were treacherous, so the kings were obliged to overwinter on Sicily. They spent Christmas together in Messina, and Philip amused himself during early 1191 by insinuating to Tancred that Richard's word was not to be trusted, and then watching the fall-out. As spring approached, however, Philip was impatient to get going and began to press for a swift departure. He had been away from France for more than half a year already and had not even reached the Holy Land yet, and both his and Richard's troops were getting bored, having little to do except eat, drink, gamble and cause trouble with each other and with the local population. But Richard continued to stall.

Eventually the reason for the delay became clear: Richard had finally dropped all pretence that he was going to marry Philip's long-suffering sister Alice, and he had already contracted another betrothal, with Berengaria, the daughter of King Sancho VI the Wise of Navarre. She was even now on her way to Sicily, being escorted by Eleanor of Aquitaine, and Richard would not leave the island until they arrived, crusade or no crusade. He, of course, had been away from his kingdom even longer than Philip had been from his, but he was not in nearly so much of a hurry to get back to England as Philip was to return to France.

Was this a bombshell? On the face of it, yes – and it was certainly a massive insult to Philip's family honour. But Philip was able to react and reprioritise so quickly that we cannot help wondering if it really was news to him. Richard had supposedly been demanding for years that his father should let him marry Alice, implying that it was the old king's fault that he could not, so once he was king himself he could have arranged the wedding straight away if he had been so inclined. But he had not done so, and someone as politically sharp as Philip knew how to interpret this. So he might well have been forewarned, and upon hearing Richard's new intentions he made no fuss at all about the breaking of the betrothal. Instead he turned his attention to gaining the greatest advantage he could out of the situation, giving Richard 'leave to marry whomsoever he should choose' but in return stipulating for the return not only of his sister but also the Vexin, which was to have been her dowry.[15] He would also get 10,000 marks in cash (2,000 per year for five years) that Richard agreed to pay in return for being released from the betrothal.

Despite his apparent acquiescence, this was a political humiliation for Philip and an affront to his family. He had matured enough, since the unfortunate episode of the elm tree, to be able to swallow his pride and anger in the short term in order to function diplomatically, but he would not forget this experience. 'From this moment,' says the French chronicler Rigord, accurately, 'disharmony, envy, and enmity began to grow between the two kings', and we can pinpoint this as the juncture at which Philip's political hostility to the Plantagenets began to turn into outright personal dislike.[16]

By March 1191 Philip could wait no longer to continue on the crusade, and he also had the added incentive that he wanted to be away from Sicily before Berengaria and Eleanor arrived. He and Richard had previously sworn that they would go to the Holy Land together, but the English king's dawdling was an acceptable excuse to break that promise, so Philip decided to leave without him — and could keep the moral high ground as he did so, saying that he was prioritising his sacred crusading vow while Richard was dealing with merely personal matters. He only just made it in time to avoid an awkward encounter: he sailed away from Messina on the morning of 30 March, only hours before the women's ship arrived at the same port.

Philip's thoughts, as Sicily disappeared over the horizon, were not very kindly towards his supposed ally, and the relationship was destined to deteriorate beyond repair once they reached the Holy Land.

Philip's voyage was made without incident, and he arrived at the great port city of Acre, which was in Muslim hands, on 20 April 1191. Acre was currently the crusaders' main target, because it was a vital hub of connection and supply that would need to be under Christian control before any attempt could be made to recover Jerusalem, which was further inland. The combined forces of the Latin kingdom of Jerusalem and visiting crusaders had been besieging Acre since August 1189 – to little effect so far, which was why the fresh impetus provided by the armies of England, France and the Empire was so eagerly awaited.[17]

Before we begin our story of Philip and Richard's sojourn in the Holy Land, we need to take a moment to acknowledge the biases of the eye-witness sources on which we rely most heavily at this point. As we might expect (and as we have seen previously), French chroniclers tended to portray Philip very positively, while English and Norman writers did the same for Richard. While the two kings were in Europe we could balance the accounts of all of these chroniclers against each other, but this is more difficult for the period of the crusade. Neither of the notable contemporary French writers, Rigord and William the Breton, was in the Holy Land, meaning that they wrote their accounts of the campaign later on and via second-hand testimony. The writers who *were* there, and who wrote detailed eye-witness testimony, were English or Anglo-Norman, and all of them were avowed fans of Richard's who sought to portray him in the best possible light – and, by extension, Philip in the worst. Richard's achievements were thus amplified while Philip's were minimised or ignored altogether.

Sometimes these writers are overt in their biases, as a few representative quotes demonstrate: 'The king of France was jealous of the king of England's success. He found his noble character unbearable, and regretted having had no part in the glory which the other had won through his own sweat and superior qualities'; 'the king of France was still seething and eaten up with envy over King Richard's noble character and success'; 'when Richard came the king of the French was extinguished and made nameless, even as the moon loses its light at sunrise'; Philip 'effected nothing' at Acre 'as he was awaiting the arrival of the king of England'.[18] We therefore need to look more carefully at the events that took place at Acre in 1191 in order to form a clearer and less prejudiced view than the one the English chroniclers sought to put forward.

Philip's arrival was a momentous occasion for him personally: the Holy Land was a place he had heard spoken of in awe for all his life, where God had taken human form and walked upon the earth and where the Crucifixion and Resurrection had happened. No twelfth-century Christian could fail to be moved by setting foot there. The part of the land he had arrived in, however, did not look particularly holy at the moment. The siege had been going on for so long that the crusaders were living outside Acre on a semi-permanent basis, and the first thing that met Philip's eye was a large, crowded and not particularly sanitary encampment some distance from the walls.[19] Two epidemics had already swept through it, in October 1190 and January 1191, wiping out large numbers of combatants and non-combatants alike.

At this time, April 1191, the crusading army was under the command of Count Henry II of Champagne, who had taken over from the rather ineffectual Guy of Lusignan almost as soon as he arrived from France in 1190. Henry was popular, and his complex family tree helped him in political terms: he was not only Philip's nephew but also Richard's, as his mother, Marie of Champagne, was a half-sister to both kings.* Numerous other French lords were also already at Acre, having set off earlier than Philip as they were not bound by his personal agreement to wait for Richard. In addition to Henry of Champagne, they included Philip's maternal uncle, Stephen of Sancerre; his paternal cousins Robert II of Dreux, Bishop Philip of Beauvais and Peter II of Courtenay; Hugh III, the duke of Burgundy; and Count Philip of Flanders. Another maternal uncle, Theobald V of Blois, had died in the epidemic of January 1191, and his men were now being commanded by his teenaged son and successor, Louis.

The German army had also arrived by this time, but it was a sad remnant of less than one-tenth of the force that had originally set out. They had suffered some losses on their overland trek and

---

* Marie, as we will recall, was the daughter of Louis VII (Philip's father) and Eleanor of Aquitaine (Richard's mother). She had one full sister and eleven half-siblings – seven maternal and four paternal – from her parents' later marriages.

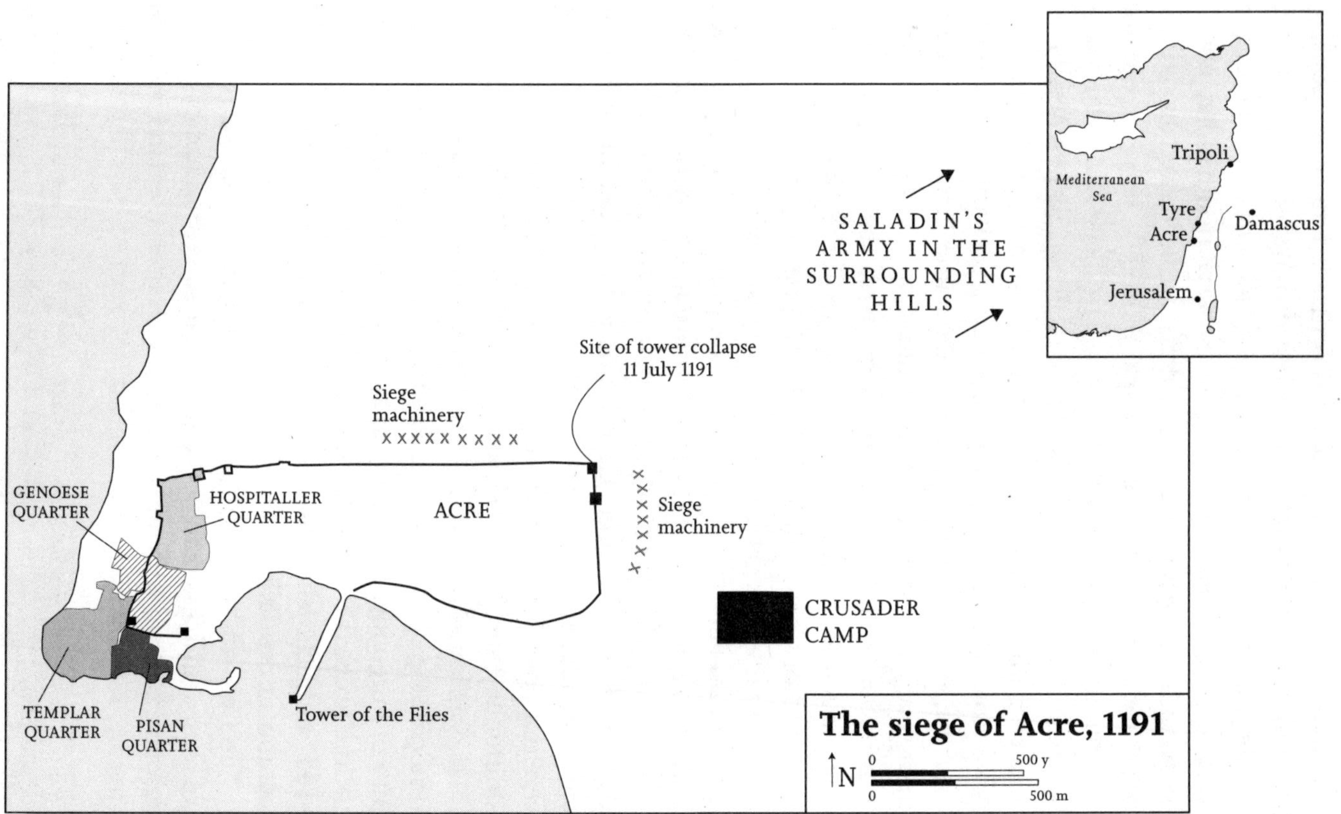

Mediterranean
Sea
Tripoli
Tyre
Acre
Damascus
Jerusalem
SALADIN'S
ARMY IN THE
SURROUNDING
HILLS
Site of tower collapse
11 July 1191
Siege
machinery
Siege
machinery
GENOESE
QUARTER
HOSPITALLER
QUARTER
ACRE
TEMPLAR
QUARTER
PISAN
QUARTER
Tower of the Flies
CRUSADER
CAMP
The siege of Acre, 1191
N
0   500 y
0   500 m

then many more in the outbreaks of disease at Acre, the casualties including Frederick, the duke of Swabia, Barbarossa's son. What was left of the imperial army was commanded by Leopold V, the duke of Austria, who was later (and completely inadvertently) to cause King Richard to have a temper tantrum that would have far-reaching consequences.

The longer-term Christian population of the kingdom of Jerusalem had also suffered numerous fatalities, among them Queen Sybil and both of her young children. This was not only a tragic loss for the royal dynasty but also a constitutional problem, because Sybil had been queen in her own right. Her hereditary heir was her one remaining sister, Isabella of Jerusalem, who was married to a nobleman named Conrad of Montferrat, but Sybil's widower Guy of Lusignan was trying to hold on to power.

Philip thus had both diplomatic and military issues to face upon his arrival, and he wasted no time. He came down on the side of Isabella and Conrad, and formed an effective military alliance with the latter which provided some very welcome momentum. Richard, predictably, favoured Guy, and made this known even before he arrived in the Holy Land.

Philip already had plenty of siege experience, and he brought it all to bear now. He rode around the outside of Acre to assess its strengths and weaknesses, and had siege machinery of all types built and positioned around the walls to the north and east. Knowing the efficacy of mining, he also set his men to filling in the moat around the city and digging under it; if they could collapse part of the walls, the crusading knights could charge through the gaps and engage in hand-to-hand combat, and the city would become almost impossible to defend.[20]

Philip made some good initial progress, but he was hampered by his oath to await Richard's arrival before making any kind of direct attack. Of course, he had also sworn not to leave Sicily before Richard did, which had not stopped him then, but he could not really be blamed for having given up and departed after waiting for Richard for more than six months. Launching an all-out assault on Acre in defiance of a promise would be a whole other order of magnitude, though, so despite his eagerness he held fire.

Richard's continuing non-appearance became an increasing problem. He had finally left Sicily some weeks after Philip, but on the way he had stopped in Cyprus, and for reasons of his own he had decided on a complete conquest of the island, even though it was Christian territory. Philip was obliged to resort to sending envoys to Cyprus in order to hurry him along, but awkwardly – and, we might suspect, deliberately – one of them was his cousin Philip of Dreux, the bishop of Beauvais. Philip was an unusual cleric, a pugnacious man 'more devoted to battles than books' who had already taken military action against Richard in the form of raids on the Norman border back in 1188, and he and Richard detested each other.[21] Upon his arrival in Cyprus Bishop Philip, with a characteristic lack of tact and diplomacy, accused Richard to his face of 'arrogantly persecuting innocent Christians when close by there were still so many thousands of Saracens whom he should be attacking'. This went down about as well as we might expect, and 'such things were said [in Richard's reply] as should not be written down'.[22]

Philip Augustus's embassy returned to Acre without Richard, who took his time completing business on Cyprus before taking ship for the last leg of his journey to the Holy Land. He finally turned up at Acre on 7 June, some seven weeks after Philip, with a great deal of fanfare. But if the wider crusading force thought that the belated appearance of the king of England was going to usher in a period of cheerful alliance that would help their cause, they were very much mistaken.

At every stage of the preliminaries and the crusade so far, Philip had arrived first, reconnoitring and making careful plans, only to be upstaged by the later and more ostentatious arrival of Richard, who brought along with him greater wealth and a coterie of obsequious chroniclers ready to give him the best PR the twelfth century had to offer. This latest example at Acre was no exception, and it is really no wonder that Philip allowed it to irk him. From the moment that they met again, every single action of both kings seemed to enrage the other, whether accidentally or deliberately.

By this time Richard was loaded down with gold and silver from his gains in Sicily and Cyprus, and he immediately irritated Philip by offering men in the host more money to serve him than Philip could afford. The French king was paying three gold bezants* a month — which had been considered generous — but Richard offered four and poached quite a few knights and men, some from right under Philip's nose. Then he ignored all Philip's military preparations and postponed any direct attack on the walls, preferring instead to send envoys to Saladin suggesting that they should meet in person.†

It was something of a relief to Philip when Richard fell ill and took to his bed, meaning that Philip was finally able to launch the concerted attack he had been planning. This took place on 3 July, and actually came close to taking the city, which would have been a bitter pill for Richard to swallow given his lack of involvement in the engagement; we might even speculate as to whether his pleasure at a Christian victory would have been outweighed by his jealousy of Philip for having achieved it without him. In any case, relations worsened even further. We can probably apportion the blame for this fairly equally, as both kings appeared to be as keen to antagonise each other as they were to take the city. At one point, a later French source tells us, Richard (after his recovery) launched an attack at a time when Philip had offered safe-conduct to a number of Muslim envoys, and Philip lost his temper to the point of considering physical assault: 'The king [Philip] was so angry that he even ordered his men to arm themselves to go and attack the king of England. He had already put on his own leg armour when the wise men in the host intervened and calmed him down.'[23]

It was not long before Philip fell ill himself, unsurprisingly given the heat and the conditions. He contracted a disease known

* A bezant was a gold coin used in Byzantium and the east; one bezant was worth two shillings.
† This did not happen; contrary to some of the legends that grew up around the Third Crusade, Richard and Saladin never met in person, though the latter did send his brother al-Adil to negotiate with the English king.

to contemporaries as *arnaldia*, which involved some very unpleasant symptoms: he suffered from a high fever, his hair and his nails fell out, and his skin peeled off in strips. The gossipy Minstrel of Reims put this down to him having been poisoned by Richard, but this seems unlikely.[24] Richard was hardly sympathetic, though, and indeed he gloated and sought to gain an advantage. Philip had recently received the harrowing news (in one of the updates he had required from Queen Adela and Archbishop William) that his son Louis was suffering with dysentery back in Paris, and Richard used this information to strike the lowest blow of all:

> King Richard conceived a great crime whereby he would kill the king of France without touching him [...] While the king of France was lying ill, King Richard went to call on him. As soon as he arrived he enquired after his illness and how he was. The king replied that he was at God's mercy and felt himself severely afflicted by his illness. Then King Richard said to him, 'As for Louis your son, how are you to be comforted?' The king of France asked him, 'What about Louis my son that I should be comforted?' 'It is for this', said the king of England, 'that I have come to comfort you, for he is dead.'[25]

Thankfully for Philip, Louis was not dead, and the little boy went on to make a full recovery, but Philip could not forget that Richard had apparently tried to kill him with shock while he was at his lowest, and he would never forgive him for it.

While he recuperated, Philip was not able to take a physical part in the siege, but he could still plan and give orders. He 'concentrated on constructing siege machines and placing stone-throwers in suitable places', arranging for them to shoot their missiles 'continually, day and night'; and he 'constructed with great determination an implement which would climb up the wall [...] called a "cat" because it clung like a cat to the wall as it crept up to seize it'.[26] The constant bombardment which the crusading forces were now able to inflict on the Muslim garrison (who were by this time exhausted and permanently on duty) meant that the siege was able to progress at a greater rate than had been the case for the last year and a half, but even this proved to be a subject of argument for the kings. The Acre garrison offered to surrender on terms, which Philip seemed inclined to accept, but Richard, scenting a more complete victory, initially refused.*

In this instance Richard was right, but it was Philip's men who tipped the scales. The French siege engines brought down a section of the city wall, and Philip's miners then caused the large tower that stood at the north-eastern corner to collapse. Acre was rendered indefensible, and it surrendered unconditionally on the following day, 12 July 1191. The English writers were quick to give Richard the credit, though the Minstrel of Reims disagreed, claiming that Richard 'felt great envy in his heart and great treachery, now that he knew Acre had been taken by King Philip'.[27]

Envy of a different sort played a part in Richard's next action, the exact reasons for which are unclear but surely related to some kind of concern about status and ego. The crusaders entered the city and flew their banners from the walls as a sign of their victory, but Richard objected to that of Duke Leopold of Austria taking its place alongside those of the kings of England, France and the Latin kingdom of Jerusalem, and had it torn down. Leopold was insulted and outraged, and left Acre not long afterwards in a spirit of bitterness against Richard.

The capture of Acre was a great breakthrough in the crusade, but it did not bring peace to the region and it still did not create accord between Philip and Richard. Contemporaries were not unaware of this, with Roger of Howden lamenting how much more could have been gained if the kings had only been able to work together:

In every affair in which the said kings [Richard and Philip] and their people had united, they were less successful than

---

* A *surrender on terms* was one that would only take place once negotiations were satisfactory for both sides. For the besieged this would mean the sparing of their lives, and possibly also that they could retain their possessions and leave in peace. An *unconditional surrender* was one in which the victorious besiegers dictated all the terms and the defeated defenders were at their mercy; this might result in summary executions, enslavement or ransom demands as well as the seizure of all property.

they would have been if they had acted separately, for the king of France and his men looked contemptuously on the king of England and his people, while he and his people did the same to the others.[28]

A fortnight after the surrender a settlement was reached over the division of the spoils from Acre, but there was still 'an enormous disagreement' between Richard and Philip over the question of the crown of Jerusalem.[29] Philip and most of the other crusaders preferred Conrad, but Richard persisted in his support for Guy, and his word carried a great deal of weight. An awkward compromise was reached, whereby Guy would retain the crown for the rest of his life, but on his death it would pass to Conrad. In the meantime, Guy would hold the south of the kingdom while Conrad would have the north.*

The convalescent Philip now made a provocative and spurious claim for half of Cyprus, on the basis that Richard had conquered it while (supposedly) on the crusade, and that they had previously sworn to share their crusade conquests equally. It would not have come as a shock when Richard refused, and it was probably at this point that Philip realised he needed to calm down and get a better grip on his emotions. He was becoming excessively petty, letting Richard get under what was left of his skin, and this was of no benefit either to himself or to France. He needed to take some time to plan his next moves properly without simply reacting badly to Richard's latest provocation, and he also needed to recover more fully from his illness, which had been severe and which would have lifelong consequences.

---

* As it transpired, this unpopular arrangement only lasted until April 1192, at which point Guy was pressured into relinquishing the crown. Conrad was then elected king, but he was assassinated only days later. His widow, Isabella of Jerusalem, queen in her own right, was pregnant with Conrad's child at the time, but this did not prevent her being immediately forced to marry again so that the kingdom could have a king. The chosen man was Count Henry II of Champagne, who was seen as an acceptable compromise candidate as he was related to the kings of France *and* England. He didn't last long, either, dying in a bizarre accident in 1197, and the unfortunate Isabella was married yet again, this time to Aimery of Lusignan, Guy's brother. Altogether she was the mother of seven children from her various unions: one son, who died in infancy, and six daughters.

In mid-July, Philip announced that he would return to France. Acre had been captured and was now in Christian hands, so he could theoretically consider his objective achieved and his crusading vow fulfilled. He was, of course, heavily criticised for this, both by the English chroniclers and by Richard himself, who made the most of the situation in a letter home in which he said that Philip had 'basely abandoned the purpose of his pilgrimage, and broke his vow, against the will of God, to the eternal disgrace of himself and of his realm'.[30]

However, Philip had a kingdom to run and he did not want to be absent from it for any longer than he could help. He and Richard had totally different priorities, which we could summarise by saying that Philip was a king who also happened to be a knight, while Richard was a knight who also happened to be a king. For Philip, France took precedence over his crusade, whereas for Richard the glory of fighting in the Holy Land and the building of his own chivalrous reputation were more important than England.

Philip sailed away from Acre on 31 July 1191.

Philip was returning home without many of those who had previously comprised the competing French domestic factions. The Capetian side of his family had survived: Robert II of Dreux, Bishop Philip of Beauvais and their cousin Peter II of Courtenay would all return from the crusade unscathed, Peter with King Philip and the Dreux brothers the following year. But the other major parties had incurred serious losses. Count Philip of Flanders had died of illness on 1 July 1191,* and the Blois–Champagne faction was all but annihilated: Theobald V of Blois had perished before King Philip even arrived, and he was followed to the grave by his brother Stephen of Sancerre and their brother-in-law

---

* The death of Count Philip opened up various possibilities for Philip Augustus, both in Flanders and in Vermandois, and it is probable that his demise was another contributing factor in the king's decision to return to France.

Rotrou of Perche. In the next generation, their nephews Hugh III of Burgundy and Henry II of Champagne both remained in the Holy Land, though the former would die there in 1192 and the latter in 1197, never returning to France. The only member of the extended family who made it back was Louis, Theobald's only son, the new count of Blois. The prosperous Champagne estates and title fell to Count Henry II's younger brother, now Theobald III, who was still a minor. Champagne would therefore continue to be ruled by King Philip's eldest half-sister, Marie, who was already its regent, and who merely swapped the name of the son she was acting for in her charters.

The effects on France would be lasting and severe, not only politically but also in terms of personal losses and mourning:

> In the whole kingdom, there was hardly a place where the people did not have some reason to cry, either for the loss of their lord, or for that of a brother or some close relative. This one had lost his children, that one his father; one lamented the death of his parents, another that of his friends; this one mourned his servant, that one his companion; one his uncles, the other his nephews; such was the disaster which hastened our great lords into the grave, when they were all struck by death at the city of Acre.[31]

Philip took a different route back to France from the one he had followed on his outward journey; his weakened state necessitated travelling in short stages, and he stopped at Tripoli, Antioch, Crete, Rhodes and Corfu before docking at Otranto (in Apulia, in Italy's heel), which was part of the kingdom of Sicily. From there he made his way overland to Rome, where he was welcomed by the elderly pope, Celestine III, and took the opportunity to complain to him about Richard's behaviour in the Holy Land.* Then Philip moved on to Milan, where he met the new Emperor, Henry VI, who had

---

* Celestine was one of the oldest men ever to be elected pope; he had been enthroned only a few months previously, in March 1191, but he was already in his mid- to late eighties.

been crowned in April 1191. Here was something of a kindred spirit: Henry was also adept at playing the game of politics, and he and Philip shared a dislike of Richard. Henry was particularly antagonistic towards the English king at this point because of the latter's recognition of Tancred as king of Sicily, and he and Philip struck up an amicable relationship.

With his new friend's permission, Philip travelled overland through the Empire before crossing the border back into France. He arrived in Paris on 27 December 1191, whereupon he gave thanks at the abbey of Saint-Denis and replaced the sacred *oriflamme* – for now. One English chronicler noted rather sarcastically that the French had no idea whether Philip's return was 'honourable, malicious or ignominious', but the inhabitants of the capital were in no doubt and gave him a joyous welcome.[32]

Given that Richard had decided to remain in the Holy Land for an unspecified amount of time, Philip would now have something of a breathing space to allow him to recover and plan his next moves. To start with he needed a period of convalescence, because he was still afflicted by the after-effects of the serious illness he had suffered on the crusade. A recurring fever seems to have been one symptom, and there were other, more permanent consequences: Philip's hair never grew back, so he was bald from this point onwards, and he also suffered lifelong psychological symptoms such as anxiety and paranoia. Being widely and publicly criticised for leaving the crusade early probably did not help his mental recovery.[*]

Philip was, of course, constrained by the oath he had sworn not to attack Richard's lands while they were on crusade (and, indeed, to protect them 'as if they were his own'). Nevertheless, he could still plan. His long-term goal – incited by what was now a virulent personal dislike – was no longer simply to protect France, but to push Richard and the Plantagenets out of their French lands

---

* It is illustrative of the way in which the eye-witness English and Anglo-Norman chroniclers portrayed both crusading kings that Philip was more heavily criticised for leaving early than Richard was for ordering the massacre of 2,700 Muslim inhabitants of Acre shortly afterwards.

entirely. This was a long game, but Philip was prepared to play it. He was helped by the atmosphere in France, where many of the holders of major titles were now young men who had known only Philip as their king, and where there was by now a deep and general distrust of Richard. In his chronicle, Rigord related a tale that was circulating at this time, that Richard was sending assassins* from the Holy Land to kill Philip, while William the Breton suspected that Philip's illness while on crusade was due to him being poisoned by the English king.[33] Neither of these accusations seem particularly plausible, but they do give us an idea of what people in France thought, or were willing to believe, at the time.

Richard's absence gave Philip time to take up the reins of power once again, to discover from Queen Adela and Archbishop William more about what had happened in his absence, and also to deal with matters in Flanders and Artois. He took the latter in hand in the name of the four-year-old Louis, who had inherited it upon the death of his mother – and who, incidentally, must have hardly recognised his father when they first met after such a long absence and so many physical changes in Philip. The king also accepted a relief payment from Baldwin V of Hainaut to become Baldwin VIII of Flanders in right of his wife Margaret, sister and heiress of the late Count Philip.

It was in early 1193, when King Philip had been home just over a year and had domestic matters firmly under control, that the momentous news arrived: Richard was a prisoner of Emperor Henry.

What had happened to Richard was fairly characteristic of all those concerned and, when we look at it in hindsight, almost inevitable. He had set off apparently without having planned an exact route in advance, but when he got as far as Corfu he realised his

* Literally: members of the sect of the Assassins, a dissident group who lived in what is now northern Syria, and who were famed – and greatly feared – for their murderous activities.

next options were limited, because nearly everyone whose lands he would have to pass through was either an ally of Philip, an antagonist of his own, or both. Emperor Henry was an enemy thanks to the Sicilian situation. Henry's vassal Leopold of Austria held a grudge against Richard following the insult he had received at Acre. North-western Italy was hostile, as it was dominated by the Montferrat family, whom Richard had opposed in the struggle over the crown of Jerusalem. Hungary was not really an option, as King Béla III was Philip's brother-in-law, and Béla's queen was Margaret of France: Richard had insulted and spurned her sister, Alice, and she herself was the widow of Henry the Young King, the brother Richard had fought against in the war which hastened his death.

Richard was, to put it bluntly, massively unpopular throughout large swathes of Europe. His only real allies were his brother-in-law Alfonso VIII of Castile and his father-in-law Sancho VI of Navarre, both of whom were much too far away to be of any help in the present situation, and his former brother-in-law Henry the Lion, duke of Saxony and Bavaria.* It is possible, therefore, that when he embarked from Corfu on the next leg of his journey Richard was aiming for a port that would offer the quickest overland route into Bavaria and relative safety. In the event, however, a storm had deposited him ashore between Aquileia and Venice in north-eastern Italy, obliging him to ride through Austria, and he had been captured by a triumphant Leopold.

Leopold had Richard taken to the castle of Dürnstein, which was about 40 miles west of Vienna, on the banks of the Danube, and informed Emperor Henry. After some haggling, Richard was transferred to Henry's custody and moved to the even remoter castle of Trifels, about 30 miles from Heidelberg in mountainous south-western Germany, there to be confined in a comfortable but ill-defined and potentially long captivity.

Henry wrote to Philip himself to apprise him of the news, addressing him as 'his beloved and especial friend Philip, the

---

* Richard's eldest sister, Matilda, had died in 1189, but her widower remained on good terms with the Plantagenets.

illustrious king of the Franks, [to whom he send wishes for] health and sincere love and affection'. After passing on the factual information, he ended his letter on a note of joint triumph:

> Inasmuch as he [Richard] is now in our power, and has always done his utmost for your annoyance and disturbance, what we have above stated we have thought proper to notify to your nobleness, knowing that the same is well pleasing to your kindly affection for us, and will afford most abundant joy to your own feelings.[34]

Richard was securely behind bars, a long way from his French domains, and in early 1193 it was doubtful whether he would ever be released.

4

A Clear Field

If we were to picture Philip rubbing his hands together in glee at this point, we would probably not be far off the mark. Richard's imprisonment was a piece of extreme good fortune for the French king, who was not directly involved in the Emperor's actions and could not in any way be blamed for them, but who could reap the benefits nonetheless.

Whether Philip's taking advantage of the situation was in any way ethical or justifiable is another question. The crucial pedantic point, given that they had now proved to be two very different scenarios, was whether the oath Philip had taken back in 1190 to protect Richard's lands was understood to comprise the period from then *until Richard returned from his crusade* or merely *while Richard was on crusade*. With the latter achieved but the former not, Philip chose to interpret his vow according to what suited him best, which might conceivably have adhered to the letter of his oath, but certainly not the spirit of it, and in hindsight it looks underhand from every point of view. But we must remind ourselves once more that twelfth-century kingship was not for the faint-hearted. Philip was criticised by some for taking advantage of Richard's absence, but others would have condemned him for weakness if he had not done so. He therefore proceeded according to his own agenda, consoling himself with the thought that Richard would have acted in exactly the same way if their positions had been reversed.

The first thing to be done was to ensure that Richard's captivity lasted as long as possible. To that end Philip sent a delegation to the

Emperor early in 1193, headed by his cousin Philip, the bishop of Beauvais. Bishops were routinely employed for this sort of diplomatic mission (there is a reason why they are important pieces on a chess board, along with knights and castles), being sufficiently educated and literate to deal with documents and correspondence and to negotiate. Naturally they all had particular secular allegiances, but they could nevertheless be considered neutral envoys because their overarching loyalty was to the international Church rather than to any one king or kingdom.[*]

Emperor Henry acceded to the first of the requests put to him by the ambassadors, which was that he should not release Richard, but he would not agree to the second, which was that custody of the prisoner should be transferred to King Philip upon payment of a fee. A second and higher-ranking delegation headed by France's most senior churchman, William Whitehands, the archbishop of Reims, was equally unsuccessful in persuading Henry on that latter point, and Philip had to accept that Richard would remain in the Empire for now. On the plus side, Henry set Richard's ransom at the almost unimaginable sum of 150,000 marks (£100,000 sterling), many times the English crown's annual income, so there seemed to be very little chance of Richard being able to raise that. He would therefore be absent from his domains for a good long time, if not permanently, and Philip could make what hay he could in the meantime.

In this, he had a willing ally.

When the original idea of John travelling with the two kings to the Holy Land had been dropped, Richard had wanted his younger brother to swear an oath that he would not set foot in England for three years. He had been persuaded by Eleanor of Aquitaine not to enforce such a provision, but in the event this had proved to be a bad move, as John then had free rein to agitate on his own behalf throughout the kingdom. Richard, he emphasised to anyone who would listen, was overseas doing something very dangerous, and

* This was the case in theory, at least — the priorities of this particular bishop might conceivably have been in a different order.

he had no children; it was surely likely that something untoward would befall him, and then his remaining brother (and the only legitimate adult male in the family)* would inherit everything. And that brother would be grateful to those who had supported him right from the off, while being rather less pleased with anyone who had hesitated.

John was able to play on the fears of the nobles, who were uncertain which way they ought to jump in order to serve their own best interests, both in the short and in the long term. Some remained loyal to Richard, but others threw in their lot with John, in much the same way as Richard had gained support back in 1189 when the barons of Henry II's continental lands realised he would not be around long and Richard would be king next. At first John was kept under a modicum of control by Eleanor, acting as Richard's official regent, but once she left England (to travel to Navarre to collect Berengaria, and then to Sicily to deliver her to Richard) his behaviour degenerated.

Philip, who was keeping a close eye on England, was well aware of all this during the year he spent back in France before he heard of Richard's captivity. He was happy to host John and even to attempt to offer him his sister Alice as a bride, conveniently ignoring the two salient facts that Alice was still being held by Richard's representatives – who had refused to hand her over without his express personal authorisation – and that John was already married.†

---

* Richard and John also had at least two illegitimate half-brothers, as Henry II had fathered sons by different mistresses both before and after his family with Eleanor. William Longespee, the youngest, was at this point still a very young man, but Geoffrey, the eldest (not to be confused with Henry II's legitimate son of the same name), was a warlike man in his early forties who had made a name for himself by remaining loyal to his father until the bitter end and attending him on his deathbed. Richard considered Geoffrey such a threat that, upon his own accession, he had obliged the canons of York to elect him their archbishop, meaning that Geoffrey had to take holy orders as a priest and was therefore ineligible to make any kind of claim to the throne.

† Alice did eventually return to France, although not for another couple of years and not to marry John. She was by that time in her early thirties and had been in Plantagenet guardianship since the age of eight. Her value on the marriage market had not quite expired, and at the age of thirty-five she was married to a French count who was half her age; she bore him two daughters and lived contentedly with her new family until her death around 1220.

Then came the unexpected, heaven-sent news about Richard's capture. Philip did not even need to invite John to his court to discuss the matter, because as soon as he heard of it John rushed across the Channel to throw himself, quite literally, at Philip's feet. He offered homage to Philip for the French lands which were now his – or soon would be – and promised he would put his wife aside and marry Alice.[*] This baffled and angered some English chroniclers, including both Roger of Wendover and Roger of Howden, who had seen it all before and who wrote of John acting according to Philip's 'pernicious counsel' or said bluntly that John 'had made a league with death and a compact with hell'.[1]

To be equally frank for a moment, we must ask ourselves why John chose to do something so unbelievably stupid. All three of his elder brothers had at various points been allies of Philip, and all three had come to grief because of it – could he really not see the pattern? The most charitable explanation is that John had been very young when the wars and rebellions of his older brothers were taking place, so perhaps he had not grasped the full extent of Philip's involvement in his family's troubles. An improbable one is that he thought he was cleverer than Philip, Young Henry, Richard and Geoffrey, and that he would succeed where his brothers had failed. But the most likely reason is that John was simply blinded by his own ambition and greed, meaning that he walked directly into Philip's trap.

In the spring of 1193 Philip invaded Normandy. The border had been fluid over the years and decades, thanks to small-scale gains and losses, but its traditional marker was the River Epte, which was protected by a line of strongholds whose circles of influence overlapped; that is, they were close enough to each other that the garrisons could cover all the ground in between them during the course of half a day's ride, making them an effective barrier.[†] Philip

---

[*] This was one of those situations in which consanguinity with one's wife came in extremely useful, as there was a ready-made excuse for an annulment.

[†] The circle of influence of a castle was half a day's ride, or about 10 miles: this allowed the garrison to emerge at daybreak, range around the countryside while it was light, and then get back behind the walls before sunset.

enjoyed immediate success when the key and well-fortified castle of Gisors surrendered to him without a fight, and then he and his siege train took Neufles, Châteauneuf, Gournay, Aumale and Eu, meaning that he had control of a 50-mile stretch of the river and its crossings, as well as the further 10 miles or so that marked the limit of each stronghold's influence.

Perhaps a little ambitiously at this stage (one chronicler calls it 'vainglorious'), Philip began a siege of the ducal capital of Rouen.[2] He was accompanied and supported by various of his senior nobles, including his cousin Peter II of Courtenay and Baldwin, the count of Flanders and Hainaut, Philip's former father-in-law. These two men had put aside any earlier Capetian–Flemish factional differences and were now allied by marriage, in one of the complex and slightly distasteful intergenerational arrangements that were not uncommon. Peter was a widower in his late thirties with one five-year-old daughter, Matilda, who was now betrothed to Baldwin's second son, Philip, who was in his late teens; and Peter himself was married to Baldwin's teenage daughter Yolande.* Simultaneously, King Philip's other cousin Robert II of Dreux, whose own county bordered Normandy further to the south (and who was coincidentally married to Baldwin's niece), captured Nonancourt in his royal cousin's name. The wider Capetian family was, it seems, much more capable of working in concert than any of the Plantagenets.

Faced with the formidable defences of Rouen and realising that any siege would need to be a long one, Philip attempted to cajole the defenders into surrender, saying that John had done homage to him for Normandy and that 'I have come hither to take possession of this city, which is the capital of the whole of Normandy; allow me to enter peaceably, and I will prove a kind and just master to you'.[3] They were having none of it, however, and he

---

* As it transpired, Philip of Hainaut's marriage to Matilda of Courtenay never actually happened, due to the political situation having changed again by the time she was old enough to marry. Much to the relief of anyone trying to draw a family tree or work out degrees of affinity, this saved Peter from becoming his brother-in-law's father-in-law, and Yolande from ending up as her elder brother's mother-in-law.

was forced to withdraw. As Philip left he burned his siege engines (all twenty-four of them), so they could not be taken and used by his foes; they were cumbersome things to disassemble and transport, so as the campaign was over for the present it was easier to destroy them and have new ones built whenever he should need them. In a slightly less explicable move, he also apparently broke open his wine casks and poured the contents away, though in this case it is difficult to see why he could not just take the barrels away with him.[4]

The withdrawal from Rouen was a setback, but not a critical one. It had been overambitious to try for the capital straight away, but even without it Philip now dominated north-eastern Normandy and controlled the frontier castles which would provide a platform for fresh campaigns in the future. Moreover, the actions of these few months had confirmed his new, broader – and now much more plausibly achievable – ambitions. Previously he had merely encouraged in-fighting or supported rebels in Plantagenet-held lands in France, hoping to cause trouble and maybe take a few bites out of the border, but now he was undertaking much deeper forays with a view to bringing large parts of Normandy under his direct control.

In a secondary campaign, Philip supported a rebellion in Poitou by Aymer, the count of Angoulême (who happened to be married to another royal cousin, Alice of Courtenay, the sister of Peter II), one of several regional lords who were taking advantage of the lack of a resident duke of Aquitaine to flex their muscles. The insurgency failed, however, due to one of King Richard's few successful alliances: his brother-in-law Sancho the Strong, the eldest son and heir of Sancho VI of Navarre, crossed the Aquitanian border from the south and, 'in anger against the French', suppressed the trouble.[5]

In sum, then, Philip had not enjoyed complete success in all his initial endeavours, but he had certainly made sufficient gains to be getting on with. And the key point, as the summer of 1193 wore on, was that Richard was still in prison in Germany; Philip had plenty of time and did not need to rush anything. Instead he could consolidate his military gains of the first half of the year while also turning his mind to other important matters of state.

Philip was first and foremost a king, and a king needed to ensure a proper line of succession. What would be the point of conquering Normandy, of expanding and empowering France, if it would all fall apart on Philip's death because he had no direct heir? His duty was to his dynasty, not merely to himself.

He did, of course, have one all-important son and heir; Louis was by now five years old and thriving.* But it was just too risky to hang the entire future of the Capetian line on one child – Philip had only to look across the Channel at the multiple deaths in Henry II's family to realise that – so he needed to marry again. Besides, a realm needed a queen as well as a king in order to achieve the proper balance, and Philip, who was still only twenty-seven, wanted a wife.

This was all very logical, but what happened next was a bizarre series of events that mystified contemporaries at the time, and which has continued to puzzle historians ever since.

Generally speaking, French kings tended to choose wives from among their own major vassals rather than seeking international matches. Philip's own first union had been with Isabelle of Hainaut, and of the seven wives accumulated by his three immediate predecessors on the throne, only two had come from outside France: Louis VI's queen Adelaide of Maurienne hailed

---

* There is a persistent myth in modern scholarship that Louis was a fragile and 'sickly' child and that Philip's concern over the succession was due to this. However, there is no contemporary evidence that Louis was ill throughout his childhood, and the idea seems to be based on nothing more than his having been struck with dysentery while Philip was in the Holy Land – which is odd, because the fact that Louis survived an illness that killed many other children is surely indicative of a robust health rather than the opposite. He was certainly able to undertake a full academic, practical and martial education, so Philip's concern can probably be attributed to the fact that Louis was his only child, and that even healthy children could die suddenly of any one of a number of accidental causes. Philip might also have feared unnecessarily for his son's life in the same way he did for his own.

from just over the imperial border in Savoy, and Louis VII's second wife, the ill-fated Constance, was a member of the Castilian royal family.* In seeking a new match now, however, Philip looked abroad, and – unusually – northwards. He sent envoys to Cnut VI of Denmark to negotiate for the hand of Cnut's sister Ingeborg, then aged eighteen and reputed to be both beautiful and pious. Philip had never met her, of course, but royal marriages were never about romantic attraction. Queens *were* expected to be personally attractive, so Ingeborg's beauty made her an acceptable consort and meant that Philip's pride would never be dented by his new wife's appearance. In practical terms, her family was fecund (Ingeborg was one of nine siblings, and her mother one of eight), so it was a reasonable bet that she would be able to bear Philip the children and supplementary heirs he needed, and her age meant she would remain fertile for the best part of two decades. Finally, her religious devotion would stand her in good stead at the French court, which was dominated by churchmen, and her personal reputation was unimpeachable.

The union was judicious in practical terms, then, but Philip's political motivation for a Danish match is more difficult to discern. It might simply have been the case that princesses of marriageable age were in short supply in western Europe at the time: he had already turned down Joanna of England, Emperor Henry had only brothers, the Navarrese royal family was out, as Richard was already married into it, and the Aragonese and Castilian royal girls were all too young to think about childbearing. The latter were also Richard's nieces, which was not the sort of match Philip was looking for.

Another possibility is that Philip's choice of Ingeborg might have been related to his long-term plans against England, although

---

* Constance had been aged somewhere between fourteen and eighteen when she was married off to the thirty-four-year-old Louis in 1154, and her life thereafter was short and unhappy. She gave birth to a daughter, Margaret, in 1157, who was taken away at the age of six months to be raised by her future father-in-law, Henry II, meaning that Constance never saw her again. Constance then fell pregnant for a second time but died giving birth to another daughter, the equally unfortunate Alice, in 1160.

if this was the case then the link was tenuous. The Danes could claim a vague hereditary right to the throne of England, dating from the time when Cnut the Great had been king of England, Denmark and Norway simultaneously, but that had been some 150 years previously, and there was little hope anyone would take it seriously against the claims of the Plantagenet dynasty and their descent from William the Conqueror. The Danes also had a fleet, and Philip's marriage negotiations touched on the use of this, but again it is difficult to see what he might gain from it. If he wanted to invade England then Normandy was the obvious embarkation point, but all the central and westward parts of it, including the coast, still held for Richard.

In the event, Cnut declined to allow use of his fleet as part of the wedding arrangements, and Philip settled for Ingeborg plus 10,000 marks in cash, which makes his political reasoning even harder to fathom. The necessary paperwork was drawn up, and here again there is something a little bit odd in the wording of the charter in which Philip specifies Ingeborg's dower. Rather than using the sort of phrases seen in similar documents, which might refer to 'our dearly beloved future wife' or similar, indicating a personal welcome to the marriage from the husband, Ingeborg is described as 'the most noble and beloved sister of the king of Denmark, whom we marry by the grace of God'.[6] This was written before the wedding, so the phraseology cannot have been influenced by what happened afterwards.

The events leading up to the big day were perplexing enough, but those that occurred immediately after it are even more baffling. Ingeborg arrived in France on 14 August 1193, and she and Philip were married the same day, having never previously met and having no common language except perhaps some Latin, for she spoke no French and he no Danish. As was customary, the couple later retired to bed to consummate the marriage, and this is where the story takes the strangest twist of all. The very next day Philip declared that he would be seeking an annulment. He attempted to hand Ingeborg back to the Danish delegation, and when they refused – instead hurrying back to Cnut to give him the news

– Philip had his new queen taken to a convent at Soissons, where she was confined against her will.

What on earth was going on? Nobody knew for sure at the time, and subsequent observers have only been able to speculate. It seems fairly safe to assume that Philip's sudden aversion was personal, given that the political situation with Denmark had not altered overnight, but further than that we cannot say with any certainty. The two principal schools of thought are that he discovered some hitherto unknown 'flaw' in Ingeborg once they were alone, or, conversely, that she was *so* beautiful and pious that he was rendered temporarily impotent (there was clearly no earlier problem of this nature, because Philip had fathered children with his first wife). The first option seems less likely, because if Philip could have blamed the situation publicly on Ingeborg then presumably he would have done, which leads us to suspect that the problem lay with him.* And the whole situation was exacerbated by Philip's ongoing problems with anxiety and paranoia (imperfectly understood at the time) as the result of his illness in the Holy Land.

Whatever the issue was, it was serious enough in Philip's mind to jeopardise his new alliance with Cnut. His repudiation of Ingeborg could not be taken as anything other than a serious insult to the Danish king – even more so, indeed, than the affront Philip himself had received when Richard had finally rejected Alice, because Philip and Ingeborg were actually married and she had been crowned queen of France. Despite these diplomatic repercussions Philip went ahead with his plans for annulment, and in November 1193 he convened a council of churchmen to consider the matter. It was hardly a fair hearing: Ingeborg was not allowed any representation, and the ten members of the council, headed by Archbishop William Whitehands, were eight men who were related to Philip and another two who were members

---

* In one of his later and more desperate attempts to rid himself of Ingeborg, Philip would assert that the marriage had never been consummated, something he had not claimed in his original bid for an annulment. This perhaps lends credence to the idea that he had been unable to perform satisfactorily on his wedding night, and that he had been too embarrassed to admit it at the time. Ingeborg always claimed that the marriage had been consummated and was therefore fully legal.

of his household. Predictably, they found in the king's favour and declared the marriage void on the grounds of consanguinity, thanks to a family tree they had drawn up which demonstrated (falsely, as it happens, due to a mistake that might have been deliberate) that Ingeborg was related to Philip's first wife, Isabelle of Hainaut. The Church's forbidden degrees of affinity included those with one's former spouse as well as oneself, so any close familial link between Ingeborg and Isabelle would have been as bad as one between Ingeborg and Philip.

This decision was not universally popular. The chronicler Rigord, normally keen to present Philip in the best possible light, wrote boldly that the clergy who had pronounced the annulment 'had become dumb dogs not able to bark, afraid for their own hide', and Pope Celestine, 'at the insistence of the Danes', was dissatisfied enough with the proceedings to send papal legates to France to investigate.[7]

On top of this, it turned out that Philip had underestimated the character and tenacity of his queen. Ingeborg did not accept her repudiation and she would spend the next twenty years fighting her cause, involving her brothers (Cnut VI and his successor on the Danish throne, Valdemar II) and two successive popes. This long-running marital conflict was to have political ramifications for Philip, so we will return to Ingeborg in due course. For now we will simply note the immediate consequences for the French king: he had no fleet, no alliance with Denmark and no means to provide himself with further heirs.[8]

By the end of 1193 Philip's period of free rein was drawing to a close.

This was due to the efforts of the one member of the Plantagenet family to whom he had not paid nearly enough attention: Eleanor of Aquitaine. She was by now in her seventies, so perhaps he thought he did not need to consider her in his wider political calculations – as an elderly dowager it would not have been surprising if she quit the stage altogether in order to retire to a convent for her final years. If so, this was a miscalculation on Philip's part, because she had done everything humanly possible to free her favourite son, approaching the task with an energy and determination that would have been astonishing had it been manifested by anyone else.

As a first step, she had sent letters of incandescent fury to Pope Celestine, styling herself 'by the wrath of God, queen of the English', and following up with some very choice words on his lack of action and his personal character:

> You cannot pretend not to know of the crime and infamy, when you are the vicar of the crucified, the successor of Peter, the priest of Christ, the anointed of the Lord [...] Henceforth the tyrant [Emperor Henry] holds the apostolic keys in derision and looks on the law of God as only words. [...] Whenever the ferment of schism is again brought forth from similar cause, God forbid, the memory of your present sloth and defects will cause some to sob.[9]

Despite this provocation, Celestine made no move to demand Richard's freedom (as he might well have been expected to do, given Richard's status as a returning crusader), because he did not want to antagonise Emperor Henry. Henry was already the most powerful man in western Europe, and his vast imperial domains bordered Rome and the papal states to the north. If he also succeeded in claiming Sicily in his wife's name – which he was now preparing to do – then the territories under his control would surround the papal states entirely. One of the reasons Celestine had been elected pope back in 1191 was that he was seen as a compromise candidate between those cardinals who supported Tancred in Sicily, and those who favoured Henry and Constance. He had walked a precarious diplomatic tightrope ever since, and he was not about to risk his neutrality by raising his voice against the Emperor.

If Eleanor wanted the support of the Church, she would need to find a different associate, so when Celestine refused to act on her behalf she allied herself with the new archbishop of Canterbury, Hubert Walter.* He was a loyal man of Richard's and had already travelled to Germany to meet with the imprisoned king and bring back his instructions – which were, unsurprisingly, that the ransom should be raised in full as quickly as possible. Eleanor did not need to be told twice, and she immediately levied a 25 per cent tax on income and on moveable property, confiscated the entire year's wool crop from the Cistercian Order in England and 'borrowed' gold and silver plate until 'there was not a single chalice or censer left in any church in England'.[10]

Richard had sent back a letter in which he requested, rather ominously, to know exactly how much each individual contributed towards his ransom, 'so that we may know how far we are bound to return thanks to each', and Eleanor used this to browbeat the major nobles into some substantial donations.[11] So successful was she that it was a mere twelve months after Richard's capture that Eleanor had the ransom ready to go; or, at least, enough in hand, with hostages to leave as security against the promise of the balance later on, to secure his release. The amount was so great that there was actually not enough coin in the whole of England to pay it in cash, so the packed wagons included various items of gold, silver and other treasure as well as barrels of silver pennies.†　Unwilling to hand it over to anyone but the Emperor in person, Eleanor travelled to Germany in the new year of 1194, reaching Mainz on 2 February.

Philip made the most of his opportunities while he still had them. In early 1194 he launched another invasion of Normandy, but the results were similar to the previous year's campaign: he

---

* Baldwin of Forde, the previous archbishop, had been one of the many casualties of the Third Crusade, dying of illness at the siege of Acre.

† The silver penny was the only coin in circulation in England at this time, which made transporting large amounts of money very cumbersome. For sizeable transactions the pennies would be weighed, not counted, which is why a pound is so named: 240 pennies weighed 1lb.

captured some castles, including those of Évreux, Neubourg and Le Vaudreuil, but his attempt at Rouen was unsuccessful. The ducal capital was going to be difficult and time-consuming to take; it would require a firmer base, meticulous planning and a longer-term campaign, but time was running out. Philip could not afford to be bogged down in a long siege while he waited for the expected news from Germany.

John, meanwhile, decided to gamble everything on being able to secure his position while Richard was absent ... and he lost. In a letter patent* of January 1194 – even as Eleanor was on her way to Germany – he declared that he had made an agreement with Philip. In return for recognition of his rights in France, he ceded to Philip 'Normandy on the French side of the river Seine to the English Channel, except the city of Rouen itself and two leagues around', as well as various other pivotal strongholds not only in Normandy, but also in Maine, Touraine and Anjou. He agreed to hold his continental lands as Philip's vassal.[12]

It is honestly quite difficult to see what John was playing at, unless he somehow believed that Emperor Henry was going to refuse to set Richard free despite the payment of the ransom and the force of nature that was Eleanor of Aquitaine appearing before him in person. And even if this had been the case, John was voluntarily giving away large concessions to Philip in return for the French king's recognition of his rights to the family's continental lands. Either way it was a recipe for disaster: if Richard returned then there was irrefutable proof that John had tried to usurp him in his absence, and if he did not then John would be only the nominal lord of his ancestral holdings in France, with Philip having already accepted what John was happy to give up and hungry for more.

The English chroniclers, wiser than John to Philip's stratagems, were not fooled. The author of the *History of William Marshal* was convinced that Philip 'thought little of his [John's] enterprise',

---

* A *letter patent* was a letter that was addressed to the public or intended for public reading, rather than a private missive to an individual.

that he was 'unwilling to assist or be of service to him' and in fact 'thought him a fool and completely pulled the wool over his eyes'.[13] Philip's political motivation in accepting John's offer is easier to understand: if Richard was going to return, as now seemed inevitable, then it suited Philip's purposes to have the English king and his brother at odds with each other. As a mark of their alliance, or possibly just as further incriminating evidence against John, Philip turned the captured Norman stronghold of Évreux over to him.

Richard was released from captivity on 4 February 1194. Philip received the news first and sent a message to John 'that he must take care of himself, for the devil was now let loose'.[14] Richard had the sense not to attempt to travel through France on his journey back to England, instead making his way, with Emperor Henry's safe-conduct, through Cologne and to Antwerp in Brabant, which was then part of the Empire. From there he took ship to England, where he arrived on 13 March.

Time was now extremely short, but Philip knew he had a little more leeway, as Richard would want to attend to matters in his kingdom as a first priority. This would surely take weeks or months, so the most useful thing Philip could do in the interim was to snatch as much additional territory as he could, and he continued campaigning. By early May he was besieging Verneuil, where 'he had not stopped for eight days in erecting petraries, nor in transporting great stones, nor in carrying machinery, nor in excavating trenches for the walls, nor in afflicting the bodies of the besieged'.[15]

It was while he was at Verneuil that Philip's time of freedom finally ran out: on 12 May 1194, Richard landed at Barfleur, the main port in Normandy.

5

War Most Grand and Cruel

The king of England's arrogance surpassed that of any other man; he did not deign to obey the king of France, his lord. The king of France could not bear his haughtiness, and nor did he want to. For this reason, and because of many other disputes, the war between them restarted, a war most grand and most cruel.[1]

As Philip might have expected, John's rebellion against Richard collapsed immediately, and he rushed to grovel before his brother, beg his pardon and make what excuses he could. Rather unexpectedly (and the hand of Eleanor of Aquitaine can be discerned here), he was forgiven straight away, although the way in which it was done was so patronising as to be a public humiliation. During his captivity, on being informed of John's rebellion, Richard had written a letter home in which he had noted dismissively that 'my brother John is not the man to subjugate a country, if there is a person able to make the slightest resistance to his attempts'. Now, in a further demonstration that he did not take his little brother seriously, he met with the married twenty-seven-year-old and 'kissed him, saying: "John, have no fear. You are a child, and you had bad men looking after you."'[2] John was able to swallow the insult if it meant he would get away with his treachery, but Richard was not completely oblivious to his brother's character and ambitions, and declined to restore him to immediate control of his English estates and incomes.

So swiftly had John turned his coat that on riding for Évreux after this episode he was welcomed into it, along with the troops accompanying him, as the garrison believed he was holding it for Philip. This had terrible consequences for them, as once he was inside John declared himself for Richard, had the garrison murdered and the town turned over to Richard's men. William the Breton adds that, in a 'monstrous action', John issued an invitation to any other Frenchmen (that is, French rather than Norman) who were in the town, then decapitated them and put their heads on poles. This might be an exaggeration on William's part, but it shows what John's reputation was already like in France: he was 'full of artifice [...] having already betrayed his father and then his brother', and therefore 'he could not do otherwise' than also betray Philip.[3] The course of events at Évreux was both an illustration of some of John's less pleasant qualities, and also a sign of the heightened tensions and the greater cruelty that would character-ise this next phase of the Capetian–Plantagenet conflict.

Philip, meanwhile, was still outside the walls of Verneuil, but his situation was becoming perilous. It is well known that, during a siege, the defenders of a stronghold might find themselves in danger of starvation – but hunger was also a threat to the attackers, who needed to raid, forage or otherwise ensure adequate lines of supply lest they run out of food before the defenders did. And this is what happened now, as the approaching Richard 'proceeded to cut off all the routes along which provisions were delivered to the King of France', forcing Philip to withdraw.[4] By this time news had reached him of the events at Évreux, which was about 40 miles west of Verneuil, so he rode straight there. He retook the town without too much trouble, then had it sacked and burned. This was partly in revenge, 'because the citizens of Évreux, having left him, had returned their duty and allegiance to their lord the king of England', and partly because he suspected he might not be able to hold on to the town (we may imagine that the defences had been weakened by the recent back-and-forth sieges) and he did not want such a valuable asset to fall into Richard's hands again.[5] The inhabitants of Évreux – and other places which were to be caught up in the primary conflict – could do nothing but count themselves unlucky that they were considered by both kings to be merely units of economic resource rather than citizens with their own lives, livelihoods and rights.

Richard, meanwhile, had not advanced against Philip in person but had turned southwards to Loches (about 25 miles south-east of Tours), where he not only attacked the garrison and the civilian population, but also 'expelled the canons of Saint-Martin of Tours, violently plundered their possessions, and did much wickedness to God's churches in those regions'.[6]

The ferocity of the conflict between the former allies was escalating, and Philip knew that this new chapter was going to tax his abilities to the limit. On an intellectual level he was certainly cleverer than Richard – better at seeing the big picture, better at the politics of governing a realm, better at reading people and discerning their motivations – but nobody was in any doubt that Richard was an exceptional, well-trained, uncompromising and ferocious combatant and military leader. Moreover, he was in France at this moment *as* a military leader, and one who was bent on revenge against those who had taken advantage of his captivity or who had betrayed him. Philip would need to have all his wits (and his allies) about him, but even that might not be enough. His next act was therefore to try to gain himself a breathing space that would allow for more in-depth planning, and in the summer of 1194 he proposed a three-year truce. However, the two kings could not agree terms, as Philip wanted the treaty to include all their vassals, while Richard demanded the exclusion of those who had rebelled against him during his absence.[7]

It is at this point that one English chronicler makes the curious claim that a suggestion was put forward that the entire dispute between the kings should be settled by a symbolic small-scale combat between five knights from either side. He implies that Philip was happy with the idea until Richard added the stipulation that the two of them had to take part in person, 'and that they should fight each other on equal terms, armed and equipped alike', at which point Philip declined.[8] As this story appears only in one minor source, written by someone who was not on the spot in France (the author was the dean of St Paul's in London), it might well be apocryphal, but it is illustrative of several important points and worth taking at least semi-seriously as a subject for discussion.

In the twelfth-century knightly eye (and certainly in the opinion of Richard's supporters), the tale shows Richard in his best light: a straightforward, honest man who wants to cut through all the politics and find a simple way forward, and who is not afraid to put his body on the line in order to do so. Richard cultivated this image of himself as a direct and forthright man, and was known to contemporaries as *Richard Oc-e-Non* ('Richard Yes-and-No', from the Occitan language used in Aquitaine), although we might put this nickname down to a reputation for bad temper and a curt manner as much as one for plain speaking. In his view he was simply offering an uncomplicated solution to a problem none of them wanted, and then everyone could call the matter closed and move on.

However, while an offer of single combat might just about have been an appropriate measure for two knights squabbling over a minor local matter, it was a hopelessly inadequate solution to a complex, wide-ranging situation involving sovereignty over large tracts of land, the borders of kingdoms and the future of the people who lived on both sides. Proposing such a thing was the mark of a foolish king who was out of his depth on the international political stage, and it would be an even more foolish one who accepted the challenge. It would be reckless in the extreme, the action of a gambler, to entrust a matter of such importance to a one-off event with a risky outcome. And besides, Philip was self-aware enough to know that he could not hope to defeat Richard in single combat, so why on earth would he be drawn into a fight he knew he could not win? Philip had no interest in performative machismo: it would be better for him to play the game on his own terms and seek to defeat Richard in the longer term.[9]

Whatever the precise circumstances, this combat – if indeed it was ever proposed in the first place – did not take place, and no three-year truce was sealed either. This meant that Philip had to be prepared for any potential incursion of Richard's into his lands, but also that he himself was free to continue planning and campaigning. One advantage he had in this was that he could see very clearly that the two of them had different priorities. Richard's was Aquitaine – the duchy that had come to him from his mother, which he had been ruling since he was in his teens and to which he was emotionally attached – while Philip's was the northern Plantagenet territories, principally Normandy. When Philip did make forays into Aquitaine, or intervene there to support rebels, it was never with the full royal army and was only intended to distract Richard's attention so Philip could make gains further north.

At midsummer 1194 Philip moved into Touraine. He was aided by the continuing unrest further south in Aquitaine, and now he benefitted from a stroke of luck. Richard's principal ally, his brother-in-law the warlike Sancho the Strong of Navarre, had been acting on his behalf in the region, but the death in June of Sancho VI the Wise meant that the younger man had to leave Aquitaine to go home for his coronation as Sancho VII, and that he would be detained by domestic matters there for some while. This left a void in Aquitaine that provided opportunities for Philip, but his good fortune there was almost immediately countered by a piece of ill luck.

In early July Philip was encamped near Fréteval, in the valley of the Loire, when Richard rather unexpectedly moved in front of him to block his route. It is not clear whether Philip's surprise was due to a failure of French intelligence, or a lightning manoeuvre of Richard's (or indeed both), but it was dangerous. Up until now the kings had avoided facing each other in a pitched battle, just as all military leaders avoided them whenever possible; such head-to-head encounters were a gamble similar to the single combat we discussed above, only on a far larger scale and with far graver potential consequences.* But now it looked as though Philip and

---

* Set-piece battles were far rarer at this time than is popularly supposed. Hattin was the most recent large-scale example (proving the point that the outcome could be disastrous and could negate the

Richard were destined to face each other with swords drawn and lances couched.

Philip's options were limited, so he played for time with a ruse, declaring that he would attack the next day. Richard apparently fell for it: 'The king of England joyously receiving his message, sent word back to him that he would wait for him, and, if he should not come, would pay him a visit on the following morning.'[10] This gave Philip time overnight, and instead of advancing, as Richard expected, he turned and retreated up the valley. The following morning Richard realised what was going on and gave chase, but only managed to catch up with the rear of the French forces. An engagement of sorts took place, which is sometimes called 'the battle of Fréteval', but in reality it was no more than a skirmish and a raid on the baggage train. The contemporary sources, as we might expect, differ in the emphasis they place on events. Rigord says only that 'the king of England with a large force of armed knights quite unexpectedly charged out of the woods and forcefully carried off King Philip's packhorses', while his English counterparts claim that 'many of the troops of the king of France were slain, and many taken prisoner', or dwell on 'the riches to be found in the midst of the army [...] pavilions, all kinds of tents, cloth of scarlet and silk, plate and coin, horses, palfreys, pack-horses, sumptuous garments and money'.[11]

Richard's men did continue the chase, but they either did not catch up with Philip, or missed him because he had gone into a church to attend Mass and the pursuit swept straight past. He therefore avoided the absolute disaster of capture; but, even as it stood, this incident was a major setback in terms of both reputation (his strategic retreat and tactic of battle avoidance could easily be spun as headlong flight) and governance. At this time kings were peripatetic, taking their court and household with them wherever they went, and so they needed to keep the apparatus of government close at hand. The slow-moving baggage train of Philip's that had

progress of months or even years), and decades could pass between such encounters. William the Conqueror fought only two battles during his lifetime, and Henry II none at all.

been captured contained not only household goods and money, but also his all-important royal seal, not to mention a list of those of Richard's men who had defected to Philip while the English king was in captivity, or who had intended to do so.[*]

Philip did not intend to let this setback turn into a calamity. Leaving one Plantagenet brother behind him, he made for the other – and easier pickings – by riding north towards Le Vaudreuil and John. It was a distance of 95 miles, normally a journey of at least a week for such a sizeable force, but Philip somehow managed it in three days, 'without dismounting or taking a moment to rest, and arriving drenched in sweat and covered in dust'.[12] His sudden appearance took John by surprise, and Philip was able to capture both Le Vaudreuil and John's siege train. After that there were some minor skirmishes and sieges, with no gains or losses of particular note for either side, until it was the end of the campaigning season. Military campaigning at this time was of necessity seasonal, running from spring to summer each year and then ceasing over the autumn and winter, because travelling was difficult for all parties, food for both men and horses was hard to come by, the dangers of disease and death from the cold were much greater, and many of the lower-ranked men in a host would be needed at home for the annual harvest.

Following the winter break, the spring of 1195 found Philip once again in Berry. The area was vulnerable following his previous campaigns there, and it was of strategic importance: if Philip could get the whole county under his control, he would be able to cut off one of the major routes between Richard's contiguous domains. Indeed, if Philip could use a conquest of Berry to then push further along the Loire, he could completely sever the link between Aquitaine and the northern Plantagenet-held territories, forcing Richard either to cross hostile territory or to travel by ship when he wanted to go from one to the other.

---

[*] The loss of some of Philip's governmental documents and records at Fréteval was a major factor in him deciding to make Paris the permanent home of French archives, and they have been based there ever since.

Neither king made any significant gains during the spring. They were still playing cat and mouse, because neither of them particularly wanted to risk everything in a large-scale pitched battle, and it was no surprise when talks were held in July, near Le Vaudreuil. But once again no agreement could be reached, and the proposed truce fell through. There were two principal reasons for this. Firstly, Philip discovered that Emperor Henry was encouraging Richard to invade France itself – that is, the lands under Philip's direct royal control, rather than the ones Richard held from him as overlord. Henry was not above playing a few games of his own, and he had kept Richard fully informed of Philip's attempts to prolong his captivity. He was by now king of Sicily as well as Emperor,[*] and with matters on the eastern side of his domains now fully under control, he evidently felt that he was best served in the west by keeping Richard and Philip at loggerheads with each other.

The second reason for the failure of the peace talks was that Philip's miners had been working under Le Vaudreuil, on the basis that he knew he would have to give it up as part of the negotiations and did not want Richard to have it intact. The idea was to hand over the town with a good grace and then whistle nonchalantly when the walls just happened to fall down once Richard had control of it, but the French miners had been rather more successful than Philip planned, and the collapse occurred while the talks were actually taking place.[13] Richard called off the conference and left.

There was more inconclusive back-and-forth for the remainder of that year's campaigning season. Realising that this could go on forever with neither of them making any significant headway, and both having other matters to attend to, the kings engaged in more serious negotiations over the winter. The result was the Peace of Louviers, sealed in January 1196, under the terms of which Philip

---

[*] Tancred of Lecce and his elder son were both dead (of natural causes) by early 1194, so Emperor Henry's only opponents when he invaded Sicily in his wife's name in August of that year were Tancred's remaining son, the eight-year-old William III, and his mother, who was acting as his regent. Henry was merciless, and the outcome for young William was predictably horrific.

would keep what he had won on the eastern side of Normandy, including Gisors and the whole of the Norman Vexin.[14] In return he ceded his gains in Berry, which meant that he could no longer — in the short term at least — aim to use that region to cut Aquitaine off from Richard's other domains. However, Philip did stay on track with regard to his number one priority: Normandy.

King Richard was a very different man to his father, but he and Henry II did have something in common, in that they ruled a vast and diverse collection of lands and they could not be in all of them at once.

Henry's advantage (albeit one that did not always function smoothly) was that he had sons who could be deployed to outlying regions to impose Plantagenet authority and quell any unrest, while he took care of core business in England and Normandy. But the childless Richard had no such back-up,* and his only real options for support were his brother-in-law Sancho VII (now unavoidably detained in Navarre) and the untrustworthy John. He therefore had to try to control everything personally, so it was inevitable that he would slip up somewhere — and that Philip would be standing ready to take full advantage of this when it happened.

Richard's priority had always been Aquitaine, but in spending so much time and expending so much effort there, he left other areas unattended. England was safe from Philip's ambitions, and Richard's deputies there were able to keep John in check, but Philip's hungry eye was always on the Plantagenet domains in the northern half of France. By the spring of 1196, with Philip's

---

* Richard had no legitimate children, which was unsurprising given that he and his wife had barely seen each other for years, but he did have at least one illegitimate son, who had been born sometime in the early 1180s. This was at a point when Richard and Philip Augustus were friends and allies, and this son was called Philip, a choice Richard might have come to regret later on. He is generally known as Philip of Cognac (a minor lordship in Aquitaine), as he became lord there when Richard arranged his marriage to the heiress. Little is known of his life, and he was not given any prominent role or favoured by his father in the same way that Henry II's illegitimate sons had been.

gains confirmed by the Peace of Louviers and the Franco-Norman border weakened to a considerable extent, Richard realised that he needed to take some kind of significant action if the duchy of Normandy were not to slide inexorably out of his grasp. He had lost a number of strong castles, which he had little prospect of regaining, so the next best thing was to build a new one.

He had his eye on a very promising site: Les Andelys, a naturally defensible position on a tall outcrop of rock overlooking a loop of the River Seine, 60 miles north-west of Paris and 25 miles south-east of Rouen. The main problem with the site was that it was of such importance to both sides that it had been the explicit subject of several clauses in the Peace of Louviers. These stipulated that Les Andelys would not form part of the domain of either king, but would instead be controlled by the archbishop of Rouen, the highest-ranking prelate in Normandy. It was also stated specifically in the terms of the Peace that the site could not be built upon: *Andeliacum non poterit inforciari* ('Les Andelys cannot be fortified') is one of the least ambiguous clauses imaginable, so there could be no room for misinterpretation.

Richard, straightforward fellow that he was, solved this problem via the simple expedient of completely ignoring the terms he had just agreed, and in the spring of 1196 construction work began on the castle he would name Château Gaillard.* Like all castles it would serve both a defensive and an offensive purpose, helping to plug the gap in the Norman border fortifications caused by the loss of Gisors, dominating the route from Paris to Rouen and possibly also serving as the base for future operations as and when Richard might want to attempt a reconquest of the Norman lands he had lost to Philip. It was a hugely ambitious project, an entire military campus rather than merely a simple castle, but Richard was prepared to throw an enormous amount of money at it,† and

---

* The word *gaillard* has overtones of impertinence, bawdiness or ribaldry, so in calling the stronghold his 'cheeky castle' Richard was very much taunting Philip and the French.

† In total, Richard spent around £11,500 on Château Gaillard. For context, that was more than he spent on all the castles in England put together during his whole reign, and it also amounted to twice the annual revenue of the entire duchy of Normandy.

the result was that the whole complex was completed in just two years, a fraction of the time that might normally be expected.

Château Gaillard was a masterclass in military architecture. Its foundation was a superb natural topographical situation: a rock 300 feet high with steep and impassable slopes to the north and east. The site overlooked and dominated the river, which protected it to the west, meaning that any attempt to besiege the castle could only come from the south and could be planned for accordingly. The fortifications combined the concentric and the linear, with a strong central keep and no fewer than three baileys: the inner around the keep, with the middle one encircling that, itself surrounded by a deep ditch and accessible only via a bridge from the third, outer bailey at the southern end of the complex. Each had its own separate high walls, with those of the middle and outer baileys incorporating cylindrical towers at regular intervals.

The defensive innovations continued. Château Gaillard was one of the first castles in Europe to use machicolations,* and the walls of the inner bailey, although having no mural towers, were of a wavy design: this meant that they were more effective at withstanding attacks from siege machinery than straight walls, and that arrows could be loosed from atop them at all angles to provide a complete field of fire with no dead spots. The gatehouse leading from the middle to the inner bailey similarly avoided blind spots in front of the gate by means of towers flanking its entrance.

Of course, castle architecture was not only about the built environment, but also the people inside it, their lives and their health. And here again Château Gaillard was well designed, with each separate bailey having its own well, so the garrison would have access to fresh water even if they had to retreat behind the next set of defences. A small town called Petit Andely was constructed to the north of the castle, lower down towards the river, that would serve as a hub for the supply of provisions and manpower.[15]

---

* *Machicolations* were stone projections at the top of a wall that allowed objects to be dropped through them on to anyone at the bottom of the wall on the outside.

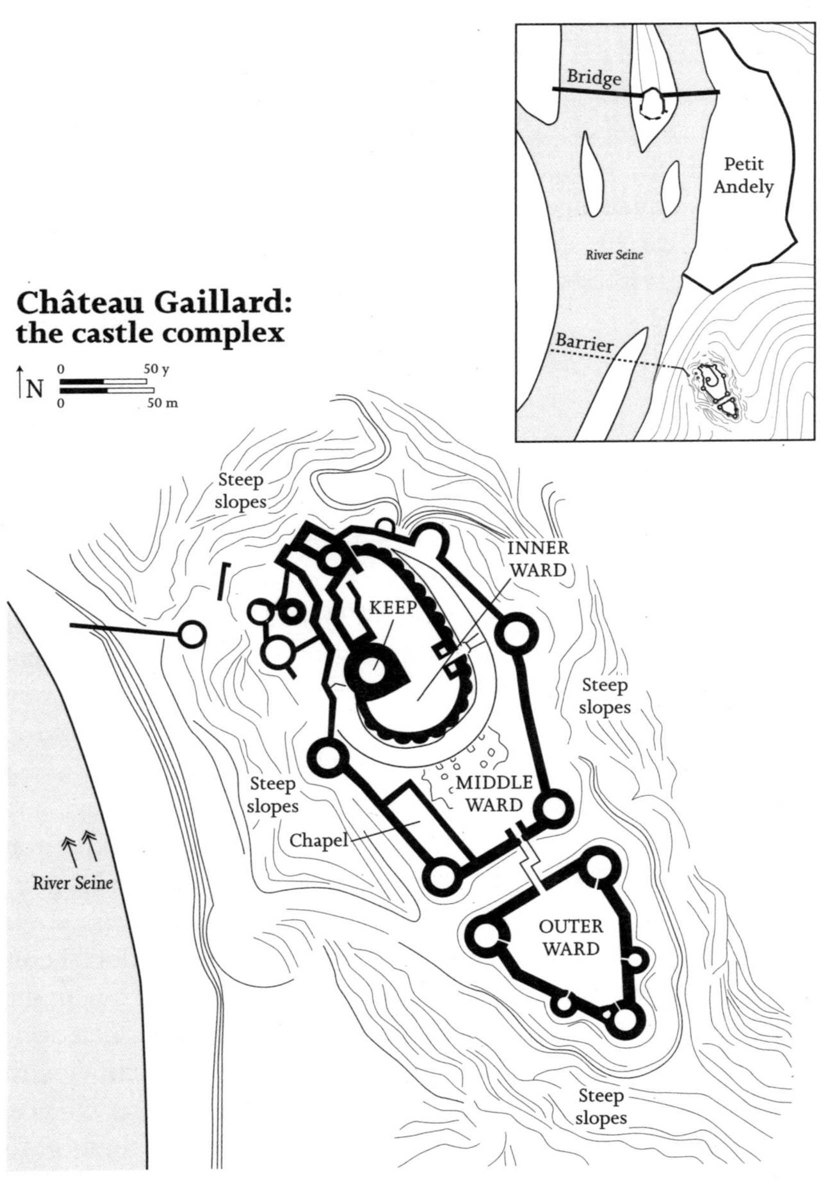

Bridge
Petit Andely
River Seine
Barrier
Château Gaillard:
the castle complex
N
0 50 y
0 50 m
Steep slopes
INNER WARD
KEEP
Steep slopes
Steep slopes
MIDDLE WARD
Chapel
River Seine
OUTER WARD
Steep slopes

Richard believed Château Gaillard to be impregnable, and boasted to that effect: 'By God's throat,' he said, 'if that castle were made entirely of butter, not to speak of iron or stone, I would have no doubt at all that I would be able to defend it stoutly against him [Philip] and all his forces.' Philip, meanwhile, however displeased he was at the breaking of the treaty and the fortification of the prohibited site, took the new and looming presence of Château Gaillard as a challenge: so confident was he that he would one day capture it that 'he said in public hearing and asserted boldly on oath that he wished that castle were made wholly of iron'.[16]

While this military construction work was going on, both kings bolstered their political positions via marriage alliances.

Philip's position in this regard was, of course, complicated by the fact that he was already married. Pope Celestine had always been sceptical about the declaration of annulment issued by Philip's tame council in November 1193, and in March 1195, after investigating the matter thoroughly, he pronounced the annulment itself invalid. As far as he was concerned, Philip and Ingeborg were still legally married. This did not necessarily mean that they had to live together as man and wife (Henry II had, after all, kept Eleanor of Aquitaine in captivity for sixteen years of their marriage, and Richard and Berengaria lived almost entirely separate lives), but it did mean that Philip was not at liberty to marry anyone else.

Philip's own view was that he was a single man, and moreover one who had to consider the demands of the succession. Louis was by this time coming up for nine years old, and had begun the sort of martial training that could easily result in a sudden accident, and Philip had no other children. His ongoing conflict with Richard also meant that he was in need of a new political alliance, preferably one with the Empire, so marriage was the solution to both problems.

He had been looking about him for some time now and, to start with, he had aimed high. Emperor Henry had no daughters or sisters, but he did have a female cousin, Agnes of Hohenstaufen, whose father Conrad had been Frederick Barbarossa's only brother. Her pedigree was eminently suitable for Philip's purposes, and she had the added bonus of being a great heiress, an only surviving child in line to inherit Conrad's title of Count Palatine of the Rhine along with other family estates. Philip had made enquiries about her in 1194, when he was twenty-eight and she around eighteen and therefore very much of childbearing age.

Unfortunately for his purposes, Philip's reputation had preceded him. He had already attempted the repudiation of two wives, so how could he be trusted not to do the same to a third? The parents of any prospective bride were right to be nervous. Plus, of course, there was the very murky ongoing situation with Ingeborg – not officially resolved at that time, as the pope was still investigating – and the consequent danger that any new marriage would be considered bigamous and its offspring illegitimate. It was just too much of a risk. Agnes's parents diplomatically made no public pronouncement about the French king's proposal, but they quietly married her off to someone else so that she was no longer available.*

By 1196 Philip was having to set his sights a little lower, and he finally found a willing accomplice in Berthold IV, the duke of Merania.† Berthold was happy for his twenty-one-year-old daughter (coincidentally another Agnes) to enter into what was now officially considered by the pope to be a bigamous marriage, if it meant she could claim the prestigious title of queen of France. Agnes herself raised no objection, and she travelled from the eastern edge of the Empire to France, arriving in June 1196. Given what she knew of the events of three years earlier, she must have been at least mildly apprehensive, but the wedding (and the wedding night) passed without incident and the couple began to co-habit as husband and wife. Ingeborg, when the news reached

---

* To add a further insult to Philip's pride, Agnes's husband was Henry of Brunswick, King Richard's nephew (the eldest son of Richard's sister Matilda and Henry the Lion, duke of Saxony), who became Count Palatine of the Rhine in 1195 upon Conrad's death.

† Merania was a duchy on the far side of the Empire, situated on the Adriatic coast in what is now Croatia.

the convent where she was confined, wrote once more to Pope Celestine to complain, but he was by now in his nineties and had less energy to engage actively in this sort of conflict. Philip, therefore, was able to think that he had got away with it.

A few months later, Richard countered with a marriage alliance of his own – or, rather, of his widowed sister, Joanna. After leaving Sicily with Richard back in 1191, Joanna had accompanied him and Berengaria to Cyprus and the Holy Land, and the two women had later made their own way back to Europe after Richard's capture. Since then Joanna had been living somewhere in Richard's French territories, still a widow, but in October 1196 she was married to Count Raymond VI of Toulouse. Raymond was Philip's first cousin (his mother, Constance of France, had been Louis VII's only sister), but this new marriage gave him a closer tie to the man who was both duke of neighbouring Aquitaine and king of England. It also meant that Richard had firm alliances all around Philip's southern borders, in Toulouse, Castile and Navarre. He had not actually seen his sister Eleanor, queen of Castile, since she was nine years old, but royal alliances did not rest on close personal connections: it was the family bloodline and loyalty to it that counted, and Eleanor and her husband Alfonso VIII counted themselves Richard's allies and friends.[17]

It was also in 1196 that the thorny question of Brittany reared its head once again, this time to Philip's eventual advantage. Constance, duchess in her own right, had been married against her will since 1189 to Ranulf, the earl of Chester, but they more or less ignored each other and the union had produced no children. The duchy's heir remained Arthur, now aged nine, with his sister, the twelve-year-old Eleanor, as the 'spare'. Now that Arthur had survived the perils of early childhood, both kings took a greater interest in him; and, in fact, Richard had never officially repealed the declaration he had made in Sicily about Arthur being his heir, so Arthur was a person of great interest all round.

In the spring of 1196 Richard summoned Constance to appear in person at his court in Normandy, an invitation she could not refuse, but as soon as she crossed the border from Brittany she was kidnapped. Ostensibly the culprit was Ranulf, with Richard claiming he had nothing to do with it, but it seems extremely unlikely that Ranulf would have acted in this way without his king's permission, and Richard certainly did not order her release. Constance was an experienced politician (and one who was rightly suspicious of Richard), so she had left Arthur safely in Brittany in the care of some of her advisors, ensuring that they would not both end up in the English king's clutches at the same time. After several months, when it became clear that Constance was not going to be released any time soon, these Breton lords renounced their fealty to Richard, swore allegiance to Arthur as their duke, appealed to Philip Augustus for assistance and managed to spirit the boy away to the royal court in Paris.

Philip, naturally, was only too glad to have the heir to Brittany in his possession as well as the opportunity to drive a further wedge between the remaining Plantagenet family members. He welcomed Arthur, who remained in Paris for a couple of years in the household of Philip's son Louis, who was the same age.* There was some talk of a marriage between Louis and Eleanor of Brittany, but it came to nothing, probably because her future status was so uncertain. She was not an heiress, and at this point it was anybody's guess whether she would end up being the sister of a duke or the sister of a king. Philip, with only one child himself and therefore only one shot at forming a strategic marriage alliance, was better off holding Louis back for now in the hope that something more prestigious would come along later.

---

* Most noble boys were sent away from home at a young age in order to serve as pages and squires with a lord who was not their father. This was not the case for royal youths, however, who instead formed their own households into which others were brought; in this way bonds of friendship and loyalty were formed between the heir to the throne and those who would grow up to be the trusted advisors of his own generation. As well as Arthur of Brittany, Louis's household also included Robert and Peter of Dreux, the two eldest sons of Philip's cousin Robert II of Dreux, who were of a similar age to him.

The pivotal year of 1196 was a busy one, but in between their political and matrimonial manoeuvring and castle construction, the kings still found plenty of time for campaigning.

Richard blithely continued to ignore the terms of the Peace of Louviers, taking Nonancourt in Normandy (without a fight, 'by trick and treason, for he paid off the garrison of knights') despite having ceded it to Philip as part of the treaty.[18] Philip, in turn, set out on the road soon after his wedding and erected his siege engines at Aumale, remaining there for several weeks. Richard arrived to relieve the stronghold, but for some reason he hesitated to fight, and was then defeated in a skirmish, whereupon 'he turned and fled'.

Aumale surrendered to Philip on 20 August. He demolished what remained of the fortifications but did not order any mass executions, instead ransoming the garrison back to Richard, 'allowing them to depart unharmed, in peace, and with their property, horses, and weapons', while gaining a useful 3,000 marks in cash. He then made his own way to Nonancourt – where by now the inhabitants must have been hardly aware of whether they were coming or going – and recaptured it, 'together with its fifteen knights, eighteen crossbowmen, many other prisoners, and an ample supply of provisions'.* He entrusted Nonancourt to his cousin Robert II of Dreux, whose own principal seat was only 10 miles away.

The usual break in campaigning took place over the winter, but the spring of 1197 found Richard making raids into the northern county of Ponthieu, where his former fiancée, Philip's sister Alice, was now the countess by marriage. Richard acted with cruelty, burning the port town of Saint-Valéry and carrying off plenty of booty, including the holy relics of the saint after whom the town was named. He found some English ships in the harbour there, despite his own recent decree (of which more in a moment) that

---

*As demonstrated by the modest size of this particular garrison, one of the great strategic advantages of castles was that they could be held by a relatively small number of men who could dominate a disproportionately large area of land.

no English merchants should trade with Flanders; he seized the cargoes, burned the ships and hanged the crews, even though they were his own subjects.

Richard next turned to raid the Beauvais area, where he scored a coup in capturing King Philip's cousin and his own long-time antagonist, Bishop Philip of Dreux. The bishop sent his brother Henry, the bishop of Orleans, to Rome with a letter for the pope complaining that Richard had imprisoned a churchman, but Celestine showed no sympathy, replying that Philip had brought this on himself: 'You have borne the shield in place of the chasuble, the sword in place of the stole, the hauberk for the alb [...] Into the pit which you have made, you have deservedly fallen.'[19] Bishop Philip made one unsuccessful attempt to escape, but was then put under closer guard, 'given harsh treatment in prison' and 'heavily loaded with chains'; he would not see the light of day again while Richard lived.[20]

In the summer of 1197 King Philip was dismayed to find that Richard was actually making some gains in Normandy, and that he had persuaded the hitherto loyal count of Hainaut and Flanders to join him. This was the young man who was Baldwin VI of Hainaut and Baldwin IX of Flanders, having succeeded to both titles following the deaths of his father and mother. His yielding to Richard was not entirely a surprise: the wealth and prosperity of both his counties depended to a great extent on trade with England, and Richard had placed economic sanctions on him by ordering English merchants not to trade in the region. Baldwin also resented the long-ago actions of his uncle, Count Philip of Flanders, in handing over the whole county of Artois to King Philip as the dowry for Baldwin's late sister Queen Isabelle of Hainaut. Artois now belonged to the young Prince Louis and was controlled by his father while he was underage, taking quite a chunk out of Baldwin's own holdings. With Richard's acquiescence, Baldwin invaded Artois.

This was a direct rebellion by a sworn vassal, and therefore a situation requiring firm and immediate action from Philip in order to reimpose royal authority. There is a difference, however, between 'immediate' and 'precipitate': Philip rode for Flanders but did so with such enthusiasm that he outpaced his baggage and found his supply lines cut behind him as Baldwin had bridges destroyed. Stranded, Philip had no choice but to agree to talks, and all three parties met in September.

But these and other domestic matters were soon overshadowed by an event of great international significance: the unexpected demise, on 28 September 1197, of Emperor Henry. He was only thirty-one, and his death – of some kind of fever, possibly malaria – threw the Empire into chaos. Both Philip and Richard now had to scramble for position and alliances there, in order to ensure that they salvaged something from the situation and made what gains they could.

In theory, the imperial throne was elective: that is, after the death of an Emperor a group of senior nobles would elect a successor from among those of suitable rank and family, who did not necessarily have to be closely related to his predecessor. In practice, most Emperors crowned a son as 'king of the Romans', and therefore the designated heir, so that succession to the Empire had become hereditary by default. But this only worked if the heir was a grown man at the time of his father's death, and in this case Henry's only child was a son, Frederick of Hohenstaufen, who was just two years old. A genuine election would therefore be needed.

In a move that surprised nobody, Philip and Richard backed different candidates. Philip supported Duke Philip of Swabia, who was Emperor Henry's younger brother and a son of the great Frederick Barbarossa, while Richard threw his weight behind Otto of Brunswick, who was the son of Henry the Lion, the late duke of Saxony – which, not coincidentally, made him Richard's nephew.* Matters grew more complicated when *both* were elected, by different and rival groups: Philip of Swabia in March 1198 by

---

* Otto's older brother Henry, duke of Saxony and Bavaria in his own right and Count Palatine of the Rhine by marriage, would have been an even better candidate, but he was at this point in the Holy Land, and claimants to the imperial throne needed to be on the spot in Germany in order to act quickly and secure the necessary support.

a party of princes mainly situated in the south of the Empire, and then Otto by a primarily northern contingent in June. Otto won the overall race – for now, anyway – when he was crowned king of the Romans at Aachen in early July.

Having Richard as king of England on one side of him and Richard's nephew as king and Emperor-elect on the other side put Philip at a great disadvantage. This was compounded when Richard made more alliances that started to bite away at Philip's borders: with Geoffrey, count of Perche, who was married to Richard's niece Richenza (Otto's sister); with Louis of Blois, Philip's own nephew (although he, at the encouragement of his cousin and close ally Theobald III, count of Champagne,[*] another of the king's nephews, changed his mind again quite swiftly and re-defected to Philip); and with Renaud de Dammartin, count of Boulogne, whose lands included the major sea ports on the Channel.

Renaud was an interesting and somewhat slippery character; he was the same age as King Philip and had been brought up with him in the royal household, but he had later wavered several times between Capetian and Plantagenet loyalties. He was the count of Boulogne by marriage, having kidnapped and forced into marriage the countess in her own right, Ida of Boulogne, in 1191.[†] This had made him enemies among the Dreux family, because he had put aside his first wife (who was Count Robert II's niece) in order to do so. Renaud's loyalties were to fluctuate again in future, as we will see.

---

[*] Theobald and Louis were first cousins twice over, as their fathers (Henry I of Champagne and Theobald V of Blois) had been brothers, and their mothers (Marie and Alix of France) had been sisters.

[†] The Boulogne succession was both female and unfortunate for several consecutive generations. Ida's mother, Marie of Boulogne (the daughter of King Stephen of England), had been a professed nun who was abducted from her convent by Matthew of Alsace (the younger brother of Count Philip of Flanders), who then forcibly married her when the deaths of both her brothers made her an heiress and a valuable prize. She never ceased petitioning for an annulment, and eventually re-entered her Order after giving birth to two daughters. Ida was similarly forced into marriage with Renaud, and would bear him one daughter, Matilda, whom we will meet later.

The year 1198 would turn out to be one of almost unmitigated disaster for Philip in France, quite apart from his disappointment at the way events transpired in the Empire. In April he promised aid to Count Aymer of Angoulême, who was rebelling against Richard again, but his attempts to form alliances with other lords in Aquitaine did not get very far, and he could make no headway against Richard there.

Worse was to come when Philip also lost his hold on Brittany. Duchess Constance had been imprisoned in Normandy for two years, but in 1198 Richard had a change of heart: she was released and her unwanted marriage to Ranulf of Chester was annulled. Constance, as we have already noted, was a shrewd politician, and her absolute priorities were Brittany and the rights of her children. It was now obvious to all parties that Richard, having turned forty and living separately from his wife, was not going to father any legitimate children, which meant that the position of heir to the English throne was there for the taking. Arthur, now aged eleven and with some governmental experience behind him already (having acted as duke, with support from his mother's advisors, while she was in captivity), had a very good claim to that position. It was therefore in his best interests for Constance to effect a switch, so following her release she and Arthur transferred their and Brittany's allegiance from Philip to Richard.

Short of invading Brittany, there was not much Philip could do about this, and then in September his year went from bad to worse when Count Baldwin of Flanders invaded Artois again. Philip was at that time busy in the Vexin, so when the besieged town of Saint-Omer appealed to him for help, he was not able to send a relief force in time. Under the prevailing conventions of siege warfare, Saint-Omer was therefore allowed to yield in order to avoid devastation, and the other major town in Artois, Aire, surrendered without a fight.

Matters in the Vexin did not go to plan, either:

The king of England with a force of fifteen hundred armed knights, many mercenaries, and a vast host of armed foot soldiers unexpectedly laid waste to the Vexin around Gisors, destroyed the fortress which they call Courcelles, and burned and plundered many rural villages. King Philip, burning with a towering rage, then tried to reach the castle of Gisors with only five hundred knights. But because of the enemy blocking the way, no route was open to him. When he saw this, his brave spirit overtook his equanimity and he launched a furious charge right into the battle lines of the enemy. With only a few knights, he fought the enemy bravely and by the mercy of God he came out unharmed and made it to Gisors, though many of his knights were taken prisoner.[21]

The tactful Rigord, who narrates this incident, omits the most mortifying part: as Philip's forces were crossing it during their retreat, the bridge over the River Epte collapsed under the weight, and many men were plunged into the river. As they all saw the incident as being of symbolic significance, those chroniclers who do mention the episode of the bridge portray it in different ways. William the Breton says specifically that Philip's horse took him safely to the other side, although others fell in the water, while Roger of Howden and Roger of Wendover are adamant that Philip himself took a tumble and that he 'had to drink of it' and 'he was rolled over and over in the mud'.[22] Whatever happened, the incident did not have any serious consequences except embarrassment: Philip was neither drowned nor captured, and made it safely inside Gisors castle.

If the contemporary English chroniclers (and, indeed, some later Anglophone scholars) are to be believed, Philip's situation at this point, late 1198, was verging on desperation. But if we look more closely we can see that this was not really the case. Since his release from captivity Richard had certainly regained some of the lands and castles that Philip had conquered in his absence, but Philip still held many of them and was, even now, in a better position than he had been before the crusade. His intelligence was holding its own against Richard's bellicosity, and Richard had not made any attempt – nor been *able* to make any attempt – on Philip's substantive French holdings.

This is not to say that Philip had not experienced setbacks during the last few years. But these were of no lasting significance, and indeed they had enabled him to learn several valuable lessons that would serve him well later on. His impetuosity, for all that Rigord tried to portray it in a positive light as 'his brave spirit' that 'overtook his equanimity', still needed to be reined in, and the instructions he needed to give himself, based on his recent experiences, could be boiled down to: remain calm and don't let your enemy get under your skin too much; don't rush; plan ahead properly; and make sure you have adequate supplies and supply lines. Philip, now well into his thirties, could take these lessons on board more thoroughly than he had done when he was a teenager, and he would not be caught unawares or unprepared again.

There was one piece of good news amid the general gloom of 1198, because it was at some point in this year that Philip's wife, Agnes, whether bigamous or not, gave birth to his second child. The baby was a girl, named Marie, which from Philip's point of view was not quite as good as having a second son, but it did prove that the couple were capable of having children together, and of course a daughter would be very useful later on in terms of forming a marriage alliance. Philip was pleased, accepted the congratulations of his nobles, and hoped for a boy next time.

And then came the final blow that was to strike him in 1198, in the form of a new international development from a recently arrived and extremely influential player.

The ancient Pope Celestine III had died in January 1198. The death of a pope was always a seismic event, and sometimes it could take weeks or even months before a successor was elected, but this was not the case here: the twenty-one (of a total of twenty-nine)* cardinals who were present in Rome at the time elected Cardinal

---

* The college of cardinals was, at this time, an almost exclusively Roman and Italian body. The twenty-one present in Rome for the election were all Italians, while the other eight were a further

Lothar of Segni to the papal throne on the very day of Celestine's death. He was the youngest among the group, only thirty-seven years old, and accepted his election and took the name Innocent III.[23] A pope's selection of a regnal name was symbolic, and Innocent's choice sent an ominous warning to the crowned heads of Christendom: Innocent II (r. 1130–43) had been unafraid to intervene in secular affairs, having excommunicated King Roger II of Sicily when he was in conflict with the Emperor of the time, and also having placed France under an interdict when he and Louis VII disagreed over an appointment to an archbishopric.

The new Innocent III wasted very little time before throwing himself into international affairs, proclaiming a new crusade to the Holy Land within months of his election. There was one very large stumbling block in the way of such a plan, however: any military campaign would require the kings of France and England (not to mention the Emperor) to be at peace with each other, so they could join or at least support it. Given that the chances of this happening were approximately zero, it was with commendable optimism and not a little self-confidence that Innocent dispatched a cardinal legate, Peter of Capua, to France in late 1198 to mediate between Philip and Richard.

Peter arrived at Christmas, with a brief that encompassed three distinct elements, none of which Philip was terribly keen to talk about: peace with Richard, the potential crusade, and the situation of Ingeborg, whose cause Innocent was already espousing. Little headway was made, although Philip did offer a further truce, which at least gave Peter something to work with as he travelled to Normandy to meet with Richard. Alas, matters then went from bad to worse for the legate. Richard, who did not see that he was in any way obliged to support a papacy that had done nothing for him while he was imprisoned in Germany, was not in the best of moods before the conference even began, and when Peter ended

six Italians – who were either absent in their own sees or abroad working as papal legates – plus the archbishop of Mainz in Germany and William Whitehands, the archbishop of Reims, in France.

it by unwisely asking Richard to release the bishop of Beauvais, the situation went rapidly downhill.

Rigord's account of the incident is rather understated, because of course he was better informed about Peter's negotiations with Philip, so of the meeting with Richard he says only that the legate was 'unable to reestablish the peace, which seemed beyond repair'. The later biographer of William Marshal has a much more entertaining vignette. Marshal was present with Richard at this time, and in later life he recounted many anecdotes to his biographer, so there is a ring of truth about the way the king is said to have reacted:

> King Richard was still so furious [about the legate's request to release Bishop Philip] that he was unable to utter a single word; instead, he huffed and puffed in his anger. Like a wild boar wounded by the huntsman, he retired huffing and puffing into his chamber and ordered the doors to be closed [...] He lay on his back on a bed, and nobody was so bold as to dare to call at the door.[24]

Peter returned to King Philip to tell him of his lack of success in the meeting with Richard (and to complain that 'he raised his eyebrows in my direction and turned as red as blazing fire, so much that I fully expected him to assault me').[25] All prospect of lasting peace evaporated, together with any of Innocent's remaining hopes of a glorious crusade led by two friendly and allied kings.

The war in the Plantagenet lands in France looked as though it would continue to grind along its attritional path; but, in the spring of 1199, 'God visited the kingdom of the French'.[26]

In March of that year Philip enjoyed something of a respite in the north, while Richard rode south to fight against Philip's allies in Aquitaine, particularly Aymer, the count of Angoulême, and his maternal half-brother, another Aymer, the viscount of Limoges.

These two men had been a thorn in Richard's side for many years, and he was glad to combine a military campaign with the prospect of financial gain; there was a popular rumour circulating that a great treasure had been found at the castle of Chalûs-Chabrol, controlled by Aymer of Limoges, and Richard was keen to get his hands on it.*

Philip was in Paris and so did not find out about events at Chalûs-Chabrol until later, but in short, on 26 March Richard was hit by a crossbow bolt loosed by one of the castle's defenders. The wound was in his left shoulder, and at first he tried to make light of it, but after a surgeon 'could not easily find the iron embedded in his very fat body'† and 'carelessly mangled the king's arm in every part', blood poisoning set in.[27] As an experienced soldier, Richard knew that death was near, so he wrote to summon his mother (rather than his wife, which probably says something about their relationship). Eleanor had for several years been enjoying a kind of semi-retirement at Fontevraud Abbey, so she was around 130 miles away, but she travelled quickly and death by blood poisoning was slow. Richard was able to cling on until she arrived, and she was by his bedside when he died on 6 April.[28]

It was spring when the news reached Paris, but all Philip's Christmases had come at once. Richard was only forty-one and might have expected to live a good many years yet, but now he had suddenly, miraculously, been removed for good. And he had left no legitimate child, which meant that there was a new Plantagenet family rift that Philip was well able to exploit.

* This is the sort of tale that sounds apocryphal, but so many chroniclers from both sides mention this treasure – even describing it as gold and depicting an emperor with his wife and family – that it is not impossible that some kind of ancient or Roman hoard had been dug up.
† We tend to picture Richard the Lionheart as a fine figure of a man right up until his death, but in fact his physical condition appears to have been waning in the same way as that of some of his other royal ancestors, who had a tendency towards obesity in middle age.

PART III

John

1199–1216

The Last of the Plantagenets

Philip needed to take a few deep breaths.

For twenty years he had faced challenging and dangerous Plantagenet opponents, a decade of Henry II followed by a decade of Richard, so the prospect of having either the feckless and erratic John or the inexperienced Arthur on the English throne was so attractive as to be intoxicating. The opportunities now unfolding were almost boundless, but he had to be careful. Although England's new king, whoever it was, would be easier to deal with than his predecessors, Philip needed to remember the lessons he had learned during the last few years: take stock, plan carefully, avoid overconfidence and play the long game. But the rewards, if he could manage all this successfully, would be great, and it was not unthinkable that he could eradicate the Plantagenet presence from France once and for all.

Philip's most important short-term goal, while he planned his longer-term strategy, was to ensure that there was as much conflict as possible between these last two male Plantagenets. The more uncertainty there was over the succession to the English throne and the family's continental lands, and the more chaos this caused, the more he and France could benefit. Philip was aided in this process by Richard's childless marriage, his failure in recent years to confirm his choice of heir and the fact that his eclectic collection of lands varied in their inheritance customs – indeed, the rules of inheritance were not even set in stone within some of the individual territories. In England, for example, there were several potential paths to the throne. As the years and centuries went by, straightforward heredity would become the defining criterion for succession to the throne, and this has continued up until the present day. This means that the order of precedence can be determined simply by looking at a family tree, and a potentially infinite line of heirs can be identified.* Various tweaks have been made over the centuries, principally on the issues of religion or of whether the crown could pass to or through a female, but birth remains the most important factor. Back in the late twelfth century, though, this was not the case. Henry II had attempted to impose strict hereditary succession, even to the extent of having his eldest son crowned during his own lifetime, but he had not entirely succeeded because there were other elements to take into account. In a world where a monarch was a military leader, the claims of an adult man held greater weight than those of a woman or child, regardless of birth order, and there were also some slightly more esoteric factors: election by, and support of, the nobility; designation as heir by the previous king; and proximity of relationship to the previous king or kings.

This last was complicated. In terms of pure hereditary right and male primogeniture,† Arthur had a better claim to the throne than John, because he was the son of John's elder brother. However, another prevalent custom was that the younger son of a reigning king took precedence over a grandson whose father had never ruled, even if the grandson came from the senior line, because the son had a closer degree of relationship to the previous king – and this favoured John. In general, Anjou, Maine and Touraine would

---

* The website britroyals.com/succession.asp, for example, has a list of the current first 100 people in the line of succession to the British throne (which contains a few surprises, not least the king of Norway, included because he is a great-grandson of Edward VII), and it has been claimed elsewhere that a line of some 5,000 individuals could be compiled.

† The custom is often referred to simply as primogeniture, but this is incorrect: *male* (or *male-preference*) *primogeniture* and *absolute primogeniture* are two separate things and need to be differentiated. The former prioritises males over females (i.e., a younger son is higher in the order than an older daughter, and a daughter can only inherit if there are no sons), while the latter prioritises absolutely by age, with no reference to sex (i.e., an older daughter is higher in the order than a younger son). In the UK royal succession, male primogeniture was replaced by absolute primogeniture in 2011.

give precedence to the grandson, and England and Normandy to the son, which just complicated matters further. And, to cap it all, there was the not-insignificant fact that John was thirty-two and Arthur had only just turned twelve.

In short, the whole situation was hopelessly unclear, open to interpretation and ripe for exploitation, and this suited Philip's purposes very well. As ever, his best tactic was to support the junior member of the family against the senior, so, as John seemed to be in pole position, Philip declared for Arthur. It seems very unlikely that Philip really believed that he could put Arthur on the English throne – a boy from Brittany who had never even crossed the Channel, and who was under the guidance of a mother who had good cause to dislike the Plantagenet dynasty and all it stood for. So it is easier to believe either that Philip was attempting to force apart the union of territories that had occurred almost by accident under Henry II, separating the Plantagenet lands in France from the English throne via different inheritance customs, or that he was simply out to cause as much trouble as possible.

Both of these explanations are logical. Philip's priority was less about who actually ended up on the English throne – he wanted someone there whom he could dominate, and either of these candidates would do – and more about his own and France's potential for gain. Having Anjou, Maine, Touraine and possibly even Normandy cut off from the resources of the English crown would be an advantage, allowing him to isolate and attack his primary targets, and any continuing intra-Plantagenet conflict at all would be to his benefit. Philip's immediate actions suggest that he was thinking along these lines: as well as declaring for Arthur, he was in the saddle and on his way to invade Normandy within days of hearing of Richard's death. There he seized the luckless Évreux once more, and devastated eastern Normandy all the way down and across the Maine border as far as Le Mans.

Philip's quick action gave him a political and military head start, but there were other players entering the game, and he needed to remain wary. In particular, it was imperative that he pay due attention to another lesson from his past and force himself to get over any residual tendency to underestimate women, because the campaigns of both principals were spearheaded by their mothers. Eleanor of Aquitaine, although in her late seventies and forced by circumstances out of her retirement, was still a formidable and much-respected figure, and she had declared for her son over her grandson.

Eleanor also acted without delay. As duchess of Aquitaine in her own right, she rendered homage to Philip for Poitou to reconfirm her entitlement – which nobody could possibly doubt – and then ceded it to John, just as she had done for Richard many years previously. John immediately awarded it back to Eleanor for the term of her life, which sounds odd but was actually such a sensible move that one suspects the idea was hers all along. John was not well known in Aquitaine, and he had seen enough of the struggles of the much more visible and capable Richard to know that he had little hope of being able to quell any unrest there while he was also fighting on several other fronts. So this arrangement meant that he would get Poitou back in due course – for even Eleanor of Aquitaine could not live forever – but for now it was in experienced and well-respected hands. Having his mother in his corner was also a great political triumph for John, as she was able to use her experience and contacts to drum up support for him, and could put the resources of her duchy at his disposal.

This effectively stopped Philip from making any direct move in Aquitaine, because he would not be able to turn any loyal nobles against the much-loved woman who had been their ruling lady for more than sixty years. However, there was a chink of hope due to the fact that Eleanor was not able to lead armies in person in the way Richard had done, something that was imperative if Aquitaine were to be kept under firm control. Philip could not make a move against her now he had accepted her homage, but that was not to say that he might not turn a blind eye to any already rebellious vassals agitating against Eleanor or John.

Matters looked brighter further north, and much of this was due to another woman whom nobody in their right mind would underestimate. Constance of Brittany was, of course, acting for

Arthur and was prepared to fight for her son until her last breath.* Richard's death had come at a bad time for Constance. From her point of view, it would actually have been more useful if he had survived another few years until Arthur was older and more politically active, which would have made him a much more viable candidate for the English throne. The situation could not be helped, though, and Constance could do nothing but face it as best she could. She was badly in need of a powerful ally against John, and was therefore happy to accept Philip's declaration of support. She did not waste any time, either, raising troops immediately on hearing of Richard's death and mobilising in even more of a hurry than Philip himself.

Events moved very rapidly.

Richard had died on 6 April 1199. It took Constance less than two weeks to march through Anjou and seize its capital, Angers, and it was there on 18 April (Easter Sunday) that a group of nobles proclaimed Arthur their lord. On the same day, Arthur issued a charter in which he styled himself count of Anjou as well as duke of Brittany, and mother and son began to plan their next steps.[1] However, there was alarm in Normandy at the prospect of being subject to a Breton, so the nobility there retaliated by proclaiming John their duke on 25 April.

John, meanwhile, with the main prize now dangling so tantalisingly close, had managed to act with great sense. Realising that baronial support and military might were the two key factors for success, and that both of these things could be bought, he had ridden straight for Richard's treasury at Chinon as soon as he heard of his brother's death. He also knew that the rite of coronation was all-important in making a king, so he sailed across the Channel,

---

* Constance's loyalty to her children was absolute. The chief reason she had remained in captivity for so long between 1196 and 1198 was that Richard had offered to release her if she would surrender Arthur into his guardianship, and she had refused as it would not be in his best interests.

headed for Westminster and had himself crowned on 27 May.* He was now, officially, both king of England and duke of Normandy.

This was a major setback for Philip, but he was not giving up yet and there were still plenty of opportunities to sow discord. He and Arthur met in person in August (accounts vary as to whether this was in Le Mans or Tours) and then an important symbolic event took place: 'The said Arthur at once did homage to the French king for Anjou, Poitou, Tours [Touraine], Maine, Brittany, and Normandy; and the king promised Arthur his assistance in gaining possession of all these places.'[2] This was a clever move on Philip's part, because homage was a two-way street: Arthur was acknowledging Philip as his overlord, but in return Philip was recognising Arthur as the rightful lord of those lands. In particular, accepting Arthur's homage for Normandy as well as the other territories signified that Philip considered John a usurper there, which in turn meant that he could legally act against John there any time he wanted to. And finally, doing all this for a lord who was a minor (and at twelve, Arthur would be a minor for some while yet)† gave Philip the opportunity to claim to be acting on his vassal's behalf while actually doing whatever he liked. And so it transpired: Philip sent Arthur to ostensible 'safety' under guard in Paris, 'and seized the cities, castles, and fortresses that belonged to Arthur, and gave them in charge to keepers appointed by himself'.[3]

It was thus in Arthur's absence that Philip met with John for talks later in August. His recent acceptance of Arthur's homage notwithstanding, Philip was well aware that the momentum was with John, who had both England and Normandy holding fast for

---

* This was the Feast of the Ascension, an important day in the Church calendar and therefore an auspicious occasion for a coronation. Ascension was always a Thursday, forty days after Easter Sunday – itself a date that could fluctuate over several weeks – so the actual date of the feast varied from year to year. As John marked the anniversary of his reign on Ascension day each year, rather than on 27 May, this meant that (in a move that could have been expressly designed to irritate later historians and archivists), his regnal years began and ended on different dates each year and were all of different lengths.

† The exact length of Arthur's minority would vary according to his eventual status. The age of majority for French nobles, including the duke of Brittany, was twenty-one; however, kings might assume full powers at an earlier age, as Philip Augustus had done himself.

him – partly as he had been crowned, and partly as the barons there saw his rule as being better for their own interests than Arthur's. So Philip decided that the best means of defence was attack, and he asked John to cede Poitou to Arthur as well as Anjou, Maine and Touraine, taking it as read that these counties were Arthur's already, although John had never actually relinquished them to his nephew. (Brittany did not form part of this discussion, as it was Arthur's undoubted inheritance from his mother and nothing to do with his paternal family.) However, confident in the support of England and Normandy, and with Eleanor and most of Aquitaine also behind him, John felt strong enough to reject Philip's demands, and 'they departed mutually at variance'.[4]

Philip had problems to face on other domestic and international fronts. John had inherited Richard's pre-existing alliances, and counts Baldwin of Flanders and Renaud of Boulogne were not yet ready to return their allegiance to the French king. Emboldened by John's rejection of Philip's terms, they reiterated their support for John in that same month of August 1199. Over in the Empire, John's nephew Otto, now the crowned king of the Romans,[*] also supported him politically, although he could offer little practical help while he was still embroiled in his own internal disputes. This was a long-term threat that Philip could not ignore completely, but for now it could be parked while he concentrated on matters nearer to home.

Constance of Brittany was by now (and probably correctly) almost as suspicious of Philip as she was of John, and she sought a new alliance of her own. Sometime between August and October 1199 she married again, this time to a man of her own choosing: a Poitevin nobleman named Guy of Thouars, who was the younger brother of Aimery, viscount of Thouars. On the

* Otto was not yet Emperor, because this would only happen when he was crowned in Rome by the pope, and Innocent III was still considering his options in the imperial dispute.

one hand, this choice was surprising, as Guy was not a rich and powerful lord who could offer a great deal in terms of resources; but, on the other, he would owe his greatly enhanced status as *jure uxoris* duke of Brittany entirely to Constance, and could concentrate his energies on her causes without having lands of his own to worry about.[*]

Arthur and Constance (but not Philip) were due to meet John for talks in November 1199, but these never took place. They were warned in advance that John intended to take advantage of the personal meeting to capture and imprison Arthur – which, given John's reputation, was entirely plausible – so they slipped away the night before the conference was due to be held. John, thwarted, had to content himself with dismissing Aimery of Thouars (Constance's new brother-in-law) from his post as the castellan of Chinon castle.[5]

John's reputation for duplicity played into Philip's hands, and the French king was able to use this over the autumn of 1199 as he flexed his negotiating muscles in talks with John's allies and sympathisers, and other notable French waverers. He proved to be very proficient at this, and by November some of them were beginning to drift – if not directly towards Philip, then certainly away from John. In that month Theobald III of Champagne held a grand tournament, at which he and his cousin Louis of Blois publicly took the cross and swore to go on the crusade that Pope Innocent was still trying to organise. Counts Baldwin of Flanders and Geoffrey of Perche saw this as an excellent get-out clause from their current predicament, and also promised to go.

Philip Augustus was getting better and better at playing the long game, and all of this turned out to his advantage later on, because none of these four men would survive the campaign later known as the Fourth Crusade. Theobald and Geoffrey died in

---

[*] In addition to political considerations, there was a prevalent thought among contemporaries (and one which is supported by most later scholars) that Constance chose her new husband at least partly on the basis of personal preference – and, we might ask, given what she'd had to put up with during her first two marriages, why shouldn't she?

1201 and 1202 respectively, while still preparing for it. Louis and Baldwin did make it overseas, but Louis was killed at the battle of Adrianople in April 1205, while Baldwin was captured in the same engagement and died in prison shortly afterwards. This left four of France's great counties simultaneously in the hands of minors who could be influenced, controlled and married off by Philip Augustus: Theobald VI of Blois (whose exact date of birth is not known, but who was certainly underage at the time of his father's death);* the seven-year-old Thomas I of Perche; the six-year-old Joan I of Flanders; and Theobald IV of Champagne, who was born posthumously to Theobald III's widow and who was count of Champagne from the day of his birth.†

By Christmas 1199 Philip could feel more confident in his domestic alliances, and in having weakened some of John's, but it was becoming increasingly clear that Arthur's cause was dying. It was time for the king to move to Plan B, which was to accept the reality of the situation and get the best out of it that he could. Once more Philip's negotiating skills were employed as he met with John in January 1200, and once more he proved adept at getting what he wanted. One immediate outcome was the release from captivity of Philip of Dreux, the bishop of Beauvais (who had been languishing in Richard's imprisonment since 1197), and he immediately rejoined King Philip, alongside his brother Count Robert II of Dreux, whose allegiance had never faltered.

The substantive negotiations were detailed and took quite some time to finalise, but eventually the agreement was confirmed in May by the Treaty of Le Goulet, the full text of which has fortunately come down to us.[6] The headline feature is that Philip *appeared* to have backed down: he recognised John as

---

* Theobald VI of Blois first paid homage to Philip in his own right in August 1212. He would have been twenty-one or slightly younger at that point, making him a maximum of thirteen at the time of his father's death.

† Theobald III's widow, who subsequently acted as regent in Champagne for their son Theobald IV, was Blanca of Navarre, the younger sister of Sancho VII and of Berengaria, Richard the Lionheart's queen. As they were both situated in France and widowed, Berengaria and Blanca were able to see something of each other in their later lives, which was unusual for royal sisters.

Richard's lawful heir, and thus accepted that Arthur would lose Anjou, Maine and Touraine. Arthur would keep his birthright of Brittany, although he would hold it from John as his overlord, not Philip.

A closer examination of the treaty, however, reveals that Philip made some very substantial gains in return – so substantial, in fact, that it leads us to suspect that his entire campaign of support for Arthur had been nothing more than a ruse in order to get him to this exact point. John agreed to pay Philip 20,000 marks in cash in return for the French king ceding direct overlordship of Brittany. Philip would keep those parts of Normandy he had already gained, and John recognised him as his overlord for the rest. Clauses dealing with the counts of Flanders and Boulogne in the north, and with the count of Angoulême and the viscount of Limoges in Aquitaine, improved Philip's domestic situation on several fronts, and his international position was bolstered by John's promise that 'we engage not to give any assistance to our nephew Otto, whether financial or military, neither directly nor by means of our vassals or any other, except by the counsel and with the consent of the king of France'.

This clause, incidentally, would later come to the attention of Pope Innocent, who eventually picked a side in the imperial dispute and decided to support Otto, influenced by the wish he shared with his predecessor, that the papal states should not be surrounded on all sides by Hohenstaufen power. Henry VI's young son, Frederick, was already the king of Sicily following the death of his mother (from whom he derived his right there), so if Philip of Swabia, Frederick's Hohenstaufen uncle, were to be Emperor, the dangers to Rome would increase. In 1201 Innocent, showing his trademark willingness to intervene in secular affairs, would write to John:

Philip, illustrious king of the French, had no power to release you from the duty by which you are bound to your nephew, the renowned King Otto, now elected to be emperor of the Romans [...] since reason prescribes, and nature demands, that an uncle should assist his nephew, undoubtedly the sworn undertaking which you are said to have given to the king of the French – namely, not to assist the said king your nephew – must be judged unlawful.[7]

This decision of Innocent's to support Otto would come back to haunt Philip Augustus later on, but for now, the treaty was agreed.

It was common for major pacts of this sort to be sealed with a marriage alliance, so it was finally time for Philip to play his card in this respect and offer up the hand of his son, Louis, now aged twelve. John had no children,* but he did have several nieces, and it was settled that the bride in question would be Blanca (or Blanche, as she was always known in France), a daughter of John's sister Eleanor and her husband, Alfonso VIII of Castile. This choice avoided any complications that might arise from a union between Louis and Eleanor of Brittany, the other principal candidate, and was of greater prestige, as Blanche was the daughter of a king while Eleanor was now only the sister of a duke. Blanche was also twelve, so the bride and groom were more well matched in age than was often the case with royal marriages.

This part of the treaty had obviously been agreed well ahead of the document being finalised, because Eleanor of Aquitaine had already travelled to Castile to fetch Blanche and bring her to France, before retiring again to Fontevraud Abbey.† John provided a lavish dowry in both cash and land, and the wedding took place on 23 May, the very day after the treaty was sealed. Philip gained

---

* As we noted earlier with regard to Richard, this is to say that John had no *legitimate* children. He did acknowledge at least a dozen illegitimate children, but they could not be used in an international marriage alliance of this import.

† That a woman of Eleanor's age should volunteer for such an arduous, mountainous, overland journey demonstrates both her continuing good health and also her enthusiasm for a reunion with her only other surviving child, Eleanor. The younger Eleanor had been nine years old when she was handed over to Castilian envoys in 1170, and she had not seen any member of her birth family in the three decades since. The two women did enjoy a brief sojourn in each other's company, but the return journey finally proved too much for Eleanor of Aquitaine; she retired to Fontevraud as they passed it on the way back, leaving Blanche to be escorted by others for the final part of her journey north.

a daughter-in-law, and also a great deal in financial terms: in yet another favourable result, it was stipulated that he would keep the dowry territories – the fiefs of Issoudun, Graçay and Bourges and their castles, all in strategically important Berry – and their incomes in his own hands until such time as the marriage of Louis and Blanche was consummated. Given the age of the children, this would not be for quite some time, and Philip would ensure that the day was postponed as long as possible.

The young people moved to the royal court in Paris, where Philip set them up in a household of their own, commensurate with the status of a married heir to the throne. Blanche was welcomed and well treated; she assimilated quickly and became thoroughly Capetian in her outlook, which would be an asset to Philip as the years went by. As his trust in the couple grew, he also confided to their care some of the very young nobles over whom he exerted control: Countess Joan of Flanders and her younger sister, Margaret, and Theobald IV of Champagne were all brought up by Louis and Blanche under Philip's eye.

During the long years when Henry II and Richard had been his principal opponents, Philip had been obliged to keep his wits about him at all times, watching out for any sudden political or military manoeuvre that might be to his disadvantage. John's accession provided him with a respite from this constant state of alert, and indeed sometimes the pleasure of the reverse: there was always the chance that John would unexpectedly slip up in some way that Philip could take advantage of. In the summer of 1200 this proved to be very much the case.

One of John's first acts as king had been to divest himself of his wife, Isabelle of Gloucester, their close blood relationship making the annulment a straightforward matter. It was thus to be expected that he would look about for a new alliance, but even Philip might have been taken aback by the ineptitude that John displayed in going about it.

Count Aymer of Angoulême was now reconciled with John, following the Treaty of Le Goulet. He was both a powerful magnate in Poitou and also a relative by marriage of Philip, as his wife was Alice of Courtenay, Philip's cousin. It was therefore in John's interest to keep Aymer on side and to attempt to weaken his ties to the French monarchy, while at the same time preventing him from making any further alliance that might jeopardise John's tenuous grip on Aquitaine. All of this was threatened when Aymer proposed to give his only daughter and heiress, Isabelle, in marriage to a neighbouring Poitevin lord, Hugh IX of Lusignan, count of La Marche.* This would create a Lusignan–La Marche–Angoulême power bloc that was just too dangerous.

John's solution to this problem was to decide to marry the girl himself. Politically this was not a bad idea, as John would prevent Aymer's alliance with Hugh while gaining it himself. The county of Angoulême lay between the Plantagenet strongholds of Poitiers and Bordeaux, and it would be very useful to have it in the hands of a close ally, and then hold it himself once Isabelle inherited it from her father. Aymer, meanwhile, was only too pleased to make the swap of intended groom if it meant his daughter would be a queen. The sticking point, of course, was Hugh IX himself, and the sensible thing for John would have been to negotiate with him calmly and to attempt to recompense him, with lands or money or a marriage alliance of equal value. What he actually did was to seize Isabelle without warning and then marry her, the wedding ceremony being held on 24 August 1200. John then took Isabelle to England, where she was crowned queen on 8 October.

There has, incidentally, been much speculation over the years that John's reasons for marrying Isabelle were based on lust, but to be fair to him this seems to be no more than blackening the

---

* This was another example of an unnecessarily intergenerational arrangement. Isabelle of Angoulême was no more than eleven years of age at the time of this betrothal, while Hugh IX of Lusignan was in his mid- to late thirties; he actually had an unmarried teenage son (Hugh X) who was older than Isabelle, and who would have been the obvious candidate for the marriage alliance. However, Hugh IX had separated from his wife, and decided to marry Isabelle himself. Hugh IX was the nephew of Guy of Lusignan, erstwhile king of Jerusalem, whom we met in Chapter 3.

already terrible reputation of 'Bad King John', especially given Isabelle's tender age. It is often said and assumed that she was about twelve at the time of her wedding (he was thirty-three), but this might only have been because that was the lowest age acceptable to the Church for girls to marry, and commentators did not wish to stir up even more controversy. It is probable that Isabelle was even younger, and indeed the fact that she was merely betrothed to Hugh IX rather than married was because she 'had not yet attained marriageable years', so she might only have been ten or eleven.[8] It is unlikely that she was any older than twelve, given that her last child was born more than thirty years later.

When the pre-marriage evidence is properly assessed there seems little real doubt that John's motives were political, rather than personal, and this impression is reinforced by his actions in the years immediately after the wedding: records show that he and Isabelle were rarely in the same place at the same time, and they do not appear to have co-habited until she was in her late teens. Isabelle would not give birth to her first child until October 1207, more than seven years after the wedding, and given how easily she conceived thereafter, for all of the rest of her fertile years, the most likely explanation for a lack of children in the first few years of the marriage is the absence of a sexual relationship.*

Hugh IX of Lusignan was predictably outraged by John's actions, but again John reacted in a very unhelpful fashion. Instead of listening to Hugh's complaints or attempting to compensate him after the fact, he dismissed all the Lusignan claims and then followed up by confiscating family property and invading La Marche. This was unwise, because Hugh took his complaints directly to Philip Augustus – who was John's overlord as well as his own in France – and Philip was very happy to hear them. In 1201 Hugh renounced his allegiance to John and married Isabelle's cousin, Matilda of

---

* Isabelle would give birth to fourteen children in total, without the detriment to her own health or theirs that would have been caused by very early childbearing. Remarkably, for a thirteenth-century mother, she did not lose a single child in infancy and would herself live to see all fourteen reach adulthood.

Angoulême, and in early 1202 Philip summoned John to appear before him to explain himself. When John failed to appear, Philip took the opportunity to declare the forfeiture of John's estates in France, which provided him with a scrupulously legal excuse to launch another military campaign. He invaded Normandy, while Arthur of Brittany – who, as we will see later in this chapter, was still staking his own claims – moved into Poitou. Hugh IX of Lusignan and several others (though not Aymer of Angoulême), joined Arthur's rebellion against John.

Philip had taken advantage of the trouble caused by John's marriage, but his own matrimonial problems had not gone away. Ingeborg had never ceased campaigning against the injustice she had suffered, and she found a more energetic supporter in Innocent III than in his predecessor on the papal throne.

In 1199 Innocent had threatened to place all of France under an interdict if Philip did not repudiate Agnes and restore Ingeborg to her position. When Philip refused to back down, the sentence was enacted in January 1200 by Peter of Capua, the legate who had by then been in France for a year to very little effect. An interdict meant that no Church services could be held in the area concerned, and that all the inhabitants were affected, not just the malefactor who had caused the sentence to be pronounced. This was an age in which the Church calendar was the rhythm of life: Mass, festivals and saints' days across the year as well as the sacraments such as baptism and marriage that marked each new personal stage for individuals. So an interdict had serious consequences, with people unable to attend Mass, marry, receive the last rites or bury their loved ones in consecrated ground. There was an almost complete disruption of life, even down to the eerie background silence caused by the prohibition of church bells, which normally sounded several times a day to mark the canonical hours.

The idea of this collective punishment was that the sinner who had prompted it would become so unpopular that he would back down. However, when this person was a king, other political and career factors came into play, with each individual bishop being obliged to decide whether, or how strictly, to enforce the sentence in his own see. In this case, some of France's prelates chose the king over the pope and simply refused to implement the interdict, notably Philip's uncle Archbishop William of Reims, his cousin Bishop Philip of Beauvais, and another cousin, Bishop Reginald of Chartres.* But many others did enforce it, including the bishop of Paris, in whose see the court and the royal palace were situated and where the densely packed population would suffer. Philip was in no mood to back down against these turbulent priests, which highlights their personal dilemmas and the consequences they might face: 'The king was fiercely angry that his bishops had agreed to the imposition of the interdict, and he threw the bishops out of their own sees, ordered that their canons and clergy be stripped of their property and thrown out of his land, and confiscated their property.'[9]

The stakes were high on the question of Philip's marriage during the spring and summer of 1200, while the interdict was in force, because Agnes of Merania was pregnant again. In September, to Philip's delight, she gave birth to a boy — finally, a second son for the king, in the month that his elder son turned thirteen. The child was named Philip, known throughout his life as Philip Hurepel (meaning 'wild hair') for the unruly brown mop like the one his father had once sported prior to his illness on crusade. Philip Hurepel was to resemble the king greatly in his physical and thoroughly Capetian appearance — in marked contrast to Louis, who was small, slim, blond and the image of his long-dead mother — and Philip Augustus would dote upon him, insofar as he was capable of doting on anyone.

Philip's major concern was now the legitimacy of his children, not that of his marriage, which meant that he had to convince the pope of his good intentions. He promised Innocent that he would

---

* Reginald was King Philip's first cousin as their mothers, Agnes and Adela of Blois–Champagne, were sisters.

put Agnes aside and restore Ingeborg to her position as queen, and even briefly released the latter from the convent where she had been living so they could both attend a council. The interdict was lifted, as Innocent now seemed satisfied, but Philip ignored the terms as soon as the pope's back was turned. Ingeborg, rather than being brought to court and treated as queen, was incarcerated again, this time in an even stricter confinement: she was locked away in Étampes castle, closely guarded and allowed no visitors. Meanwhile, Agnes was soon pregnant again, but she died in a possibly premature childbirth in July 1201, and the baby (another boy) died with her. Philip mourned her loss, but it had to be admitted that this tragedy did simplify his situation to a great extent. As he now had three healthy children, two of them boys and one already married, he decided not to risk taking another wife, although he was still only thirty-six. Ingeborg remained in Étampes, but Pope Innocent, his eyes now firmly on crusading plans, was content as long as she and Philip were married in name and the king did not attempt bigamy again.

In November 1201 Philip achieved his major objective as Innocent pronounced Agnes's children, Marie and Philip Hurepel, legitimate. This seems at odds with his insistence that Philip and Ingeborg had been legally married all along, but the fudge was accomplished due to Innocent's declaration that the late Agnes (to whom he could be more sympathetic now that she would cause him no further trouble) had entered into the marriage in good faith.

Despite the general esteem in which the king was held by his subjects, this was not an entirely popular decision, and Rigord noted that 'this deed dissatisfied very many people at that time'.[10] There was a great deal of sympathy for Ingeborg, and she did not take either the legitimation or her continuing imprisonment lying down. She wrote to Pope Innocent from Étampes, styling herself as 'queen of France in name only' and detailing her ordeals:

My lord husband persecutes me [...] You should know, holy father, that in our prison I have no comfort and I suffer innumerable and unbearable harms; for no one dares to visit me there except some religious person to console me, nor can I hear the word of God from any mouth to restore my soul, nor do I have the means to make confession to any priest; rarely can I hear mass, never other offices. Moreover no person or messenger from my native land is permitted to come or to speak with me, with or without letters. My food is given sometimes very scantily [...] I can have no one to counsel me about the health of my body, or to do what would be good for me. [...] I fear from my appearance that serious infirmities will develop.[11]

Philip's purpose in this was presumably to make Ingeborg's life so miserable that she would give up and either take the veil or seek an annulment herself. But once again he had underestimated her strength of character: she would maintain her position and he would make further fruitless attempts over the years to dissolve the marriage.

The motherless Marie and Philip Hurepel were placed in the household of their older brother and sister-in-law, where Blanche saw to their education alongside that of other children despite being only in her teens herself.* Philip Augustus wasted little time in playing his new cards in the marriage game. Philip Hurepel was not even one year old when he was betrothed in August 1201 to the (equally young) Matilda de Dammartin, daughter and heiress of Renaud, the count of Boulogne – by now the only major magnate still not reconciled with the king – as part of negotiations. Marie was betrothed to the future Alexander II of Scots while they were both toddlers, and when this was broken off in 1202 she was switched immediately to Arthur of Brittany, a decade her senior.[12] This union never happened, either, for the reasons we will explore

---

* Blanche was by this time the first lady of the French royal court, as Agnes was dead, Ingeborg was imprisoned and Queen Mother Adela – shocked at what she saw as her son's immoral marital behaviour – preferred to live away from court. This rift would never be mended: Adela would die in 1206 and would choose to be buried in her own ancestral lands rather than in Paris.

below, and in the end she would not walk down the aisle until she married the marquis of Namur at the grand old age of eleven.

King Philip never married again, although he evidently did enjoy at least one discreet dalliance as he recognised an illegitimate son, born to a mother whose name is unknown to us, sometime in the second half of the decade. The boy was named Peter Charlot and was destined for a life in the Church.

As part of his grand strategy, Philip had supported Arthur of Brittany when it suited him, but had shown no hesitation in dropping him as soon as it was more convenient to do so. Arthur had been the biggest loser from the Treaty of Le Goulet, his cause all but stopped in its tracks by Philip's withdrawal of support, but he and Constance had continued their fight. In reality, they had little choice: John would always see Arthur as a threat, even if he retired quietly to domestic life in Brittany, so his life would always be in danger. The only way Arthur could defend himself, therefore, was to gain as much power as possible.* He and Constance could also keep at the back of their minds the knowledge that John, due to the age of his wife, was unlikely to father any legitimate children any time soon. Even if they were not victorious now, and did not succeed in deposing John, if they could just keep going long enough then Arthur might yet outlive his uncle and succeed him as the only possible heir to England and all the other Plantagenet lands.

Initially Constance was able to continue pressing her son's cause, but the marriage which she had hoped would help actually turned out to be one of her few tactical mistakes. It was personally happy, and Guy of Thouars acted on her behalf as he had been expected to, but the couple might have been a bit *too* blissful: immediate pregnancies and births put Constance out of action for two years, as she bore two daughters in swift succession and

---

* It really was true that when you played the game of thrones, you won or you died.

then fell pregnant again. And then, in September 1201, she died, probably from complications related to this third pregnancy or a premature labour.

This left Arthur with no protector other than his stepfather, who had few resources of his own to call upon, so he was obliged – at the age of fourteen – to take charge of his own campaign. At Easter 1202 he was summoned by John to pay homage to him once more, but Arthur's distrust of his uncle was such that he instead changed tack and fled to Philip's court. This was at the same time as Philip declared John's lands forfeit, following John's failure to appear in response to Hugh IX of Lusignan's complaints, so the time was right for Philip to consider using Arthur once more for his own ends. He agreed to lend his support, and it was now that he betrothed his daughter Marie to the young man.

Arthur, now officially and somewhat ambitiously styling himself 'duke of Brittany and Aquitaine, count of Anjou and Maine', did homage to Philip.[13] Philip also knighted him, which was another symbolic move.* A young man's knighthood was generally conferred on him by his overlord, so in bestowing it himself, instead of leaving it to John, Philip was subtly implying that Arthur held his lands directly from the French crown, and was not merely the duke of Brittany who owed allegiance via the duke of Normandy. Arthur's homage for the multiple territories also meant that Philip recognised him, rather than John, as duke of Aquitaine, which was legally dubious given that Eleanor of Aquitaine was still alive.

Unrest against John was still ongoing in the Poitou region of Aquitaine, led by the Lusignans and joined by others, and not quelled by any preventative action of Philip's. The rebel cause was bolstered in June 1202 by the death of John's father-in-law and ally Aymer of Angoulême, and the subsequent power vacuum caused by the absence from the region of John and Isabelle. With Philip's encouragement, the strife turned into a full-scale revolt in Arthur's name, and Arthur rode to Poitou in person. He was by now fifteen,

---

* One English chronicler places Arthur's knighting by Philip earlier, in 1199, when Philip first espoused his cause, but all other contemporary sources agree that it took place in 1202.

and the king evidently considered him old enough to fight his own battles – for had he not been forced to do the same, at the same age? Philip provided Arthur with men and money but did not join him; instead, and predictably, he headed for Normandy.

Arthur was welcomed by the rebellious barons, while Eleanor of Aquitaine, who had now reached the age of eighty, was forced out of retirement yet again to deal with the situation. She moved from Fontevraud to tour the duchy, and stopped at the castle of Mirebeau, on the border of Poitou and Anjou. Arthur moved to assail her there, and the fact that he was attacking his own grandmother only demonstrates that the intra-Plantagenet struggles were just as ferocious as they had been for the last twenty years. However, Arthur was surprised by a relief force mustered very quickly by John, and on 1 August 1202 he was defeated and captured.[14]

When the news reached him, Philip was at Arques, deep into Normandy, having already made gains there by taking Conches, Le Vaudreuil and Gournay.* Arthur's capture threw his plans into disarray, and he was forced to abandon the siege: 'The King of France was angry [...] He was not inclined to wait a minute longer: immediately he had his tents taken down and all his machines of war cut into pieces.'[15] Philip moved southwards towards the Loire valley in order to limit the damage.

Arthur was taken to Falaise castle in Normandy, and for some while there was uncertainty about his fate. The wording of some of Philip's charters between August 1202 and March 1203 reflects this, with awards being made or homage offered conditionally only. A lord named Maurice de Craon, who owed service to Arthur, paid homage instead directly to King Philip in March 1203, this allegiance to last 'for so long as Arthur should remain in prison [...] if Arthur is released, Maurice will be his liege man [...] or if not, Maurice will be the liege man of Arthur's sister

---

* Philip's success at Gournay was due to an effective manoeuvre that demonstrated once again his intellectual capacity for besieging castles. Noting that its defences relied on deep moats created from a man-made diversion of the River Epte, he did not assault the stronghold directly but instead broke the dam that lay higher up the river. This resulted in a huge flood that crumbled and swept away the walls, so the defenceless garrison had no choice but to surrender.

[Eleanor] as long as she marries according to the king's will'. By October of the same year, the wording 'if Arthur is released' had changed in Philip's charters to the rather more ominous 'if Arthur is still alive'.[16]

By that time, Arthur was almost certainly dead. In January 1203 he had been moved from Falaise to Rouen, where he simply disappeared, never to be seen again, and by April there was general agreement among commentators on all sides that John had had him murdered, or had possibly even carried out the deed personally.[17] John completed his sweep of potential rival heirs by also capturing Arthur's older sister, Eleanor of Brittany, and sending her to England for what would turn out to be a lifelong imprisonment.[*]

John's treatment of Arthur backfired on him badly. If Arthur had been killed on the field of battle, that would have been bad enough, but in that sort of situation John could have got away with claiming that Arthur had known what he was getting himself into, despite his youth, and that battlefields were dangerous places however much one attempted to avoid killing one's principal opponent. But the deliberate, cold-blooded murder of a nephew, a boy of fifteen, was something entirely different, and John would never be trusted by anyone again. Medieval kingship, as we have already had cause to note, was a tough business, but there were some actions that were beyond the pale even in the early thirteenth century.

Philip's part in this tragedy is also inexcusable. Obviously he was not the one who actually killed Arthur or who ordered his murder, but his callous disregard throughout the years 1199 to 1202 for a boy who was meant to be under his protection contributed in great part to Arthur's death. It is just possible that Philip believed that Arthur would come to no harm if he was captured – that he could be bargained for, and his custody bought or passed around as part of the political game, as had happened to others before – but it is implausible that a man as shrewd and

---

* Eleanor of Brittany was eighteen when she was imprisoned by John in 1203. She did not die until 1241, having spent thirty-eight years, the entirety of her adult life, in captivity.

as talented at reading people as Philip did not know what John was capable of. Philip must therefore shoulder some measure of responsibility for Arthur's dark fate.

***

By mid-1203, then, Philip's lifelong campaign of turning one member of the Plantagenet family against another finally came to an end, because there were simply no more of them left to exploit. That is, no more living: Philip was well able to use the uncertainty over Arthur's fate, and the rumours and accusations against John, for his own purposes. Any time he wished to challenge the English king, he could simply demand that John produce Arthur, safe in the knowledge that it could not happen, and that everyone would be reminded of John's wickedness. Not that Philip really needed this additional leverage, because the last of the Plantagenets was by no means the equal of his father or his brothers, and he was certainly no match for Philip either intellectually, politically or militarily.

Philip Augustus had weathered the storm of the first few years after Richard's unexpected death. He had been patient, resisting any temptation to act impetuously, and had prepared the ground well. His manner and his actions had become colder and more calculating, as he showed little remorse for effectively delivering a teenage boy into murderous enemy hands, but in terms of his own kingship, his strategy had worked. And now, after twenty-four years of defence – aggressive defence, but defence nonetheless – the French king was ready to go on the offensive.

7

Philip the Conqueror

It was time.

Philip had been taking sporadic bites out of eastern Normandy for some years, but now was the moment to launch a full-scale campaign to conquer the entire duchy, a region of vital importance to his long-term plans in several respects. Having Normandy under his personal control would naturally be a defensive advantage: at its closest point the Norman border was only 40 miles from Paris, so as long as the duchy was in hostile hands there was always a potential threat to his capital.* But there were also important offensive opportunities. As it stood, Philip had no direct access to the Channel coast, which ran from the imperial border with the Low Countries in the north, via the county of Flanders, through the duchies of Normandy, Brittany and Aquitaine down to the Navarrese border in the south. Success in the forthcoming campaign would give Philip lordship over the established Norman ports, which would open up a whole world of possibilities for further conquest and also for trade, either overland or via the Seine, the banks of which would be under his control on both sides all the way from Paris through Rouen to Le Havre. He would have a

---

* The threat of Paris being attacked via Normandy was no idle one: Philip Augustus's grandfather Louis VI had once been caught out by the wily Henry I of England doing just that. Louis was campaigning in Flanders when Henry slipped behind him and advanced towards the capital – he did not assail it, but set up camp between Paris and Chartres and remained there with his troops, untroubled, for eight days. His point was made, and Louis was obliged to withdraw back to his own domains.

vastly expanded royal domain, a great deal of additional revenue and – significantly, from a personal point of view – the satisfaction of having torn a gaping hole in the Plantagenet holdings in France.

The most important thing, as he had learned to his cost over the years, was not to rush. If this campaign were to succeed where smaller ones had failed, it would need to be well organised, methodical and thorough. It would also be expensive, as all military campaigns were: troops needed to be retained and paid, men and horses fed, and siege machinery constructed and transported. Castellans might need to be offered financial inducements, which was cheaper in the long run than having to rebuild a destroyed castle, but meant additional upfront costs. Fortunately, Philip was in a very healthy financial position at this time. This was due not only to his territorial gains in recent years and the cash payments he had received from John (although these certainly helped), but also because of the careful financial management and administration in which he had engaged throughout his reign. As we noted earlier, Philip was not afraid to employ and promote officials based on aptitude rather than birth, and many of his best administrators were loyal and clever men of lower status who had taken this career route.

Chief among them at this point was Brother Guérin, the keeper of the royal seal. Guérin was not a monk, as his title might imply, but rather a Hospitaller knight of some renown who had returned to France sometime after the Third Crusade, in which he had fought with distinction.* We know almost nothing about his origins, but he is assumed to have been of sub-noble rank and born sometime in the mid-1150s.[1] His name starts to appear in governmental records around 1201, and he rose in prominence in 1202 following the death of the ageing William Whitehands, the archbishop of Reims. William had been a pivotal figure in King Philip's administration, as well as France's leading prelate, and Guérin filled the

---

* The Order of Knights of the Hospital of Saint John of Jerusalem, to give it its full title, was a military order based in the Holy Land. It was somewhat akin to the Templars, in that its members were warriors who took quasi-religious orders.

first of those gaps admirably. Despite his new role, he retained his Hospitaller title and continued to wear the Order's habit, and contemporary records show that he ran an extremely efficient chancery and exchequer.* He kept the money flowing into the royal coffers and ensured it was ready for the king's use whenever he needed it. Philip was thus able to begin his preparations safe in the knowledge that he would not have to pause the campaign for lack of funds, and that he could take to the field himself because he left a smoothly functioning administration behind him. And, of course, Normandy was not exactly the Holy Land: it was close enough to Paris that frequent communication could take place.

In the late spring of 1203, just after the date at which it seems to have become common knowledge that Arthur of Brittany had been murdered, Philip started with something of a feint, moving through the Loire valley into Anjou, in a strike into the ancestral Plantagenet heartlands. This did enough to attract John's attention, and he sent troops and began to organise some kind of defence, although he himself remained in Normandy during the spring and summer, at Rouen or Falaise. But the distraction had worked well enough, so Philip immediately left that theatre of operations in the hands of others and returned to Normandy.

The Franco-Norman border was the most heavily fortified part of the realm. This was going to be a war of sieges, and it was not going to be over quickly: each castle would have to be subdued individually, as Philip could not afford to leave any behind that were held against him. If possible, he also needed to take each one without damaging its fabric too much, because it was in his own best interests to garrison these strongholds himself, rather than destroying them. This was going to prove an intellectual, as well as a military, challenge for Philip: although we might sometimes refer to 'standard' siege techniques, each castle was unique in its topographical situation, its fortifications and the character of its castellan, so different individual tactics would be needed.

* Given Guérin's background and military reputation, one imagines that nobody argued with him too much about their bills.

However, it was a challenge for which the French king was exceptionally well prepared.

The composition of the army that Philip took into Normandy was tailored to the task ahead. He had several of his major vassals with him, including the Dreux brothers Count Robert II and Bishop Philip, his other cousins Peter II and Robert of Courtenay, and Renaud, the newly loyal count of Boulogne. The host comprised knights, mounted and foot sergeants, crossbowmen, engineers, miners and plenty of ancillary staff such as grooms and cooks; in total, probably around 2,500 men.* The proximity of the campaign to Philip's own domains meant that supply lines were secure. Siege machinery had been constructed in advance and could be assembled at each location, then disassembled, packed away and transported on baggage carts to the next site, and in the expert hands of Philip's siege engineers this would become a slick operation, much more efficient than constructing machinery anew in each place.

Philip's political and military position was aided by John's extreme unpopularity in most of his French lands. The Bretons held John responsible for the death of their young duke, and they renounced him to rally behind King Philip under their new leader, Guy of Thouars. Following Arthur's assumed murder and the imprisonment of his full sister, Eleanor, the ducal title had passed to the elder of Constance's two daughters by Guy, Alix, who was at this point still a toddler, so Guy was acting as regent in her name. The Poitevins' resistance to John had also hardened. Many of the rebel lords of that region had been captured at Mirebeau along with Arthur, and they had been imprisoned in such harsh captivity that twenty-two of them had subsequently died, which understandably angered their families and friends. Philip made agreements with the major barons in Brittany and Poitou, as well as in parts of Maine, Anjou and Touraine, which had the effect of

---

* Contemporary chroniclers generally loved a bit of exaggeration about troop numbers, but in reality medieval armies were much smaller than they would have us believe. This makes sense when we consider the logistical difficulties of transport, food and so on.

cutting off John's path between Normandy and Aquitaine, should he ever decide to take it.

Nor did the Normans themselves have any particular reason to love John. Back in 1199 they had declared for him over Arthur because they did not want to be ruled by a Breton, but John's ineptitude was costing them dearly in terms of constant warfare, which was debilitating, dangerous and expensive. Arthur was out of the picture so there was no longer any threat of Breton over-lordship, and some of the Norman barons were recalling that the duke of Normandy owed allegiance to the king of France anyway, so it might just be in their best interests to cut out the middle man. And even among those who still held for John, there was suspicion and distrust: if John could murder the duke of Brittany, a high-ranking noble and his own vassal, then who could count himself safe?

If there was one person who knew how to prey on these fears, it was Philip Augustus. He now advanced into Normandy, past the revised border that had been agreed in the Treaty of Le Goulet three years previously, and began by taking Conches and a number of smaller fortifications with ease. Then he turned his attention to Le Vaudreuil, scene of much conflict already in the previous two decades, which was held for John by two barons who were of English, rather than Norman, extraction: Robert Fitzwalter and Saer de Quincy. The idea of John appointing English defenders for Norman castles was understandable up to a point, because it avoided the possibility of any Normans wavering because they felt too French, but it also had its disadvantages, in that Englishmen with no local connections had much less to lose.

John's hope was that Philip would get bogged down in a lengthy siege at Le Vaudreuil, and he had already re-supplied and strength-ened it with this in mind. Philip evidently thought that it was going to be a long haul, too, as he made camp and spent time erecting siege machinery. As it transpired, though, not one single blow needed to be struck: Fitzwalter and de Quincy 'surrendered it very quickly, for which they were much blamed', and 'the least stone of that castle was not damaged, so not one hair of the heads of the garrison was hurt'.[2] This action by the two defenders baffled contemporaries, and has never been satisfactorily accounted for since, but we might hazard a guess along the lines we have just mentioned – that is, that Fitzwalter and de Quincy were more concerned about their own interests than John's, and they felt that these were better served by surrendering Le Vaudreuil to Philip.

This new war came to the attention of Pope Innocent, who wrote to Philip in an attempt to intervene. The early parts of his letter are an exercise in guilt-tripping: 'You realise,' he wrote, 'what evils have come into the realms of France and England, and generally to Christian people everywhere' because of the dispute between the two kings. This meant that 'churches are destroyed, the rich are impoverished, the poor are oppressed [...] religious men who used to devote themselves to prayer are now forced to beg their bread' – and so on and so on – at home. Innocent was still concerned with his forthcoming crusade, so he added that the conflict between Philip and John had also resulted in Muslim gains in the Holy Land. The missive ended with an entreaty and a threat:

> We exhort you in the Lord, we charge you as you hope for remission for your sins, to make an enduring peace with King John in response to our warning, or to arrange a suitable truce so that in the interval the question of restoring a lasting peace between you can be freely and safely discussed [...] Otherwise, however great our love in the Lord for both of you, we shall not be able for any reason to avoid giving inviolable sanction.[3]

John, already beleaguered with threats from several directions, would probably have taken the offer of a truce (he received his own letter from Innocent at around the same time, urging him 'devoutly to consider the things which pertain unto peace'), but Philip was not to be deterred.[4] His opinion, a reasonable one under the circumstances, was that matters between secular overlords and vassals were none of the pope's business. He was supported in this by his senior nobles, more than a dozen of whom wrote to him – in suspiciously identical wording – confirming that they advised him not to let the pope force him into a peace with John.[5]

Some 9 miles away from Le Vaudreuil, on the other side of the River Seine, lay the castle of Radepont. This was Philip's next port of call, and 'having set movable wooden towers and a large number of other engines around the town, he vigorously attacked and seized it'. The operation took him three weeks, but he captured the fortification more or less intact along with twenty knights, 100 sergeants and thirty crossbowmen.[6]

Le Vaudreuil and Radepont were valuable strongholds in their own right, but they were also satellite castles, preliminary lines of defence and potential sources of relief for Château Gaillard. That mighty complex was the real key point of the whole campaign, as it protected all the main routes towards the Norman capital, Rouen; if it fell, the duchy would be cracked wide open. Château Gaillard was reputed to be impregnable, but if anyone was going to conquer it, it would be an experienced, intelligent, well-prepared siege expert who still bore a determined personal grudge against the dead man who had built the castle as a taunt to him.

The site was already fortified by nature, but Richard made it even more impregnable. He enclosed it in a double wall and built high towers all round, equally spaced [...] He fortified the summit of the rock and built a citadel. The position, beauty and fortifications of the place had made the name of Château Gaillard renowned throughout the world.

Gaillard had no reason to fear being taken in a siege, both because of its ramparts, and because it is surrounded on all sides by valleys, sheer rocks and hills, whose slopes are steep and covered with stones, so that even if there were no other fortifications, its natural position alone would be sufficient to defend it.[7]

Thus did William the Breton – whose works indicate that he was present in Philip's host at this time – describe the formidable defences of Château Gaillard, with its keep and three baileys built on solid rock 300 feet above the River Seine. The Minstrel of Reims echoes the sentiment in his dramatised account, having Philip declare, 'By the spear of Saint James, I have never seen a castle so well fortified and so well situated as this one! It would clearly take all my available means to capture it by force.'[8]

Château Gaillard stood more or less exactly as Richard had left it when it was completed, except for one small addition: John had erected a new building on the inside wall of the middle bailey, containing a chapel above and a latrine below. In 1203 the complex was under the control of an Englishman, Roger de Lacy, who had previously been the constable of Chester. He was 'noble and warlike' in his demeanour, and – unlike Robert Fitzwalter and Saer de Quincy, who were barons in their own right with landed estates in England – he owed absolutely everything to John's patronage.[9] He therefore had the greatest of incentives to defend Château Gaillard for his king with all his might, and he was well prepared to do so: he had ample stores and a garrison of forty knights and probably around 200 other fighting men, a mixture of sergeants and crossbowmen.

Philip arrived at Château Gaillard in late August 1203. He was well aware that his army would be there for some time, so his first tasks were to ensure that his siege camp was properly arranged and sanitary, and to secure his supply lines while also cutting off any further provisioning of the stronghold itself.

Just below the castle, the river split in two and there was an island in the middle, upon which stood a fortified building that guarded the crossing. Bridges led from the island to both banks of the river, but Roger de Lacy had already prudently destroyed the one to the west, on the opposite side from the castle, meaning that Philip's host could not be supplied from that direction. An additional defence was a barrier that had been constructed in the river itself, which would prevent provisions being sent by boat. This issue required some lateral thinking, but that was not a problem for Philip. After assembling his siege machinery and using it to keep the defenders of the castle and island fort occupied, and therefore less able to loose missiles of their own, he sent a group of young men to swim out to the barrier. They carried axes with them, and once they reached it they were able to hack an opening wide enough to allow the passage of large boats, so Philip could make use of the Seine for transport.

Next he had to deal with the missing bridge. Bridge-building was an exercise requiring a great deal of time and technical skill, so it was unlikely that anything as good as the old one could be constructed at short notice. Philip solved this problem by gathering boats — wide, flat-bottomed barges that were used for river trade — and having them lashed together across the width of the river to form a floating bridge. Piles were driven into the river bed, to which the boats were tied at intervals, and the finished structure, although temporary, was actually strong enough for two small towers to be built on it.

This meant that Philip's host could attack the island's fortification from both sides, and they began to do so. John, who was at this point in Rouen, sent a relief force under William Marshal with some very (perhaps overly) complex plans for simultaneous land- and water-based attacks to seize the floating bridge and reinforce and re-supply the two garrisons in the main castle and the island fort. However, this operation was a complete disaster, achieving nothing but some unnecessary civilian deaths before being seen off by a rapid counter-attack by the French.* The unrelieved island fortress soon fell to Philip's forces, after which they turned their attention to the town of Petit Andely, which lay in the shadow of the main castle.

The civilian population of around 1,500–1,600 people knew they would not be able to withstand any attack, so they took the obvious course of action and fled up to the castle for safety. This was only to be expected — one of the main functions of a castle

---

* William Marshal survived but was obliged, ingloriously, to flee the scene. This is presumably why his biographer fails to mention the episode at all, despite being generally very keen on relating engagements in which Marshal participated.

was to protect the local area – but such an eventuality had either not been factored into Roger de Lacy's calculations at all, or his reckoning had been based on the assumption that he would be further re-supplied, which was now looking unlikely. The castle contained enough provisions to feed the garrison for a full year, but adding another 1,500 mouths, most of whom were not able to fight and were therefore of little practical use to him, was another matter, especially in the light of the defeat of the relief force.

The next thing on Philip's methodical list was to blockade and isolate the castle, to ensure that there was no chance whatsoever of further relief or re-supply. Once de Lacy knew he was on his own, and that he and his men faced slow starvation, he might be persuaded to surrender with no damage to the fabric of the castle, which would be greatly to Philip's benefit. The French king was in no hurry and he began some substantial earthworks, flattening slopes and digging a double line of deep trenches to surround the landward side of the castle – and also, wisely, extending these ditches behind his own camp to avoid being taken by surprise by any relieving force arriving from the opposite direction. The camp itself took on a more semi-permanent character, the tents being replaced with sturdier buildings of wattle and thatch that would be better able to withstand the weather over the forthcoming winter. Some of the French troops could also be accommodated in the island fort and in the houses of the deserted town of Petit Andely, so they were well protected against the worst of the conditions.

Roger de Lacy, meanwhile, upon examining his stores, came to an unsatisfactory conclusion about how long he would be able to hold out. He therefore picked out some 500 of the citizens of Petit Andely – the so-called 'useless mouths' of the old, the young, the weak and the sick – and expelled them from the castle. They were no threat, wanting only to escape, so the French host let them pass unharmed.

In October, Philip, satisfied with progress so far, left the siege in the hands of subordinates. It was going to be a very long business, and it would not do for the king to be static in one place for so long; he needed to retain his momentum and to keep an eye on other areas. Soon after this, de Lacy sent out another batch of 500 civilians; they were also allowed to pass through the French lines unharmed, but when this news reached Philip (who was at that time only a few miles away at Radepont), he gave orders that no more were to be allowed free exit. He intended to starve the garrison out, or at least weaken their resolve through hunger, so the more people eating their way through the castle stores, the better.

Here we can recognise another example of commoners not really being considered people deserving of safety and protection in their own right, but only as assets belonging to an opposing lord. Elsewhere and at other times, they might have been units of wealth production who needed to be prevented from exercising that function; but here and now they were units of food consumption who needed to be used for that purpose. In giving his order, Philip believed that de Lacy would be forced to keep the remaining civilians inside the castle, but he had underestimated the castellan's ruthlessness and devotion to his own and John's interests. One of the great horrors of the Middle Ages was about to unfold.

The final group of civilians, probably numbering around 500–600 people, was expelled from the castle. But the French had their king's orders, so instead of letting these people through their lines, they met them with a hail of missiles that drove them back. So far, so good: the plan was working, and the besieging army expected to see the gates open to re-admit the refugees. However, they did not, and the unfortunate souls were met with another barrage of missiles from the garrison to whom they had looked for protection. Driven away from the gate and the castle walls, and fearful of approaching the French again, they had no choice but to take up a position in the no-man's-land on the steep slopes outside the castle. And there they stayed, exposed on the desolate hillside with no food and only the shelter of hollows or overhanging rocks, throughout the long months of a bleak winter.

Where the fault for this situation lay can be debated up to a point, but the only real conclusion under the prevailing contemporary customs is that the defenders bore the greatest share of the responsibility. Philip, as the antagonist, had less of a duty to the citizens of Petit Andely, and if he let them go then he would gain a reputation for weakness that would make the rest of his campaign much more difficult: any place he was besieging would send out its non-combatants and therefore be able to hold out against him for longer. The situation was different for Roger de Lacy and his overlord, John. The accepted deal was that the people of a region were subject to a lord for whom they worked, produced food, goods and wealth, paid their taxes, and so on, but in return that lord was supposed to protect them. William the Breton, looking on in shock as the situation unfolded, reminded his readers of this duty:

> We should not be surprised that their enemy did not receive them; but we should be both surprised and grieved at those who expelled them, because these people were their friends and relatives. Who would not be moved by indignation at seeing them expose to death those to whom they owed a share of their food, however small that was![10]

The additional irony was that the citizens of Petit Andely, living as they did in the shadow of the most strongly fortified castle in France, probably felt *more* confident than usual in their safety. But all their hopes and expectations were dashed. Roger de Lacy steadfastly refused to open the gates, and John either did not care or word of the situation never even reached him because de Lacy knew what his answer would be: prioritise the defence of the castle over all else. Philip, meanwhile, was in receipt of regular reports and cannot have been totally unaware that a group of people was now stuck between his force and the castle, but at a distance the human cost was less visible to him, so he did not change his mind. In short, each side seemed to be waiting for the other to blink first, but neither of them did and it was the pitiful group of civilians who paid the price.

William the Breton gives some incredibly distressing details that still have the power to shock and appal some eight centuries later. A chicken that had managed to get loose from the castle to wander outside was ripped to shreds and wolfed down raw, feathers, bones, excrement and all. Roger de Lacy had expelled all the dogs from the castle, on the basis that they would need feeding (perhaps not thinking that his men might have been glad of the extra meat when they got really desperate), and these too were devoured, meat and skin, on the desolate slopes outside. And then the ultimate horror: one of the women in no-man's-land was pregnant when she was trapped, and during the course of the winter she gave birth out in the open, only to see her newborn immediately ripped from her by ravenous men and eaten. We might fervently hope that this episode is an exaggeration for effect on William's part, but it is, unbearably, all too plausible.[11]

These occasional scraps, plus a few roots and plants gathered from the hillsides, would not have been enough on their own to save the refugees, but they also had access to water from the river, which sustained them just enough to keep them alive. Or rather, in a state of mere existence, for their lot was so wretched that they 'neither lived nor died; being unable to hold on to life, they could not quite lose it either'.[12]

In December 1203, while all this was going on, John seemed to give up on Normandy completely, returning to England with so little fanfare that it was almost done in secret. He announced that he was going to raise money for a fresh campaign in the spring, but nothing actually happened, and in fact he would never set foot in Normandy again. Philip remained absent from the siege during these long winter months, spending some time dealing with affairs in Paris and then engaging in helping his Breton allies, whose lands were being ravaged by the troops John had left on that side of Normandy.

Philip had left his orders at Château Gaillard, and progress was made while he was away. There was no direct assault, because that was not the plan at this stage; more preparations were needed before such a thing could be contemplated. Instead, further extensive engineering works took place, with the French host levelling the approach to the outer bailey on the southern, landward side and starting to fill in the moat. This provided a path for heavy machinery to be brought closer to the walls when necessary. While the engineers were busy with this work, the fighting men of the host spent their time plundering the surrounding countryside. This had multiple benefits (for them, that is – not for the local inhabitants) in that it alleviated boredom, gave the men and their horses some exercise, and brought in further supplies to complement the regular shipments arriving by river. The besiegers therefore remained in a state of good health and vigour, while the castle garrison were penned in and had only their dwindling stock of stored provisions to consume. By now there was very little fresh food available to them, which began to take a toll on their health, and their morale would soon begin to suffer correspondingly.* With this in mind, frequent messages were sent to the castle offering surrender terms, but Roger de Lacy refused them all, calling out defiantly that he would never give up the castle 'until he had been dragged out of it by his feet'.[13]

Philip arrived back at the siege in February 1204. Almost the first sight that met his eyes was that of the emaciated survivors trapped between his forces and the castle, who recognised him crossing the bridge from the island and called out to beg him for mercy. This was the first time that Philip had seen the situation in person, and he gave immediate orders that the refugees should be let out. William the Breton puts this down to the king's great 'compassion' and his desire to 'save the unfortunate', and there may well have been a substantial element of personal pity in Philip's response, as well as the knowledge that he had a reputation to keep up as *rex christianissimus* and as a merciful man.[14] Nonetheless, it is also worth noting that such a course of action was also to his own benefit. These people might be sick as well as starving, in which case he wanted them sent well away from his siege camp – such places being notorious vectors for disease – as quickly as possible. He also wanted them out of the way ahead of the direct assault on the castle walls that he was now planning. Besides, the tragic situation had served its purpose, in that hunger had been used as a weapon at Château Gaillard – not

---

* Or, to be more precise, morale would suffer further: it cannot have been particularly high at any point, given what was happening immediately and visibly outside the castle walls.

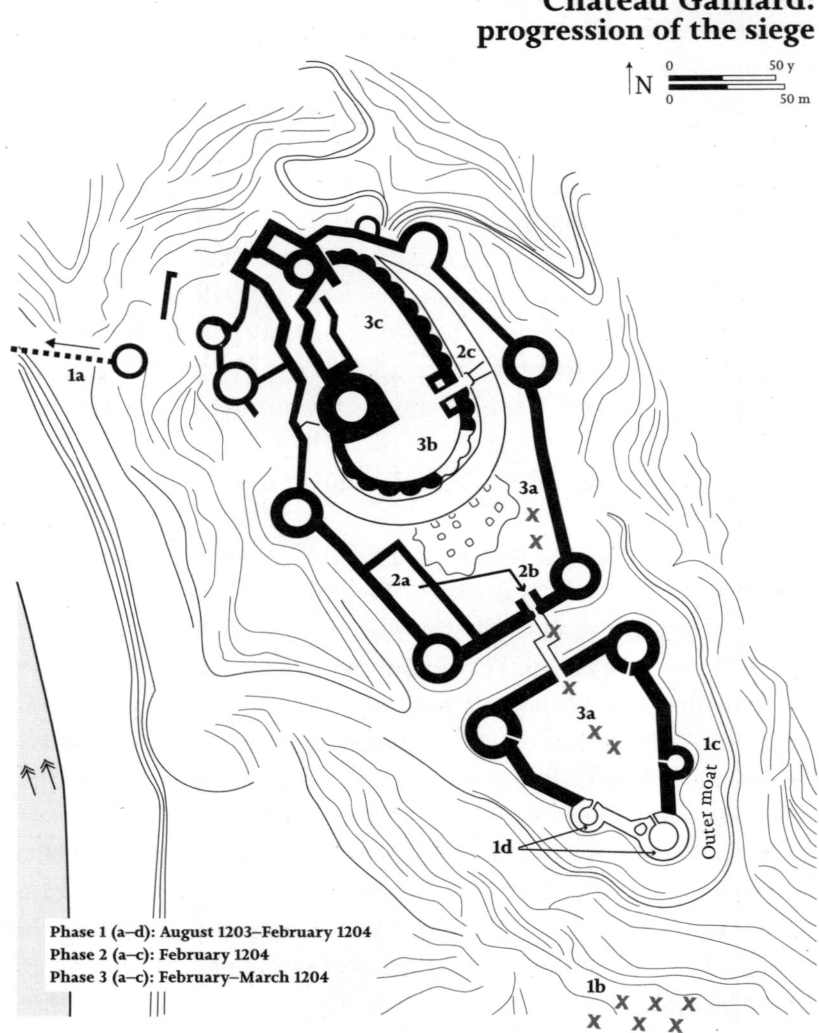

necessarily in the way Philip had originally envisioned, because these civilians had not been his intended target, but their plight *had* served as an object lesson to the garrison of what would happen to them if they persisted in holding out.

Roger de Lacy continued to display a heart of the flintiest stone, and he watched the surviving civilians depart while still refusing

Phase 1: August 1203–February 1204
1a. *River barriers destroyed. Pontoon bridge built.*
1b. *Siege camp erected. Major earthworks undertaken. Siege machinery built.*
1c. *Outer moat filled in.*
1d. *Miners bring down towers.*

Phase 2: February 1204
2a. *Small group enters via chapel building.*
2b. *They enter the middle bailey and lower the drawbridge.*
2c. *Miners set to work under cover of stone bridge*

Phase 3: February–March 1204
3a. *Siege machinery dragged inside bailey.*
3b. *Inner wall collapses.*
3c. *Hand-to-hand fighting in inner bailey and final surrender.*

---

to surrender the castle.* But by now his garrison was weakened by hunger, by the monotony of a diet containing little fresh food, and by their long confinement, and Philip judged that it was time to pounce. This was still a gamble, because an all-out assault on a heavily fortified stone castle always was, but kings did not win by hanging back when there was a viable opportunity before them, and his calculations told him that he had done enough to tip the odds in his favour.

In addition to wearing down the garrison, Philip had also made progress against the fortification itself. His engineers had done sterling work over the winter, flattening and widening the landward approach to the outer bailey, so he was able to bring his siege machinery much closer, making it proportionally more effective. His stone-throwing machines were complemented by a tall belfry, which, when dragged as close to the wall as possible, enabled the French crossbowmen and archers to shoot downwards at the garrison inside – always an advantage when compared with standing back from the walls and having to shoot up and over them

---

* We would probably like to think that these wretched people recovered and lived happily ever after, but sadly their sufferings were not yet over. Sympathetic French soldiers offered them food, but many of them (understandably) gorged themselves after their months of starvation and then died from the effects of overeating on an empty stomach.

from a distance. All Philip's sieges included an effective mining component, and this one was no different: sappers had been set to work on the foundations of the outer bailey's towers, and at some point in February these fell, allowing access via the breach for hand-to-hand combat. As an additional advantage, the rubble from the collapsed towers helped to fill the moat, meaning that the French fighters had easier access as they did not have to clamber down into the ditch and then up again.

As the overall commander of the besieging forces, Philip needed to be able to see the big picture, so he was not one of the first to throw themselves through the gap in the wall. He was, however, in the front rank of those on the outer edge of the ditch. With his banner flying and probably wearing a heraldic surcoat, Philip was an obvious target.* William the Breton tells us that the king was hit several times by arrows or other missiles, but that he was unharmed because he was wearing armour and a helmet, and carrying a shield – an indication that Philip was more circumspect than his old foe Richard the Lionheart, who had been overconfidently unarmoured when he was hit by the crossbow bolt that had killed him.

Roger de Lacy was nothing if not pragmatic, and it was not long before he realised that the outer bailey had become indefensible. He therefore ordered his garrison to retreat, and they torched the buildings in the outer bailey as they went, so the French could not benefit from them in any way. The defenders fell back to the middle bailey and hauled the drawbridge up behind them.

Philip was now able to get a first and closer look at this new obstacle, and to weigh up the best way of approaching it. Here he was aided once more by the military incompetence of King John, as the construction of the new chapel-and-latrine building meant that there were now two openings in the previously solid stone wall: a window above and a latrine chute below. Again, William

---

* The wearing of a 'coat-of-arms' emblazoned with a specific heraldic device – that is, one that identified an individual rather than simply being a generic picture or pattern – was first noted in western Europe in the 1170s, and by 1204 it was common practice. The French royal arms were a particularly distinctive blue field covered in gold fleurs-de-lys.

the Breton's eye-witness account gives us plenty of detail. A small group of intrepid men moved forward and then down into the ditch below the wall. They had no ladders, but one stood on the shoulders of another and managed to reach up and grasp a hand-hold where the building protruded, 'remaining suspended there for a long time until, with astonishing agility, he [swung himself up and] entered, then threw a rope down to his companions to haul them up'.[15] We might hope for his sake that this entry was effected via the chapel window rather than the noisome chute, but in either case the men made it into the new building.

From there they ran out into the bailey, shouting as loudly as possible and setting fire to a door to cause a distraction. The surprised garrison thought the sudden attack was much larger in scale than it actually was, and in their confusion and semi-retreat the members of the French party were able to open the gate and lower the drawbridge by cutting its ropes. A much larger group of knights and foot soldiers was standing ready, and they poured across. The middle bailey was secured, and the garrison forced to retreat once more, this time to the inner bailey and keep.

The besiegers were faced with yet another ditch and wall, the latter this time in curvilinear waves that allowed the defenders to shoot from all angles. Having got this far, and surprisingly quickly, Philip was not about to do anything rash, so he paused the attack while he considered the best approach. Again, he spotted the one potential design flaw: the bridge between the middle and inner baileys was a permanent one of stone, not a wooden drawbridge, so the defenders had not been able to destroy it during their retreat. This offered excellent cover for Philip's miners, and he set them to work under it on the foundations of the wall of the inner bailey. This was, of course, both a noisy operation and an obvious one, so de Lacy was ready for it. He had a counter-mine dug, and his men forced the French to retreat before they could complete their work.

Mining was therefore paused, but with the outer parts of the castle and all the surrounding area under his control Philip was able to take his time. Instead of attempting a direct assault straight away, which could have been costly in terms of lives, he had his siege machinery dragged inside the bailey. With so much rubble lying around everywhere, as well as any ammunition remaining from his own original stocks, there was no shortage of missiles. The petraries bombarded the inner wall – which was already weakened by the French mine and the garrison's counter-mine – with great force at short range. Inevitably, it fell, creating another breach through which Philip's confident knights and men could enter. Astonishingly, given the hopeless circumstances, Roger de Lacy *still* did not surrender, and vicious, desperate hand-to-hand fighting ensued. But the garrison men were weak, hungry and outnumbered, and it was not long before the French were victorious. Château Gaillard surrendered to Philip on 6 March 1204.

The achievement was almost beyond belief. Philip had captured the supposedly impregnable castle of his greatest enemy, and he had done it in little more than six months and in the most glorious manner, by storm. He knew that the news would fly to John, and we could not blame him if he felt that it was almost a shame that Richard was dead and had not seen his pride and joy fall to the man he had always considered a very inferior warrior to himself.

According to the prevailing customs of war, after taking a castle by storm the victor was entitled to treat the defeated garrison however he wished, even to the point of having them executed en masse. But Philip did not order one single killing after the fall of Château Gaillard; even the obdurate Roger de Lacy was spared. As ever, Philip's motives were probably mixed. There might have been a hint of magnanimity and respect for an opponent who had put up a tremendous fight in the name of loyalty to his overlord, but this was coupled with pragmatism: living men could be ransomed, while dead men were worth nothing. This siege had been expensive – and there would be more to come – so the cash generated by ransom payments would go some small way to recompensing Philip's campaign costs. He could not, however, resist one particular gesture that might be seen as either triumphantly merciful or hugely petty: Roger de Lacy had declared many times that he would never surrender the castle until he was dragged out by his feet, and this is exactly how he was removed from it.[16] He did survive the humiliation — which was better than execution or mutilation, even for a man as hard-bitten as Roger de Lacy — and he was then imprisoned, along with the surviving thirty-six of the castle's original complement of forty knights, and 120 other members of the garrison.[*]

It is worth emphasising that Philip's success at Château Gaillard was not due to luck. The castle was taken because there was an effective combination of preparation, planning and execution, carried out by an army whose composition was precisely calculated for the task, and because Philip was happy to put his trust in the common men who were part of his host — engineers, miners and intrepid sergeants who could swim and climb — and not just in knights. The fact that he was also at the forefront of the newest technical developments in siege machinery was also very helpful.[†]

He had, therefore, achieved a great victory, but he did not waste time resting on his laurels. The momentum was with him, and now the way to Rouen and the rest of Normandy lay open.

Despite the temptation, Philip did not head immediately for Rouen. He had made two relatively half-hearted and unsuccessful attempts to take it in the past, and this time he was going to make absolutely sure that he prepared the ground properly. He proceeded, therefore, with a methodical ruthlessness, sweeping round Normandy to the south and west to ensure that Rouen was completely cut off. This would make the city and its fortress easier to deal with, and it also minimised the chances of Philip getting

---

[*] Roger de Lacy's extreme devotion to the cause impressed even John, when he heard about it; the English king contributed £1,000 towards de Lacy's ransom and, on his release, appointed him sheriff of Yorkshire and Cumberland.

[†] Philip's enthusiasm for the latest developments in siege machinery also, and conversely, meant that he was well versed in the science of castle architecture, designing any new builds so that they could withstand exactly the sort of assault he would launch. He was at the forefront of the introduction of round (rather than square) towers for castles, which fared much better against stone-throwing engines and mining.

stuck there for so long that John would have time to muster and send an army from England.

Oddly, throughout Philip's campaign in Normandy in the spring and summer of 1204, John seemed detached from the situation – uninterested, even, and stricken by some kind of lethargy:

> All the holders of castles in the transmarine territories [i.e., the Plantagenet lands in France], with the citizens and other subjects of the king of England, sent messengers to England to tell him in what a precarious situation they were placed, and that the time, according to the terms of the treaty, was near, when they must either give up the cities and castles to the king of the French, or consign to destruction the hostages which they had given him. To which message king John answered; and intimated by the same messengers to all of them, that they were to expect no assistance from him, but that they each were to do what seemed best to him.[17]

Yet again we have to wonder what John was playing at, and how Philip was supposed to deal with an opponent who was so erratic. In this instance, although we should obviously be wary of attempting any kind of medical diagnosis, it seems possible that John was afflicted by despair at his situation, and by the constant stream of bad news, to such an extent that he could not summon the physical or mental energy to do anything about it.

While all this was going on, there was a death of great political significance: Eleanor of Aquitaine passed away on 1 April 1204, aged in her early eighties. She had lived just long enough to hear of the fall of Château Gaillard, and to know that her last remaining son was defeated and the family empire on the verge of being broken up, but by that stage there was little she could have done about it. Philip, when he heard the news, probably did not shed too many tears; indeed, Eleanor's death was to his advantage, as John had lost his most widely respected supporter – and, along with her, any remaining hope that he might be able to hold on to the duchy of Aquitaine in any meaningful manner.

It was also in April, and at the urging of Pope Innocent, that John made a somewhat desperate play for a truce. The catalyst for this was probably the arrival of the shocking news of the fall of Château Gaillard, which hardly anyone in England had thought possible, never mind that it could have happened so quickly. A high-ranking delegation including the archbishop of Canterbury, the bishops of Norwich and Ely, William Marshal and a papal legate was dispatched to France. Philip was happy to listen to their messages – if only to avoid antagonising Pope Innocent by refusing to see his representative – but as he very much had the upper hand, he was in no mood to make concessions. He would agree to a truce, he said, only if John would hand over Arthur of Brittany, alive, and surrender all claim to Plantagenet lands in France.[18] John could not do the first and was unwilling to do the second, so the delegation had no choice but to decline on his behalf and withdraw.

Philip proceeded on his sweep around Normandy, making judicious decisions as he went regarding exactly whom to threaten with what. He wanted the duchy under his control, there was no question about that; but there would be little point in a pyrrhic victory that would only add hundreds of square miles of charred wasteland to his domain. He therefore offered both carrot and stick. The threat of violence always hung in the air – he brought his siege engines with him to each new place and had them erected, and word of the horrific fate of the civilians at Château Gaillard soon got round – but he also announced that any town that submitted to him unconditionally would not be sacked and was guaranteed to keep its existing rights and privileges. Moreover, any Norman baron who was prepared to leave John's service and recognise Philip as his overlord would be allowed to keep his lands. Philip was also able to point out to all and sundry that he was acting within the law: under the terms of the Treaty of Le Goulet, John had recognised him as his overlord for Normandy, and it was in that position that Philip had subsequently declared the duchy forfeit. Therefore any lords, castellans or citizens who changed sides were morally and legally correct to do so.

Philip's methods proved successful, and Normandy's major strongholds fell to him one by one, as well as towns. Argentan, in the south of the duchy, was a significant Plantagenet royal holding, and one of the great hubs of trade and arms manufacture; Philip arrived there in the first week of May and took it with minimal effort. Falaise, the birthplace of William the Conqueror, was subdued within seven days of his arrival. He initiated a bombardment and then persuaded the garrison and citizens to surrender, 'because they preferred to hand the castle over whole, saving their freedom and their possessions, rather than taking their chances in war and risking being conquered'.[19] Philip was then able to make unprecedented progress into the western half of Normandy, where the submissions came thick and fast. Sometimes he did not even need to unpack his siege engines: Caen surrendered three days before he got there, and Bayeux did likewise when the citizens heard that the royal army was approaching. Coutances, Domfront and Lisieux offered little resistance. Philip's Breton allies worked on his behalf from the other direction, and Guy of Thouars took Mont-Saint-Michel and Avranches in Philip's name before moving to meet him at Caen.*

And so, finally, to Rouen. The ducal capital was extremely well defended, with a double wall and deep triple moat, but it was by now isolated, with nowhere to turn for re-supply or re-garrison. Philip began with intimidation, arriving at the end of May with his entire army and his siege machinery, but once there he acted within the accepted conventions. Those inside the castle and city were allowed to appeal to John for help, and Philip would not attack before an agreed deadline for reply. On 1 June the castellan and citizens issued a formal document to that effect:

> The lord king of France has given us an indulgence from the first day of the present month of June, for thirty days, on such condition that if John the king of England does not make peace with

* Mont-Saint-Michel is better known as an abbey, but John had fortified the site to make a royal stronghold. Guy's attack destroyed much of the island by fire, but Philip was fair in his subsequent dealings: he ordered the remains of John's fortress razed, but paid the abbot compensation so that the ecclesiastical buildings could be rebuilt.

the aforesaid king of France within the said thirty days [...] we surrender to the same king of France, or by his command, the city of Rouen, complete with all its forts, and we take an oath to observe these agreements.[20]

John either could not or would not help; he sent back a similar reply to all the others, saying only that the people of Rouen could do as they saw fit. Once this message had been received, there was very little to weigh up, for the advantages were all on one side. Their old overlord had shown no interest in helping them, and could offer no protection. Their potential new overlord could be ruthless when the need arose, but he was also true to his word: after Falaise had surrendered he had, as promised, left the place and its people unmolested, and confirmed their existing privileges. The citizens of Rouen opened their gates to Philip on 24 June, a week before the thirty-day truce had even expired.

In less than two years, Philip had, 'with a minimum of cost, fatigue and time', conquered the whole duchy of Normandy, something 'which nobody had thought possible'.[21]

Normandy had been a duchy for almost 300 years, since the king of what was then West Francia ceded the area to a Viking leader named Rollo in the year 911. Rollo had been succeeded by a line of thirteen further dukes, with John being the unlucky thirteenth and, as it now transpired, last. For Philip's first and most momentous decision about his new acquisition was that there would no longer be a duke of Normandy at all: instead, he would subsume the duchy into the royal domain and rule it personally from Paris. Normandy was thereby transformed at a stroke from a quasi-independent region (and a key part of the Angevin empire) to nothing more than a simple province of France.

There was surprisingly little resistance to this decree, for a number of reasons. First came the fact that the various towns and castles had been surrendered voluntarily, so the population could hardly complain about the result; and, besides, most of them were more concerned about their crops and their trade and simply wanted peace. But there was also a large-scale redistribution of local and regional power, because every baron was offered a stark choice to jump one way or the other: they could stay loyal to John and lose their lands in Normandy, or they could submit to Philip and keep their Norman estates, although that would involve losing their English lands as part of John's retribution. Many – especially those who had significant holdings in England – chose John, which enabled Philip to seize the confiscated Norman lands and use them to reward his own loyal men. There was a profound upheaval, with perhaps up to one-third of Normandy's geographical area changing hands, but it resulted in an even smaller chance of any rebellion against the new royal rule. Normandy was not only under direct French royal control, but also finally at peace. And, pertinently for Philip's future plans, the border between him and England was no longer the Vexin, just 40 miles from Paris, but the Channel.

8

The Battle to End All Battles

As soon as he was satisfied that the new administration in Normandy was bedding in properly, Philip turned his attention to the Loire valley, southern Anjou and northern Poitou. He arrived there in the spring of 1205, and was aided by the fact that Gascony (the southern part of Aquitaine) had been invaded by Alfonso VIII of Castile, who was both John's brother-in-law and the father of Philip's daughter-in-law. This was an entirely separate issue: Alfonso was claiming that Aquitaine had been promised to him as far back as 1169, as the dowry of his wife, Eleanor, to be handed over to him when her mother died. There was no official written record of this, and indeed Aquitaine had been publicly designated as Richard the Lionheart's inheritance from his earliest youth, so the scenario seems unlikely. Given that everyone involved in the marriage negotiations was now dead except Alfonso himself, so there were no other witnesses to what might or might not have been said, his claim would appear to be little more than opportunism brought about by the instability following Eleanor of Aquitaine's death. Alfonso could see John's weaknesses as well as anyone.

Philip was not in military alliance with Alfonso, but the Castilian king's actions served as a very useful distraction and Philip was able to take the city of Poitiers, the region's capital that was both the ancient ducal seat and the birthplace of Eleanor of Aquitaine. He also brought the might of the French royal army to bear on the castles of Chinon and Loches, which had been doggedly holding out in John's name for an entire year while the rest of Anjou and

Touraine collapsed around them, and both were in his hands by the end of the summer.

The dual threat to Aquitaine finally jolted John out of his lethargy, and in the spring of 1206 he mustered an army and a fleet, sailing from England and landing at La Rochelle to be met by those Poitevin barons who were still loyal to him. Realistically, he could not hope to regain everything that Philip had already taken, but he had to make some kind of show; he did this by supporting and relieving those places still holding out for him against Philip's forces, which was easier than attempting any recaptures. Then John made his way further south into Gascony, managing to take Montauban (which lay about 30 miles north of Toulouse) back from the Castilian forces that had seized it.

Philip was kept informed of John's activities. By now he was aware that any successes of John's would probably be followed by self-inflicted disasters, but he was taking no chances and did not wish to be caught out by underestimating his foe. He therefore marched his own army to the border of Anjou and Poitou, where he made a point of situating his headquarters at the erstwhile Plantagenet stronghold of Chinon. He had no intention of overreaching himself, though: he was not there to attempt any further conquest but only to defend the borders of what he had already gained. Normandy, most of Anjou and Maine and a few northerly parts of Poitou were enough for now – the rest of Aquitaine could wait for another day.

John did not push his luck, either, and requested peace negotiations. The result of this was a truce agreed in October 1206, to last for two years, with each king retaining the lands and the baronial allegiances in Poitou that he held already.[1] This naturally favoured Philip, who got to keep his gains, but his advantage was balanced by a stroke of good fortune for John: Alfonso VIII was recalled to Castile by the threat of Muslim incursion on his own southern border, and he made no further attempt on Gascony.

After 1206 there was something of a hiatus in direct confrontation between Philip and John: partly due to the truce, of course, but also because both were embroiled in other, separate concerns. John (as Philip was glad to hear) was busy becoming very unpopular with his barons, and he was also getting into conflict with the pope regarding the appointment of a new archbishop of Canterbury following the death of the incumbent, Hubert Walter. To summarise, John had a preferred candidate for the role and tried to force through his choice, but the right to elect new archbishops lay with the canons of Canterbury, who chose someone else. There was an impasse and both sides appealed to Pope Innocent, who overruled everybody and appointed a third candidate, Stephen Langton, an English cardinal then in Rome. Innocent consecrated Stephen as archbishop of Canterbury and sent him to England, but John refused him entry. Part of this was pique at not getting his own way in the business, but John was also suspicious of the appointment of a man who had formerly lived and taught in Paris: Langton was 'a man altogether unknown to him, and who had been for a long time familiar with his declared enemies in the French kingdom'.[2] John's obduracy in continuing to refuse the new archbishop entry led to Innocent pronouncing an interdict on England in May 1208 and, when this had little effect, excommunicating John personally in November 1209. Many bishops fled from England to France, where Stephen Langton was himself residing, and Philip made a show of welcoming them.

Issues with the Church were not restricted to England, however, and in early 1208 a shocking event occurred in France that would have significant and lasting repercussions. This was the murder, in Saint-Gilles, in the county of Toulouse, of the papal legate Peter of Castelnau, who had been sent to France by the pope to address the growing problem of the Cathar heresy. Innocent held Count Raymond VI of Toulouse responsible for the death – although there was no evidence he was directly involved – and excommunicated him, demanding at the same time that King Philip launch a campaign, a crusade, to wipe out the heresy. Philip declined to do so personally but said that his vassals might take action if they so wished, and so began the Albigensian Crusade, which was to be a feature of France's internal politics for the next two decades.

Philip had other domestic concerns to deal with, one of which was his first attempt at establishing a navy of his own. Seafaring was an area of expertise in which he was well behind his English rivals, who had the service of a fleet from the Cinque Ports and whose family had been crossing the Channel frequently since the Anglo-Norman realm was formed in 1066. Philip had rarely needed ships, and when he did (for setting off on crusade in 1190, for example) he had either requisitioned or hired vessels. But now, with his increased access to the sea, having a fleet of his own would be a significant improvement. And fortunately, although he was unfamiliar with naval matters, there were plenty of skilled shipbuilders in the Norman part of his newly expanded royal domain, so it was simply a case of having them work for him rather than John. As ever, Brother Guérin's efficient chancery and exchequer were able to supply funding adequate to the purpose.

Philip was also active during these years in promoting his own interests via the marriage arrangements of his vassals and wards, and four unions in particular, all of them involving scandalously young heiresses, would have a profound impact on the future course of events.

First came the marriage of Philip's younger son, Philip Hurepel, with Matilda de Dammartin, daughter of the count of Boulogne. They had been betrothed since their infancy, and would normally have expected to wait a little longer before the actual wedding, but Philip Augustus decided to expedite the ceremony in order to bind the vacillating Count Renaud to him more tightly, so the bride and groom were just nine and ten when they walked down the aisle. Matilda, at least, could console herself with the fact that she had been bound for life to a husband of her own age, but this was a comfort denied to the other three girls, who, as ever, had no choice but to acquiesce. In a further move to strengthen Dammartin family loyalties, Renaud's brother Simon (aged twenty-eight) was also offered a bride of royal blood. King Philip's only daughter was already married, so the selected candidate was the nine-year-old Marie of Ponthieu, the daughter and heiress of Philip's sister Alice and the husband she had married after being released from her long confinement in England.

Also up for grabs in the north-west of France was the rich county of Flanders, whose twelve-year-old Countess Joan had been in the king's guardianship for some time. Her new husband came from further afield: he was Ferrand (aged twenty-four), the fourth son of the king of Portugal. He had little expectation in his home country, and he had previous ties to Flanders, as he was the nephew of Theresa of Portugal, the second wife and surviving widow of Count Philip of Flanders who had been so influential at the beginning of Philip Augustus's reign. Theresa was active on Ferrand's behalf in helping to arrange the match, and he became count of Flanders, *jure uxoris*. And finally, for now, Duchess Alix of Brittany was married to a man of guaranteed family loyalty: Peter of Dreux, the second son of Count Robert II, the king's cousin. Peter was only about ten years older than Alix, for which she was probably grateful under the circumstances, and he supplanted Guy of Thouars, her father and regent, to become duke of Brittany by marriage.*

Meanwhile, Philip Augustus had been disappointed to hear that John was no longer the last male Plantagenet, as Isabelle of Angoulême had given birth to two sons: Henry in October 1207 and Richard in January 1209. The family line would continue for one more generation at least, and Isabelle would follow up with three daughters to add to the mix. There was also some good dynastic news in France, because – oddly, given that they were almost the same age – Philip became a grandfather not long after John became a father. In September 1209, when she was twenty-one, Blanche of Castile bore Prince Louis a son, who was somewhat inevitably called Philip. It probably says something about the scale of previous upheavals, the early deaths and fertility problems in the

---

* Guy, coincidentally, died the year after the wedding, so Peter did not have to deal with a father-in-law aggrieved at losing his position. Guy's death seems to have been from natural causes (he was probably around sixty by this time), and he was buried alongside Constance at Villeneuve Abbey, near Nantes in Brittany, as had been their joint wish.

family, and the stability that Philip Augustus now represented, that with this birth he became the first king in the 222-year history of the Capetian royal dynasty to have two direct heirs, a son and a grandson, alive during his own lifetime.*

Dynastic success brought its own travails, however, and what to do with Louis was fast becoming one of Philip's most pressing issues. This was not because his heir was troublesome; far from it. Louis was a model of loyalty to his father, despite the numerous provocations aimed at him by the latter. Philip had always been of a suspicious nature – and this had been ever more marked since his return from the Holy Land – and even the faithful Louis was on the receiving end of his paranoia. For example, every previous king of the Capetian dynasty had crowned his heir as 'junior king' during his own lifetime, in order to ensure the continuity of the succession, but Philip did not do the same for Louis, even when he reached his majority. And there were other personal trials. Louis was extremely keen on martial pursuits, and might have expected an early knighthood given his rank and position, but Philip would not sanction the ceremony until Louis was almost twenty-two, which was so late as to be verging on an insult. Finally, Louis was supposedly the count of Artois in his own right (via his maternal inheritance), but Philip refused to confirm him in the title, because this would give him a landed power base of his own.

One of Philip's problems was that there was no recent precedent for an adult heir to the French throne, as there had not been one for a hundred years.† There was ample precedent on the other side of the Channel, of course, but this was not exactly a model

---

* Blanche had previously borne a daughter, in 1205, which indicates that the marriage had been consummated when she and Louis were around sixteen. Sadly this baby had died at or shortly after birth, and, given that Philip was not born until 1209, it is possible that Blanche suffered miscarriages in the intervening years that we do not know of. She and Louis were certainly a fecund couple after this point: in total they were the parents of ten sons and two daughters, although tragically only five of these children (four boys and the younger girl) would live to adulthood.

† Philip, as we know, had been fourteen at the time of his coronation and fifteen when he became sole king. His father, Louis VII, had inherited the throne at the age of seventeen, meaning that the last adult heir had been Philip's grandfather Louis VI, who had been around twenty-seven at the time of his accession in 1108.

Philip wanted to emulate, so he had to find his own way forward. On the one hand, he wanted to keep Louis under tight control; but on the other, he did not want to replicate Henry II's mistakes by giving his heir no authority or autonomy at all, and then either ending up with a rebellion on his hands or leaving a successor who had no idea of the duties of kingship.

Louis did not resemble Philip either in appearance or in character, being less politically astute but much more bellicose and a very capable warrior and military tactician.[3] Happily for all concerned, as time went by Philip realised that their differing personalities and interests could work to his advantage: if he could only force himself to allow his son some autonomy, they could become an effective team. In 1212 the now twenty-four-year-old Louis was able to cut his military leadership teeth with a short unsupervised campaign of his own in Flanders, seeking to regain the towns of Saint-Omer and Aire, which had been seized by the late Count Baldwin IX before he set off for the Fourth Crusade and never returned. These towns were actually in Artois (Louis's own county) rather than Flanders, but the question of their ownership had been put to one side while both Louis and Countess Joan were underage.

Louis's majority and Joan's marriage to the ambitious Ferrand changed the situation. The new count refused to cede the towns, and in short order he found himself on the receiving end of an extremely well-planned and well-executed campaign that captured them both with little trouble. A treaty was then agreed, under the terms of which Louis would keep Saint-Omer and Aire in return for not making any claim to, or invasion of, the rest of Flanders.[4] Ferrand was forced to assent, but he was not happy and began making overtures to King John. This suited John, who was already colluding with the slippery Renaud of Boulogne, the dual Dammartin French royal marriages notwithstanding. Renaud had managed to fall out with Philip Augustus again, and this was exacerbated by a quarrel with the king's loyal cousins of the house of Dreux, Count Robert II and his brother Philip, the bishop of Beauvais. This did Renaud no favours at the French royal court, and in 1212 he formally renounced his allegiance to Philip and paid homage to John.

Philip had thus lost two disaffected counts to John – and, moreover, two counts whose lands were contiguous and bordered the Channel. This was the first intimation of a new danger and of renewed direct conflict with the Plantagenets, and unfortunately the situation soon got a whole lot worse, thanks to new developments in the Empire. The next phase of the ongoing struggle was going to pull in actors from far beyond Philip's own borders.

The Empire had not been a peaceful place for some time, and several of the events of the early 1200s had been positively Byzantine in their complexity and violence.

Otto of Brunswick's coronation as king of the Romans in 1198 had superseded the election of his rival Philip of Swabia a few months earlier,* but Philip had continued to press his claims for the next decade, so Otto could never quite consider his position settled. However, Philip was murdered in 1208 while attending a wedding, which settled the question in a definitive manner. Otto always maintained that he had nothing to do with it, and fortuitously for him the killer himself was murdered less than a year later, before he could be brought to justice to explain himself. Philip of Swabia left no son, so his male line was extinct, but he did have four daughters. In order to further cement his position, Otto immediately betrothed himself to the eldest, Beatrice, then aged ten (he was thirty-three). With no remaining rival his path was clear, and he was crowned Holy Roman Emperor by Pope Innocent in 1209. Otto married Beatrice in 1212, as soon as she turned fourteen, but – in another astonishingly coincidental piece of luck for him – she died in mysterious circumstances just three weeks after the wedding, leaving him free to make a new choice of wife.

---

* As we saw above, in Chapter 5.

While all this was going on, a third candidate to the imperial throne arrived on the scene. This was Frederick of Hohenstaufen, the only son and heir of the previous Emperor, Henry VI. He had been overlooked at the time of his father's death because he had been only two years old at that point, but by 1212 he was seventeen, already the king of Sicily, and ambitious for more. Furthermore, he had succeeded in getting the influential Innocent III on side, as the pope had fallen out with Otto soon after his coronation, and had excommunicated him in 1210.* As King John was firmly in the camp of Otto, his nephew, it was no surprise that Philip Augustus should favour the young Frederick, and he declared his support. Frederick had himself proclaimed king of the Romans, and was crowned as such in December 1212. By that time he and King Philip had already agreed a treaty, which had been brokered by Louis, the prince having done the travelling on his father's behalf. The gist of this agreement was that neither Philip nor Frederick would make peace with John, Otto or any of their allies.[5] Frederick could not yet be an active collaborative partner for Philip, given that he needed to cement his own position in the Empire before he could turn his attention to foreign policy, but it was a start.

Philip was able to make one further ally in the Empire in early 1213 by arranging the marriage of his daughter, Marie, to Henry I, duke of Brabant. Henry was a useful ally to have, as his duchy bordered the French county of Flanders (it encompassed what is now northern Belgium and the southern part of the Netherlands), but Marie was even unluckier in terms of the age difference between herself and her new husband than the girls we mentioned earlier. On paper the couple were similarly situated as they were both widowed,† but she was still only fourteen, while he was nearly fifty and had children older than she was. But Marie's personal

---

* Otto had rather ill-advisedly attempted to insist that the pope should recognise the Emperor's right to appoint bishops, rather than this being a privilege of the Church. This was an age-old question in the Empire, and one that had been the subject of generations of imperial–papal conflict, so Innocent was not about to let it raise its head again.

† Marie had been married at a young age to Philip I, marquis of Namur (who was the younger brother of the late Count Baldwin IX of Flanders and of Isabelle of Hainaut, King Philip's first

happiness, or otherwise, was a much lower priority for King Philip than forming a strategic alliance that suited his purposes, so she (like the other women in his life) would just have to make the best of it.

And so the pieces were almost in place, with the board of the new game encompassing England, France, the Low Countries and Germany. John had the incumbent Emperor on his side and the resources of England behind him, as well as alliances with counts Renaud and Ferrand that gave him access to the coasts of Boulogne and Flanders. Philip had some support of his own in the Empire, plus the backing of nearly all the major French vassals, and his territorial domains and overlordship included both Normandy and Brittany. Moreover, and before the first move could be made, Philip tipped the odds in his favour by forming one more alliance. This one had been a very long time in the making, but it was the most important of all, for his new friend was Pope Innocent III.

The catalyst for this reconciliation was Philip's realisation, after twenty long years, that he was not going to get the better of Ingeborg in the question of their marriage. It was not going to be dissolved, she was not going to give up, and he had better learn to accept it. In practice, he only really needed to make one minor step, because all that was required was for him to release her and declare that they were properly married. There was no necessity for the two of them actually to co-habit as man and wife, as long as Ingeborg had the public status of queen. Royal couples often did lead separate lives, especially when their childbearing years were over, and Philip had long given up on the possibility of more children. The succession was secure enough without them: he had two sons, and his heir, Louis, had a son of his own and would surely have more in due course. Indeed, Blanche had given birth again in January 1213, and although both babies (she had borne twin boys) had died, there was no question that she and Louis were fertile and that more pregnancies would ensue.

wife), but he had died when she was still only twelve. Duke Henry's first wife had been Matilda of Boulogne, another member of the extended family of Flanders, Boulogne and Hainaut.

Ingeborg was thus brought back to court and restored to her rights, and Philip was restored to the pope's good graces. Even better for him was that the same could not be said of John, with whom Innocent was growing increasingly irritated. The excommunication had proved as ineffective as the interdict in getting John to change his mind about the appointment of Stephen Langton, and the titular archbishop of Canterbury was still living in France along with all but one of England's bishops.* In early 1213 Innocent took a drastic step:

> The pope then being deeply grieved for the desolation of the kingdom of England, by the advice of his cardinals, bishops, and other wise men, definitively decreed that John king of England should be deposed from the throne of that kingdom, and that another, more worthy than he, to be chosen by the pope, should succeed him. In pursuance of this his decree, our lord the pope wrote to the most potent Philip, king of the French, ordering him, in remission of all his faults, to undertake this business.[6]

There is a great deal to unpack here. The first question to ask is whether or not this formal deposition actually happened at all; this quote is from the work of Roger of Wendover, but none of the French writers mention it, and we might expect that William the Breton at least would do so, if he knew of it. There is also no written record in the French royal archives. But Innocent was certainly making noises about deposing John at this time, regardless of whether he actually issued official documents to that effect, and if we assume that there was at least some impetus from the pope, we can see that double standards abound. Under other circumstances, Philip would have argued vociferously that Innocent had no jurisdiction in secular affairs, and it is easy to imagine what he would have had to say if the pope had made any such declaration about the crown of France. But, because it suited his own purposes to

---

* This exception was Peter des Roches, the bishop of Winchester, who was a staunch adherent of John and almost as pugnacious as the bishop of Beauvais.

have Church backing in his war against John, Philip said nothing, not even arguing with the idea that John's successor should be 'chosen by the pope'.

An explanation for this lies in Roger of Wendover's next line, which follows on directly from the quote above: 'and declaring that, after he [Philip] had expelled the English king from the throne of that kingdom, he and his successors should hold possession of the kingdom of England for ever'. The idea that the pope could depose a crowned and anointed king at will, and then bestow the crown on someone unrelated, was an incredibly dangerous precedent to set, but in this specific instance it gave Philip the legal excuse he wanted. He could position himself not as the king of France seeking to dethrone the king of England in an unjustified manner, but rather as a Christian king fighting on behalf of the Church, on behalf of all those exiled bishops and of the people of England (still suffering under the long interdict), against an excommunicate who had forfeited his right to the throne. William the Breton certainly believed this, crediting Philip's motives as being that 'he wished to return to their churches all those bishops who had been expelled long ago and were in exile in his realm; and to re-establish divine service in England, which had been forbidden for seven years'.[7]

John's deposition in England had not been part of Philip's plan in the short term. We can see from his careful consolidation in Normandy, and the prudent moves he had made since that conquest, that he was engaged in a long-term strategy that involved standing on demonstrably firm ground before each subsequent step forward was taken. But although the present circumstances might involve getting ahead of himself, it was an opportunity that Philip could not turn down once it had arisen: to strike directly at John in England, his strongest point, now. If this strike were to be successful, it would make Philip's task in Aquitaine and in John's other remaining French lands all the easier, and he could still achieve his lifelong aim of wiping the Plantagenets off the map.

A second advantage to this unexpected opening was that it would solve the Louis problem. Philip had no particular desire to sit on the English throne himself; he just wanted the Plantagenets off it. He was already the king of France, a position he considered far superior, so the new title would add nothing to his status while making his workload considerably heavier as he grew older. It would be better by far to have England in the hands of a loyal subordinate, so his avowed intention was that Louis would become king there – but, crucially, he would hold that title as an apanage from Philip and would be obliged to defer to him as overlord.[*] In April 1213 Philip even went so far as to have a formal document drawn up between himself and Louis to this effect.[8]

With the pope's backing, and in the knowledge that John was unpopular with his barons in England, Philip was able to begin his military and naval preparations, and he mustered at Damme the large fleet he had been building and requisitioning. However, John – ever the gambler – now made a move so totally unexpected that it threw even Philip off balance. John had realised, as Philip had done before him, that being in conflict with the pope was a significant hindrance to any monarch in western Europe, and that in his particular circumstances it might even prove fatal to his kingship and his dynasty's future. He therefore needed to address this, and he needed to do it now, before Philip's ships could set sail. He might even have been inspired by Philip's own recent experience: it was encouraging to John to see how readily Innocent had accepted Philip back into the fold following the latter's climbdown

---

[*] An *apanage* was a system used in France whereby a lordship or grant of land was made to a younger son, sourced perhaps from his mother's inheritance or an additional gain by conquest, or by carving a small lordship off the main patrimony. It was a kind of compromise between equal inheritance of all sons (which would result in a holding being subdivided into ever smaller and eventually untenable fractions) and primogeniture (which kept the holding intact, but created frustration and anger among younger sons who received nothing and who might therefore rebel). The best-known contemporary example of this practice in France was the county of Dreux, which had been given to Count Robert I, Louis VII's younger brother, as an apanage; Philip Augustus would later bestow the county of Clermont upon his own second son, Philip Hurepel, in the same way. In both cases the apanage was the grantee's to hold and to pass on to his heirs, but if his line ever became extinct then the title and lands would revert to the crown and could be awarded to a younger son of a new generation in the same way. In positioning the kingdom of England as nothing more than an apanage to be bestowed at the will of the French king, Philip was emphasising the superiority of one crown over the other.

over Ingeborg. The pope, as it happens, had not been particularly keen on Philip's plan to set Louis up as king of England (because he wanted the prince to lead the Albigensian Crusade), so he was open to discussion with John.

As it transpired, Innocent had no need to negotiate, because what happened was John's immediate and total capitulation. John had been refusing for more than five years to accept Stephen Langton's consecration as archbishop of Canterbury, but in May 1213 he performed an abrupt *volte face* and said he would do so. This was perhaps only to be expected, and Philip might have seen it coming, but he could hardly have predicted what else John would do at the same time: he ceded England as a papal fief.

The enormity of this action should not be underestimated. John was, in effect, surrendering his crown to the papacy, which would be England's overlord in perpetuity. He would continue to wear that crown for now, but only as the liege man and subordinate of the pope, and his kingship could be rescinded at any time by Innocent or his successors. It is no wonder that Philip Augustus was taken aback, for who could possibly have predicted that John would do something so startling and extreme?

Pope Innocent, with his ambitions for widespread secular as well as ecclesiastical control, was certainly not going to turn down such an opportunity. He wrote immediately to John (who, in marked contrast to recent papal missives, was now addressed as 'the illustrious king of England' and an 'exalted prince') to confirm and accept that 'you have put your person and territory under apostolic suzerainty – by right of lordship making over in perpetuity to the Holy Roman Church your kingdoms of England and Ireland, to be held through the Church and of the Church'.[9] He could probably hardly believe what he was dictating to his scribes. Innocent then performed a U-turn even more screeching than John's own, cancelling all Philip's invasion plans – 'for the whole realm of England was the pope's fief' – and even threatening to excommunicate the French king if he persisted in doing the very thing the pope had been urging him to do up until about five minutes ago.[10]

Philip was livid. But what could he do? He had made much of the idea that he was in the right against John because he was acting on the pope's behalf, so to continue with a campaign now, against Innocent's express prohibition, would be futile. It would do nothing for his reputation and would result in a further breach between himself and the papacy — a breach so recently healed, after so long, that Philip did not want to risk opening it again. He therefore cancelled his plans, much to Louis's disappointment as well as his own. They allowed themselves to take out some of their frustrations on Ferrand of Flanders, who, as a rebellious vassal, was a fair target. Philip made sure that he was acting within the letter of the law by summoning Ferrand to appear before him, and only giving the order for his lands to be ravaged when he failed to turn up, and Louis took up the burning torch with alacrity.

Alas, this action, satisfying as it might have been in the short term, turned out to be counterproductive. Ferrand appealed to John for help, and John responded by sending his own fleet across the Channel, under the command of his illegitimate half-brother William Longespee, the earl of Salisbury.* These ships arrived at Damme on 30 May 1213 to find that Philip's fleet, which lay at anchor, was only sparsely guarded, as the French forces were engaging in ravaging further inland. William Longespee and his men were able to 'cut the cables of three hundred of their ships loaded with corn, wine, flour, meat, arms and other stores, and sent them to sea to make for England; besides these they set fire to and burned a hundred or more which were aground'. The conflagration was such that the burning ships were 'belching forth smoke as if the very sea were on fire'.[11] The English forces landed and might have made incursions further inland, but Philip was not all that far away and, with the assistance of Louis and of Peter

---

* William Longespee was the youngest of the illegitimate children of Henry II. As a bastard he had no inheritance of his own, and was thus both dependent on his half-brothers' generosity and entirely loyal to them for that reason. He was by now in his late thirties and greatly resembled Richard the Lionheart at the same age: the 'long sword' of his epithet refers to the outsize weapons he wielded due to his height and strength. Richard had arranged William's marriage in 1196 to Ela, countess of Salisbury in her own right.

of Dreux, the young duke of Brittany, he was able to launch a counter-attack that chased the raiders back to their ships and out to sea. This limited the immediate damage, but the English fleet remained a looming danger, and it was Philip himself, seeing what a great disadvantage it would be for his ships to fall into enemy hands, who gave orders that the rest of his recently constructed fleet should be burned.

This very first idea of invading England had run a course similar to Philip's initial attempts on Rouen many years previously: an unexpected opportunity had led him to get too far ahead of himself, resulting in a campaign that was not as well planned as it could have been, and one that was too rushed to succeed. But he had learned his lesson back then, about patience and the necessity of thorough preparation, and he would do the same again now. Fleets could be rebuilt and plans re-laid.

William Longespee's success at Damme led John into overconfidence. He fancied that he had Philip on the run and that he could exploit this, so he pushed his coalition into action, planning a two-pronged attack to take place in the spring and summer of 1214. John himself was to invade Poitou, to the south of Philip's royal domain, aided by his remaining loyal barons there, while Emperor Otto and Counts Renaud and Ferrand – supported by further English forces under William Longespee – would attack in the north. Their idea was that Philip would be caught in the middle and crushed, and so confident were these allies that they were apparently already dividing France up between them: 'Count Ferrand wanted Paris; Count Renard [sic] wanted Normandy; the emperor wanted Orleans, Chartres, and Étampes.'[12]

Philip Augustus had other ideas. Facing enemies on two fronts was not easy, but now he could reap the rewards of having an adult and warlike son: Louis was dispatched south to deal with John, while Philip would face the others in the north. Louis engaged John's forces at La-Roche-aux-Moines, in Anjou, on 2 July 1214, although John was not there himself, as he had fled at Louis's approach – so quickly, in fact, that most of his army did not even know he had gone. The result was leaderless chaos and easy pickings, with Louis winning a resounding victory; a significant number of John's men were killed or captured in the fight, or drowned as they tried to escape across the river, and Louis seized much useful booty in the form of armour, weapons, provisions and valuables.[13] He then sent word of the triumph to Philip, letting him know that the southern threat was no more, but it is doubtful whether this message had reached the king before the second army of his foes appeared in the north.

Set-piece battles, as we know, were generally avoided by medieval commanders, as their outcomes could be both unpredictable and all too decisive. But sometimes avoidance was not possible, and sometimes a battle was actually the least worst option available — and this is what Philip realised as he was pausing to eat lunch, on a hot summer's day, in the hitherto unremarkable village of Bouvines in Flanders. This recognition was going to be significant, because the repercussions of the battle that would take place there on 27 July 1214 would reverberate through western Europe for decades.

It was inevitable that the coalition forces were going to attack at some point, and Philip was not unprepared. He had mustered a royal army and collected the *oriflamme* from Saint-Denis, and he was extremely well supported by his nobles — they were fully cognisant of the fact that this was no petty conflict but a defence of their kingdom, their homeland, and they flocked to the king's banner. Almost every loyal senior vassal was present in the host: Philip's vastly experienced Dreux cousins, Count Robert II and Bishop Philip (both by now in their early sixties), along with the count's youngest son, John of Dreux, then aged about sixteen; Philip's brother-in-law William, the count of Ponthieu; Thomas, the eighteen-year-old count of Perche;* Odo III, the duke of Burgundy;

---

* Thomas of Perche might have found himself in an awkward position, as he was both Philip Augustus's cousin and Emperor Otto's nephew: his mother was Richenza of Saxony, who was Otto's

and Walter II de Châtillon, the count of Saint-Pol.* Those who were not in the royal host were absent for good reasons: Prince Louis, of course, was still in Poitou; Peter of Dreux was defending Brittany against John's incursion there, while his brother Robert junior had recently been taken prisoner by John in the same campaign; Theobald IV of Champagne was only thirteen, and his regent was his mother, so neither of them would be expected to take the field in person; and Theobald VI of Blois, although now of age, was suffering from leprosy.

One family of close royal relations was unfortunately split. Peter II of Courtenay, Philip Augustus's first cousin, fought 'virtuously' for the king, as did his younger brother Robert, but Peter was married to Yolande of Flanders,† which made their children first cousins of Joan, the current countess of Flanders.[14] Peter's eldest son, Philip, had chosen to fight for Count Ferrand and therefore took the field against his own father.

There was a significant Church presence in the royal army. Any French host, of course, contained its fair share of priests and clerics as non-combatants, and Philip was well supplied with men to bless his army and pray for his victory. One of these was his chaplain and clerk, William the Breton, whose eye-witness testimony is invaluable, and who notes his own presence in his work: 'At this time there was stationed behind the king, not far from him, his chaplain who is the writer of this account.'[15] But this particular army also included two representatives of the more militant arm of the Church, because the bishop of Beauvais fully intended to fight alongside his brother, and Brother Guérin had left his chancery and donned his armour so that the king could benefit from his extensive military experience.

---

sister and King John's niece. However, he remained loyal to Philip and France throughout his life and never showed any hint of divided loyalties.

* Odo was the son of Hugh III, the duke of Burgundy who had died at Acre during the Third Crusade after being left in charge of the French troops following King Philip's departure. Walter was a nephew of Robert II of Dreux and Bishop Philip, as his mother was their sister.

† As noted above in Chapter 4.

The army was an effective one, composed of different types of combatant. There was no need for miners or siege engineers this time, but Philip had 'collected an army of earls, barons, knights, and soldiers, horse and foot, together with the commoners of the cities and towns', which meant that he was prepared for most eventualities.[16] The size of medieval armies is notoriously difficult to gauge, but in this case we are aided by Philip's administration keeping such efficient records, so we can say with relative confidence that his force comprised around 1,300 cavalry (mainly knights, but a few lightly armoured mounted sergeants) and between 4,000 and 6,000 infantry.[17] There were also clear lines of command: each separate contingent reported to its own count or duke, who would be with them in the field, but they in turn understood that they took their orders from Philip, who was in undisputed overall command.

Against Philip was ranged the army of the coalition, which was slightly larger than his, at around 1,500 cavalry and 7,500 infantry. However, it was less well organised and led, with Otto, Renaud, Ferrand and William Longespee all claiming superiority over the others on the various bases of rank, local knowledge, provision of the greatest number of men or the greatest financial contribution. They argued among themselves on the question of whether or not they wanted to engage Philip in the field, but they eventually managed to agree that the best outcome would be Philip's swift death or capture, which was much more likely to happen in a battle than anywhere else. If they got bogged down in a war of sieges, Philip would have the upper hand.

The village of Bouvines lay on the road from Lille to Tournai, about 130 miles north of Paris and 65 miles south-east of Calais, and was the site of a bridge across the River Marcq. At around noon on 27 July 1214, Philip was marching westwards through it, in the direction of Lille, and his army was in the process of crossing the bridge. This was a long process, because the way was narrow, and Philip himself had paused for a simple meal of bread and wine while he waited his turn. He was still eating, and about half of the troops had crossed, when Brother Guérin, who had been with the rearguard, galloped up to say that the coalition host was behind them and advancing from Tournai. They were so close that there had already been some attacks on his rearguard.

This put Philip in an extremely dangerous predicament, because the last thing he needed was for his host to be caught half on one side of the river and half on the other side, with a bottleneck in between. So he had two choices: keep going, and hope the rest of them could cross in time to get away, or turn back and face the enemy. In the circumstances, the second option was the better one, because he was going to have to face the coalition forces at some point anyway, so he might as well do it now, while he had the time to form up properly and they were still straggling along the road towards him. He recalled the part of his force that had already crossed the river, destroyed the bridge behind him so none of his men could flee, and then moved well away from the marshy ground surrounding the bridge to a firmer, flat area. Unfortunately for the local villagers, this was one of their grain fields that was almost ready to harvest, but they were not in a position to object.

It was a testament to the good order and discipline of the French troops that they were able to turn round and get back so quickly, and Philip ended up with ample time to form them up, in three divisions, before the full coalition force had arrived. The main initial question for the king was, where should he place himself? He was faced with the inevitable commander's choice between stationing himself at a distance, where he could see the big picture, and being the inspiring leader who led his men personally in the field. Philip was decisive on this point, and he placed himself and his sacred *oriflamme* banner front and centre, in the first rank of the middle division. With him were around 200 mounted knights, mainly from his own household, who knew each other, had trained together and who 'had been put in the king's battalion specially to protect his person and because of their great loyalty and reputation for outstanding prowess'.[18] Also in the

Plan of the battle of Bouvines

	The French		The Coalition
Left	Robert, count of Dreux Philip, bishop of Beauvais William, count of Ponthieu	**Right**	Renaud, count of Boulogne William Longespee Henry, duke of Brabant
Centre	Philip Augustus Royal household knights	**Centre**	Otto, Holy Roman Emperor Imperial household knights Imperial infantry
Right	Odo, duke of Burgundy Knights of Champagne and Saint-Pol Brother Guérin	**Left**	Ferrand, count of Flanders

central division were around 2,000 of the infantry, and behind them all Philip stationed a rearguard of some 150 sergeants to guard the remains of the bridge.

The division to Philip's left was commanded by counts Robert of Dreux and William of Ponthieu, and comprised the men of their own counties – including the bishop of Beauvais – along with some Bretons who had been sent by Robert's son Peter. To the king's right were the knights of Burgundy and Saint-Pol, and also of Champagne, furnished by their underage count and his mother although they could not be present in person. This wing was commanded by the duke of Burgundy, the count of Saint-Pol and also by Brother Guérin, who 'rode rapidly among the men, encouraging them to fight vigorously for the honour of their king and kingdom [...] and telling them to guard at all costs against a more numerous enemy outflanking and surrounding them'.[19] Philip had deliberately posted Guérin there, instead of keeping him at hand in the central division, and this was probably to stiffen the backbone of Odo of Burgundy, who was apparently 'very fat and of a phlegmatic disposition'.*[20] This wing was supported by a small force of mounted sergeants and a number of militia groups summoned from Paris and other towns and cities under royal control.

The coalition army also formed up in three divisions. Emperor Otto placed himself in the centre, facing Philip, along with a small elite bodyguard of knights and supported by infantry from the Empire, all under the imperial banners of a dragon and an eagle, which were mounted on a golden cart. To Otto's left (and therefore facing the men of Champagne, Burgundy and Saint-Pol) was Count Ferrand with knights and infantry from Flanders and Hainaut; to Otto's right, facing the Dreux brothers, were Count Renaud and William Longespee with English knights and Brabançon infantry. Duke Henry of Brabant had very much hedged his bets during the last year, following up his wedding to Philip Augustus's daughter by marrying off his own eldest daughter to the widowed Otto. When eventually forced to jump one way or the other he had chosen Otto, although we do not know what his wife might have had to say about this. On the extreme right flank of the coalition army was a small group of English archers, who would have nothing like the influence of their counterparts in later centuries.

---

* William the Breton's insinuation here about Odo's military prowess turned out to be erroneous: the duke fought with distinction in the battle and had two or three horses killed under him.

In placing his divisions, Philip had managed to gain one small advantage. The plain was flat, so there was no hill to form up on in either direction, but he had positioned his army facing more or less east, meaning that the bright summer afternoon sun was behind them. When the allied forces arrived, therefore, they had the sun in their eyes.

Position was one thing; morale was another. It was necessary for Philip to make a stirring speech, and in it he chose to emphasise the religious aspects of the French cause, while giving a nod to patriotism. They were being attacked and invaded by an army led by an excommunicate, so God would be on their side:

> Now, the Lord Himself is giving me what I wanted [...] He will turn us into cutting instruments; He will hit and we will be the hammer; He will lead the whole battle and we will be His ministers [...] Show yourselves to be the enemies of the enemies of the Church. May your fighting prevail, not for me but for you and the kingdom.[21]

After that it was time for Philip to take his place in the host and prepare for imminent combat. We cannot know exactly what was going through his mind as he sat there on his restless warhorse, surrounded by other mounted and armed men, but it would be reasonable to guess that he experienced a combination of thoughts and feelings. He would hardly have been human had there not been an element of the deeply personal: *What will happen to me in the next few hours? Will I be injured or killed?* And, as a field commander, some wider questions: *How will my army fare during this encounter? How will they fight, and how will I know? Who will I lose?* Such worries would be enough for anyone in a similar position, but Philip was first and foremost a king, so there were issues of even greater significance to contend with. *What will happen to France if I am defeated?*

There was some small crumb of comfort in the answer to that final question. When Philip had embarked on the perilous business of the crusade, more than twenty years previously, the succession had been hanging by a thread and a civil war might well have erupted if he had died. Now he had an heir of proven character who was in his twenties, and who had two sons of his own (Blanche had given birth to another surviving son, Louis, in April 1214) and further back-up in the form of the teenaged Philip Hurepel. But, although this might assuage his worries about his kingdom, it did nothing for Philip's personal situation. He intended to survive the day – he *needed* to survive it – because he was not finished yet. He was just shy of forty-nine years old, with years of life ahead of him, and there was still so much to accomplish before his life's work was complete. As he said his last-minute prayers, as he made sure his sword was loose in its scabbard, as his helm was lowered and positioned, shutting him in, and as the lance was put in his hand, Philip Augustus was determined to win this battle – for God, for France and for himself.

The first action, as agreed, was taken to Philip's right by Brother Guérin, who led a charge against the Flemings facing him. He was followed by the mounted knights of Champagne, Burgundy and Saint-Pol, with these last actually breaking right through Ferrand's line so they could, with exemplary discipline, turn and attack again from the rear. Buoyed by what they could see of this early success, the French left then engaged the coalition right, and the two opposing centre divisions charged.

Philip was cut off from the big picture, his field of vision narrowing both metaphorically and literally to what he could see directly in front of him from inside the helm. When we look back on battles in overview – exactly as we are doing now – we might see a neat diagram of the formations and movements of armies, but the reality on the ground was very different. There it was the feel of the ground underfoot or beneath horses' hooves, the effort of seeing and hearing, of gulping in enough air, of controlling and wielding weapons. It was the sudden heart-stopping glimpse of the enemy approaching, and the almighty smash when the two sides slammed into each other at speed ... everything was an over-whelming sensory jumble of noise and fear and action and blood and pain.

William the Breton's vivid account of Bouvines brings some of
this atmosphere to life:

Lances are shattering, swords and daggers hit each other,
combatants split each other's heads with their axes, and their
lowered swords plunge into the bowels of horses [...] The
combatants are engaging each other over the whole plain
in such a close melee that those who are striking and those
who are being struck are so close to each other that they
barely have room to raise their arm to strike another blow
[...] Loose horses are running here and there across the field,
some giving out their last breaths, some with entrails spill-
ing out of their stomachs, some kneeling and falling to the
ground [...] There is hardly one place where you cannot see
dead men and dying horses.[22]

Philip was in the midst of all this, a marked man with his banners
flying above him, and the obvious target for every enemy blade.
The allies had 'planned on killing the king as soon as they captured
him, with the intention, once the king was slain, of easily defeating
the rest of the army', and this plan was soon put into action as the
two central divisions moved forward to engage.[23] First there was
the charge of the imperial knights, many of them aiming directly
at Philip, but this had been expected, and a counter-charge by the
French held them off. But once these organised advances lost their
initial momentum and disintegrated into smaller pockets of individual encounters, the German infantry were able to push their
way through the melee.

Philip, engaged with opponents on horseback, could not see
everything that was happening on the ground in his immediate
vicinity, and a group of foot soldiers managed to get through the
thick of the press, all aiming for him and wielding long polearms
with blades and hooks. One of these, 'a man more daring than
the others, pierced his [Philip's] armour between the chest and
the head [...] precisely below his chin'. Kings were able to benefit from the latest up-to-date armour, and Philip was saved from

instant death by the strength of his hauberk and collar, but the hook of the man's weapon caught in the mail links, causing disaster: 'As the king pulled again with all his strength, pushed at the same time by the crowd which surrounded him, he fell from the height [of his horse's back] and was knocked down to the ground, head first.'

This was an incredibly dangerous moment, for Philip and for France. Falling to the ground could easily prove fatal: there were flying and stamping hooves all around and the danger of being crushed or suffocated by a collapsing horse, to say nothing of the sharp weapons stabbing down at him with murderous intent. Fortunately Philip was not prone for long, as 'his natural strength helped him to get up, and he found himself on his feet'. But the hook was still stuck in his armour, and it took the combined efforts of several of his household knights to free it.[24] By that time they were all in a thick press, with Philip still on foot and in danger from the mounted enemy cavalry above him as well as the hacking pole weapons of the imperial infantry.

Philip's household knights had been hand-picked for their heroism and loyalty, and one of them, Peter Tristan, demonstrated that now. In a valiant act of self-sacrifice – and one that ensured his name would be remembered eight centuries later, when others were long forgotten – he dismounted, offered his horse to Philip and then threw himself bodily between the king and his attackers to enable the former time to escape the press. He was killed, but his king survived.

As soon as Philip was clear he rallied, turned and continued to fight. His survival and reappearance in the fray heartened his troops, and the tide began to turn in this central part of the battle. The French pushed forward, and soon it was Otto's turn to be attacked in person as a party of knights reached him. It is unclear (and possible that they did not even know themselves) whether they were trying to capture or kill him; one knight seized his bridle, in an attempt to drag him away, but another aimed a stab at his chest. This had unintended consequences, as Otto's mount reared up at that exact moment, and the knight's thrust pierced

the horse's eye rather than the Emperor's armour. The scream-
ing animal managed to stagger away a little before collapsing and
dying, and this gave one of Otto's bodyguard a few extra moments
in which to dismount and offer Otto his own horse. This could
have been a repeat of Philip's experience, but it was different in
two respects: the heroic knight survived, and Otto did not turn
and rally. Instead he fled the field, leaving his knights to cover his
retreat and abandoning the imperial standard to be captured by the
jubilant French.

With the Emperor now in flight, the momentum was with the
French. We lose sight of Philip for a short while here, but it is
possible that he had enough respite from the combat to hear the
news from the flanking parts of the battle. First to arrive were
the heartening tidings from the right: Ferrand of Flanders was
surrounded and captured, and with the loss of their leader the
Flemish forces collapsed. Some managed to flee, but the rest were
killed or captured.

The battle over to Philip's left was a whole other story on its
own. Fierce fighting had been going on for some time when
the imposing figure of William Longespee came face to face
with Philip of Dreux. As a bishop (and one, moreover, who had
sworn an oath on his release from captivity back in 1200 that he
would never again shed the blood of Christians), Philip was not
carrying a sword. However, he did 'happen to have a mace in his
hand' and he was not afraid to use it, especially on an opponent
who so closely resembled his old foe Richard the Lionheart. He
bludgeoned William Longespee – a huge man some twenty years
his junior – and caught him such a mighty blow on the head
that William's helm was crushed and he was sent flying from
his horse, tumbling to the ground with a thump and making an
earl-of-Salisbury-shaped dent in the ground as he did so. The
dazed William had no choice but to yield, and Bishop Philip
took him prisoner.[25]

Time was also soon up for Count Renaud, the only coalition
leader still fighting. His physical courage could not be doubted:
he formed the dwindling remains of his infantry into a circle of

two ranks, pikes and axes facing outwards, from which he and his mounted companions made sortie after sortie. But before long he was both exhausted and vastly outnumbered, as fighting elsewhere ceased and more of Philip's army could be sent to surround him. After one sortie too many he was knocked from his horse and trapped underneath it, unable to move. There was a scramble to attack him, and he was nearly killed, rescued only by the timely arrival of Brother Guérin, to whom he surrendered. William the Breton saw this, noting of Renaud that 'his face and all his members are covered with a stream of blood; he can barely lift his body to climb back on a horse; [Brother Guérin] places him on it'.[26] The foot soldiers who had been forming the ring around Renaud had no monetary value and were all killed; Renaud survived the day, although he would later wish that he had not.

The whole battle was over within three hours of the first blow being struck, and it is difficult to pin down the exact point at which Philip realised that he had won. But now, with Otto gone and Renaud, Ferrand and William Longespee all captured, there was no question about it: Philip had gained a spectacular victory. In an admirable display of restraint, he did not set out on a wild chase after escapees, nor allow his troops to do so. Instead he regrouped, ensuring that he was prepared in case there was further danger from fleeing enemies turning round and re-forming, and then he gave thanks to God in a nearby chapel.

The Emperor was defeated. The king of England was defeated. Domestic resistance against Philip's rule had been crushed. It was going to take a long time for the ramifications of such a resounding victory to sink in, not only for Philip but for everyone else in France and the major players elsewhere. In the meantime the exhausted king could disarm, wash and eat, letting the fatigue sweep over him and beginning to feel the aches and pains from blows he might not even have noticed at the time. Perhaps he relived, or tried not to relive, his own near-death experience, but he could also remind himself that he had survived, and could additionally congratulate himself on not having lost a single commander of note.

His victory had been resoundingly complete. As he spent the evening of 27 July 1214 in a tent near the village of Bouvines, Philip not only remained the undisputed king of France, but also the pre-eminent monarch in western Europe. Nobody could touch him now, and he could plan his next moves with confidence.

Thinking the Unthinkable

Philip Augustus was not a vindictive man. He had demonstrated this after the capture of Château Gaillard back in 1204, when he had spared the entire garrison despite taking the castle by storm, and he proved it again now in his treatment of the prisoners taken at Bouvines:

> On that same evening all the noble men who had been taken in battle were brought to him: five counts and twenty-five men of such high nobility that each carried his own banner in battle, and a great number of other prisoners of lesser position. Although they were all from his kingdom and were his liege men, although they had conspired against him and made every effort to kill him, although they were guilty and deserved to be beheaded according to the customs of the land, the king (I tell you) showed himself to be gentle and merciful; he spared all their lives.[1]

Not only did Philip not order a single execution, but some of the prisoners of lesser rank were actually set at liberty. Upon releasing one Flemish knight to his family, Philip was upbraided by the duke of Burgundy, but his reply was that the man in question 'never did like war, and he advised his lord against it every day. He never wanted to do homage to the king of England, even when the others did; and if he has caused damage to me by serving his lord loyally, I hold no ill will towards him because of it.'[2]

With no danger of further rebellion or counter-attack against him in Flanders, Philip was free to return to Paris. He entered the capital amid scenes of jubilation comparable to the ones that had taken place at the time of his own birth nearly half a century earlier, as William the Breton described:

> The citizens and all the scholars, the clergy and the people, came to meet the king singing hymns and canticles, and showed by their actions the great joy in their hearts. It was not enough for them to celebrate by day; they prolonged their revels into the night, for seven nights, by the light of so many torches that night was as bright as day.

In his other account, William added that 'the king was more beloved than ever, because it was through his efforts that they [the people] could enjoy peace and live in safety'.[3]

The captured enemy leaders were put in a cart and paraded through the streets amid general opprobrium and taunts, but were otherwise unharmed, and then Philip turned his mind to their individual fates. William Longespee was an offshoot of the Plantagenet dynasty, but he was not a vassal of Philip's and was therefore a simple foe rather than a traitor. The bishop of Beauvais had handed Longespee over to the king after the battle, but Philip awarded the earl's custody back to the Dreux family, in recognition of their service and with the intention that they could negotiate an exchange of prisoners with John in order to free Count Robert's heir, the future Robert III, who had been captured during John's southern campaign. This was eventually achieved, but only after so long a delay on John's part that there were suggestions he was deliberately stalling.[*]

The two rebellious counts, Renaud and Ferrand, were in the most serious trouble and, as William the Breton's quote at the start of

---

[*] Rumours that John was delaying his half-brother's release on purpose, because he was having a liaison with William's wife, began to circulate; we ought to be able to dismiss these as scurrilous gossip, but with John one can never really be sure.

this chapter indicates, Philip was perfectly entitled to have them executed after they had made a pact with a foreign king and taken up arms against their sovereign. But he did not, instead deciding on imprisonment. Of the two, Ferrand was treated a little more leniently, probably because his brother Afonso II was the king of Portugal and Philip did not want to cause a diplomatic incident; he was incarcerated, but it was a simple confinement with no additional punishment. The multiple-turncoat Renaud, however, was a different matter. He had been a boyhood companion of Philip's, so the betrayal felt by the king was all the greater. He confronted Renaud in person, 'possessed by anger and resentment', and 'began to reproach him for all the favours he had granted him and said that, as he was his liege man, he had dubbed him into knighthood; as he was poor he had made him rich; and, for all these privileges, he had returned ill for good'. Renaud was not only thrown in a cell, but also shackled there to a heavy log ('which two men could barely move each time he had to go and relieve himself') by a chain so short that he could not move more than half a pace in any direction.[4] And there he would remain, at the king's pleasure.

Ferrand and Renaud both held their counties and titles only via marriage. Given that wives were legally subordinate to their husbands and thus presumed to be acting under orders, Philip had no cause to imprison them as well, and they were left at liberty. The young Joan of Flanders, still only fourteen or fifteen, was allowed to continue her rule, but under much closer royal supervision. She petitioned the pope for the annulment of her marriage, claiming it had never been consummated, but she was unsuccessful; she therefore remained married to Ferrand but unable to produce an heir for her county while he was in prison, which was an additional bonus for Philip Augustus.

Ida of Boulogne, meanwhile, was only married to Renaud because he had abducted her against her will, years before, and she might well have been glad to see the back of him.* Renaud was

* Ida had been an unwilling bride, and certainly not party to any sort of faux 'abduction' in which she could be suspected of being complicit. At the time of her kidnap she had actually been planning

obliged, and Ida encouraged, to abdicate in favour of their only daughter and heiress, Matilda – who was, of course, married to Philip Augustus's son Philip Hurepel. As the couple were both still well underage, this gave the king direct control of the county of Boulogne for the next few years.

Ferrand and Renaud would remain in prison for the rest of Philip Augustus's reign, Renaud in chains the whole time and wishing he had died a heroic death on the field at Bouvines. Ferrand was eventually released in 1227, in the early part of the reign of Philip's grandson Louis IX, when the prevailing situation in Flanders made it politic to do so.* No such offer was extended to Renaud, as it would have been counterproductive to royal interests: Philip Hurepel was by then ruling Boulogne in person and Louis IX did not want to cause any trouble for his uncle. It was at that point that Renaud gave up all hope of ever being released, and somehow managed to commit suicide in his cell.

The final coalition leader, Otto, had made it back to Germany following his flight from the battlefield at Bouvines. He was therefore out of Philip's reach, but it did not matter: Otto was finished. His reputation was in tatters, his support evaporated, and he was forced to retire to his family lands in Brunswick, while Frederick of Hohenstaufen made gain after gain. Otto was deposed in 1215 and would die, still in seclusion and disgrace, in 1218, leaving no children. Philip Augustus *had* captured Otto's imperial dragon

to marry someone else, a man of her own choosing, and she managed to smuggle out a desperate message to him from her imprisonment. He set out to rescue her but was captured by Renaud's men, and the situation did not end happily. It would not be surprising if Ida had never forgiven Renaud for this, even after twenty years of marriage.

* Flanders was the scene of some bizarre upheavals in the 1220s. Joan's younger sister, Margaret, rebelled against her, together with her erratic and only quasi-legal husband (who was twenty years older than her, had formerly been her guardian, and had taken holy orders). Joan managed to quell the revolt, but then, in 1225, an imposter turned up claiming to be her long-lost father, Baldwin IX, saying he had been captive in the east all this time rather than having died in 1206 as reported. A sufficient number of people in France and Flanders believed him – or pretended to do so – for the episode to become troublesome, but he was eventually unmasked and executed. Ferrand's release put a grown man in charge of Flanders once more, deterring anyone else from trying to take advantage of Joan.

and eagle standards during the battle of Bouvines, and shortly afterwards he sent them to the young Frederick, with his compliments. This was both a gesture of friendship and alliance, and a reminder about as subtle as the mace of the bishop of Beauvais that Frederick owed his newly enhanced position in great part to the king of France. Frederick would be crowned Emperor in 1220, and France was safe from any attack from that direction for the rest of Philip's reign.[*]

Much of this still lay in the future, but even in the immediate aftermath of the battle of Bouvines, as Philip surveyed the domestic and international situation from his lofty position at the very pinnacle of kingship, the signs were all positive. In August 1215 he celebrated his fiftieth birthday, and he had the leisure to ask himself: what next?

The answer to that question was an obvious one, given that there was still a Plantagenet on the English throne who controlled some areas of France. And, now that he had the time and opportunity to prepare properly, Philip could genuinely begin to contemplate something that had seemed unthinkable when he had ascended the throne thirty-six years earlier, when he was just a boy and Henry II had reigned supreme: the overthrow of the king of England.

John was actually doing much of the groundwork for deposition himself, having become so unpopular with his barons that a substantial proportion had rebelled against him, resulting in civil war. By the summer of 1215 these rebels thought they had succeeded in restraining the excesses of John's rule when they forced him to agree to the terms of Magna Carta; however, he immediately reneged on his word and appealed to Pope Innocent,

---

[*] Frederick was far too busy to worry much about France, in any case. Not satisfied with his existing workload as king of Sicily, king of Germany and Holy Roman Emperor, he also went on two crusades and would additionally become the king of Jerusalem in 1225, all while fathering at least twenty children by three official wives and a dozen mistresses.

who was, of course, now his overlord for England. Innocent annulled the charter in August, at which point the rebellious barons decided that if John could not be controlled, he needed to be overthrown. That, in turn, meant that they needed a new king, so a representative group was empowered to make the offer. These men sailed across the Channel and reached Paris sometime in the late autumn.

Philip Augustus was ready to receive them, and to accept their offer regally and graciously without gloating *too* much, but he was taken aback by the delegation's message. They did, as expected, come with a proposal regarding the English throne, but it was not for him; instead, they offered the crown directly to Louis.

From the barons' point of view, this was an acceptable compromise. Certainly they wanted a new king, who had to be a man of royal blood, but they were also concerned with their own self-interest, and inviting Philip Augustus to depose John and take the throne of England would be like chasing the fox away from the hen house by bringing in a wolf. Louis seemed to them a much more reasonable option, his blood just as royal as his father's but his character not so authoritarian.

The shock of the barons' offer required a swift political rethink on Philip's part, but fortunately there was nobody more mentally agile in such a situation, and he was able to come to terms with the altered situation very rapidly. On the one hand, he was entitled to feel put out. He was the king, he was the senior, and he might have expected that any offer would be made to him so that he could then confer it on his son. It had, of course, been Philip's own intention back in 1213 for Louis to take the English throne, but that was the point: it had been Philip's *own* plan, in which England was his to bestow as he saw fit, and Louis would remain officially subordinate to him. As the situation now stood, Louis would be Philip's equal as a fellow king. But there was no point in sulking about it; the thing to do was to identify the potential advantages of the new proposed arrangement so they could be exploited.

Philip had always been something of a stickler for the letter of the law, and in terms of a legal right to the English throne (as opposed to a mere war of conquest), Louis's claim was better than his. Either of them might assert the right of election, if invited to do so, but Louis also had a hereditary claim, because he was married to Blanche of Castile, Henry II's granddaughter and King John's niece.* A campaign led by Louis could therefore assume more of the legal and moral high ground than one led by Philip, which would be to both their advantages.

There was also the spiritual dimension to take into account, which was radically altered since Philip's first planned invasion of England back in 1213. At that point, Philip had been able to position himself and Louis as good Christians acting as the champions of the pope and the religiously deprived English people against an excommunicated king. But now it was the other way round: they would be acting at the behest of a group of barons who had rebelled against a king who was not only legitimate but under the pope's specific and personal protection. England was a papal fief, with Innocent as its overlord, and Innocent wanted John to remain king. Any attempt to depose and replace John, therefore, was certain to involve conflict with the pope and also to jeopardise Philip's reputation as *rex christianissimus*.

Philip, so recently reconciled with Innocent after so long, did not wish to enter into such open dispute, but now he did not have to, because he would not be the one who sailed for England. Instead, the barons' offer to Louis meant that Philip was able to enter into a double game, one he played with exceptional political skill, hoodwinking all those around him. His poker face throughout the whole episode was so good that it has held up

---

* This was still a fairly tenuous claim in hereditary terms. Even if we discount King John's own children, there were six more grandchildren of Henry II who were higher in the queue than Blanche: Eleanor of Brittany (the daughter of Henry II's son Geoffrey); Henry and Otto of Brunswick (the surviving sons of Henry II's eldest daughter); and Henry, Berenguela and Urraca of Castile (Blanche's own younger brother and older sisters). However, the barons of England needed someone who was in a position to act quickly, and all of these were very impractical choices from that point of view: Eleanor was in John's captivity; Henry of Brunswick had vast estates in Germany and no interest in England; Otto was in disgrace; Henry of Castile was only eleven and already the king of Castile, with the divorced Berenguela acting as his regent; and Urraca was the queen of Portugal.

over the centuries, and even now there is room for debate about his motives and actions, but a close examination of the available evidence shows that Philip was almost certainly manipulating the situation in his own best interests.

In the first instance, Philip made no public pronouncement, but instead let Louis have his say, so that the responsibility was his. Unsurprisingly, Louis accepted the barons' offer straight away, even before he could put his case to an assembly of nobles, as was customary, and in December 1215 he sent 140 knights across the Channel.* This hardly constituted an army of invasion, but it was not meant to be one. No large-scale military campaign could be begun in the winter, but Louis was eager to show his immediate support and intent via the dispatch of a token force.

It was also difficult to summon a council of all France's major nobles over the winter, so this did not happen until April 1216, when it took place at Melun, about 25 miles south-east of Paris. Louis put his case to the assembled lords, to ask if they would support him in his endeavour, and a counter-case was offered by Guala Bicchieri, a papal legate. The meeting was under Philip's authority, but he ostentatiously elected to preside without taking a position for or against either side; instead, he would let the two factions do the talking while he analysed their cases and observed the reactions of the assembled nobility. When Guala objected to Louis's case even being heard, Philip was ready with an answer:

'I have always been a devoted and faithful ally of our lord the pope and the church of Rome, and in all transactions have until this time effectually promoted their welfare; neither shall my son Louis now have my advice in attempting anything against the church of Rome. However, if Louis can prove any claim that he has to the kingdom of England, let him be heard.'[5]

* Louis had recruited these knights privately, not via royal summons, a point to which we will return later in this chapter.

Louis's argument was exactly the one Philip had expected: he claimed that John had forfeited the English throne by his crimes, referencing such long-ago actions as rebellion against his brother King Richard and the murder of Arthur of Brittany, as well as more recent events such as the fact that John had not consulted his nobles before ceding England as a papal fief. He added that John's misdeeds also barred his heirs from inheriting, so that the English throne was now vacant and the barons were entitled to elect a successor. And that successor, naturally, should be himself: the barons had chosen him, and he could also claim the crown in right of his wife. And finally, because John's kingship was illegitimate, he had not actually had the right to cede his kingdom to the pope in the first place, so neither Innocent nor his mouthpiece Guala had any jurisdiction over the matter.

So far, so expected. It did not take a man of Philip's acumen to see that these arguments were weak. But that was not the point: what mattered was how his senior nobles would react and, more pertinently, what arguments Guala, and by extension the papacy, would put up against Louis. Philip allowed the legate the floor.

Guala's case was also not terribly surprising. John had not been deposed, because only the pope had the right to depose him; and even if he was, this did not debar his heirs, so if a new king *were* required it could only be John's eldest son, Henry (currently aged eight). Finally, and Guala evidently considered this his trump card, John had taken the cross, so his lands were under the protection of the Church. But this was not the killer argument the legate intended: John had indeed taken a vow to go on crusade at the same time he had ceded England to the papacy, in order to further curry favour with Pope Innocent, but nobody was under any illusion that he actually ever intended to fulfil it.

All of this gave Philip some clues as to how best to react. Louis was determined to go, and the nobles overwhelmingly supported him, but the papacy was implacably opposed to it. It seemed a binary choice, therefore, with Philip having to decide between his wish to keep on the right side of the pope and his lifelong goal of destroying the Plantagenets, but now he was able to take advantage of the fact that the crown had been offered directly to Louis rather than to himself. He could, in fact, have his cake and eat it. Philip declared loudly to Guala that, as a loyal son of the Church and a friend of Pope Innocent, he would not support any attempt of his son's upon the English throne, he would not give it royal sanction, and he would not allow Louis to recruit in the name of the crown. He was convincing enough that William the Breton noted approvingly in his chronicle that Louis, in pressing ahead, acted 'against the will of his father'. Indeed, William even went so far as to say that Philip actually confiscated Louis's French lands as a punishment for disobedience, but there is no record at all of this in the royal archives, so possibly William was just enthusiastically toeing the official line that Philip was acting in accordance with Pope Innocent's will. Innocent suspected Philip of 'favouring his son', and was threatening to excommunicate him if this were truly the case, so he needed to be convincingly persuaded otherwise.[6]

What was left unsaid, but is nevertheless glaringly obvious, is that — despite his public protestations — Philip made no real attempt to *stop* Louis from going. The king could certainly have forbidden the enterprise if he wanted to, but he did not, and the reason was that he sensed a win–win situation. If Louis achieved his goal, John would be ejected from his place on the English throne; and, although Louis would not be officially subordinate to Philip as per the plans of 1213, he was certainly a much better proposition as king of England, from Philip's point of view, than any Plantagenet. But if Louis were to be unsuccessful then it would be his own failure, not Philip's, and the French king would lose no face because he could simply reiterate that he had never supported the campaign in the first place. Moreover, in either of those scenarios he would stay on the right side of Pope Innocent.

With Louis determined to proceed, Guala departed from the French court in a fit of pique and headed for England. Philip was glad to see the back of him, but was careful to ensure that the legate had a courteous safe-conduct as long as he was on French soil. The king's scrupulousness and his convincing act at the assembly were rewarded: once Guala reached England he excommunicated Louis, but not Philip, and Pope Innocent made no further move to sanction the king himself.[7]

Not all contemporaries, incidentally, were fooled. William the Breton might well have been – or possibly he was just loyally reflecting what Philip wanted him to say – but another chronicler saw through the ruse. The Anonymous of Béthune, as he is known to us, was a member of the household of a lord who was one of Louis's most ardent supporters in the campaign, and he wrote an astute eye-witness account of events in England as they were happening. His take was that Philip 'publicly made it appear as though he did not want to be involved because of the truce he had granted [i.e., reconciliation with the pope]; but privately, it was believed that he had advised him [Louis].'[8] We can never know exactly what father and son said to each other behind closed doors, but it is a fair bet that Philip and Louis discussed the matter in some detail when no churchmen were present. And, as we noted earlier, the most compelling evidence of their collusion is that Philip could have stopped it all if he had wanted to, but did not.

Philip's manipulation of the situation in order to further his own interests did, however, cause Louis some serious issues. The main one was that he was obliged to undertake the enterprise privately, so he could not summon all those lords and men who owed military service to the French crown; he could only recruit by using his own personal contacts and persuasive powers to seek volunteers. What transpired was a sort of generational divide. Philip and his senior lords, the men of his own generation, would remain in France and have nothing to do with the campaign; after all, they had estates to govern and a pretence of obedience to the pope to keep up. It was predominantly the younger nobles who volunteered to go with Louis, either because they were adult heirs to great titles who did not yet have any ruling responsibility and wanted something to do in the meantime, or because they were younger sons who had little or no expectation at home and who joined up for the adventure and the prospect of gain.

A fleet was assembled, and Louis sailed away from the Flemish coast on the Feast of Pentecost, which fell that year on 20 May 1216.[9]

The royal court was a quieter place. Louis and Philip had never exactly lived in each other's pockets, but still, they functioned as something of a team and the prince's absence must have been felt, not to mention the additional sudden disappearance of the household of young, boisterous male companions who had gone with him. Blanche remained, of course, and she was pregnant once more, so we might suppose that Philip spent some time with her – as one of the few people around who was on his own intellectual level – or at least that he kept an eye on her welfare and that of his soon-to-be next grandchild. The king could certainly be content in his family situation at this point, with his second son Philip Hurepel now in his mid-teens and engaged in the sort of martial training common to boys his age, and a couple of young grandsons of whom he was fond. The elder of these, Philip, the future king, was also just coming to the age where he would leave the female-dominated royal nursery and start his own military and political training, which would bring him more closely under Philip Augustus's eye.

Philip could be satisfied with the condition of his realm as a whole, as well as that of his family. His crushing victory at Bouvines meant that he now had nothing to fear either domestically or internationally, because 'no one dared to wage war against him, and he and the whole of his land lived in great peace for a long time'.[10] With no threats looming over him Philip could concentrate on the business of governance, and he continued to issue charters at a great rate, as he had done throughout his reign, on matters both great and small. Extant documents from the year 1216 show the king dealing with an eclectic variety of subjects, bestowing grants on the Church or on loyal supporters, making concessions regarding woodlands and mills, settling disputes between neighbouring lords, and so on. Some things never changed, though: in one letter Philip 'invites' the bellicose bishop of Beauvais to make peace with a rival with whom he had been in conflict.[11] Meanwhile, Brother Guérin's chancery (to which he had returned after the military interlude at Bouvines) continued to function efficiently, and the king could watch his treasury filling up in a most satisfactory manner.

A brief sketch of Philip at this point shows the ways in which he had, and had not, changed since we first examined his character at the age of twenty-two.* In some respects there had been little alteration: for example, despite his on–off conflict with the pope, he remained just as devoted to the wider Church as ever, and the number of his charters that give donations to various foundations, or announce that he is taking specific abbeys under his personal protection, show that this was not merely lip service. Another constant was that he persisted in his refusal to co-habit with Ingeborg, though he did at least treat her with greater outward respect than he had done for many years.

Physically the passage of nearly three decades, for a man known·to be fond of good food and fine wine, had caused an entirely predictable change in Philip's appearance: he had put on weight, although evidently not enough to prevent him taking a very active part in the battle of Bouvines or from hunting on horseback. He was slowing down a little by now, though, as not even a king could expect to be in the same physical condition in his late forties and early fifties as he had been in his twenties. Possibly Philip looked a little older than his true age, as much due to his lack of hair as to the stresses and strains of his position, although of course he had been bald so long (since his serious illness in the Holy Land back in 1191) that everyone around him was used to it.

Mentally, the changes in Philip over the years were for the better. He still had the same acute intelligence, but he could now add to it many years' worth of ruling experience and the ability to plan

___

* See the pen-portrait above, in Chapter 2.

ahead coolly for the long game. All the impetuosity of youth was long gone, and it is almost impossible to imagine the Philip of 1216 losing control of himself to the extent that he would order the elm tree between Gisors and Trie to be hacked down. Some of the sharpest edges of his personality had also been worn away by time, and, although it is perhaps a step too far to say that he was actually softening, Philip does seem to have been able to create and maintain close family relationships more easily than he did as a young man.

Given his very comfortable and advantageous situation post-1214, it would be both understandable and forgivable if Philip became complacent, but he did not. He kept his wits about him as much as ever, and the reins of power firmly in his hands. Very little that happened in France escaped his attention, and he was also in receipt of regular reports on events in England, now that Louis was prosecuting the family feud. Philip knew that Louis had landed unopposed in the south-east, and had then ridden for London (which was already in rebel hands), where he was proclaimed king. The idea of his own son wearing the English crown in place of the offspring of Henry II must have been an overwhelming delight, allowing Philip to feel as smug as he could ever permit himself to be, especially as John was now a hunted fugitive in his own land, being chased further and further westwards and away from his centres of power in the south-east of England. But, unfortunately for Philip and for Louis, the son suffered from a lack of official advice from the father. Louis was a superb warrior but not as astute a politician as Philip, and he failed to grasp the political and symbolic significance of having himself crowned. Following an acclamation as king in London, there is little doubt that Philip would have organised a coronation, but Louis decided to skip the ceremony in favour of an immediate military campaign to subdue those still holding out against him. And this allowed resistance to strengthen, because John was still able to claim that he was the only crowned king in England.

It is not easy to discern exactly what Philip was thinking as each subsequent report reached him. Disappointment?

Frustration? Indecision over whether to throw greater resources at the campaign, pope or no pope? Or possibly even a hint of *Schadenfreude*, as Philip thought how much better things would be going if he had been the one in charge, if the barons had offered the crown to him? We can extrapolate a few hints from his actions, and these tell us that getting rid of the last adult Plantagenet was still the French king's overwhelming priority. Louis's military offensive in the summer of 1216, like most others of the period, was characterised by a series of sieges, and he took a number of smaller castles but made little headway against major fortifications, especially the key stronghold of Dover. Breaking reputedly impregnable castles was something Philip knew a thing or two about, and after all his years of campaigning he had amassed a great deal of equipment relevant to such a task. He had made many public protestations about not supporting Louis, so of course the English campaign was no concern of his, but somehow, when the pope was not looking, a large trebuchet from the French royal armoury made its way across the Channel to assist Louis's efforts at Dover.[12]

As it happened, Pope Innocent's attention was elsewhere for good reasons: firstly, because he was trying to organise yet another crusade, and then because he was dying. During a visit to Perugia, in central Italy, in the height of summer, he was struck down with a virulent fever, and he succumbed to it on 16 July 1216. He was only fifty-five, but he had been on the papal throne for an almost unprecedented eighteen years and – as we have seen – exerted a huge influence on the international politics of Europe, secular as well as ecclesiastical. The upheaval caused by his death, and any potential or protracted uncertainty over the identity of his successor, might have been an opportunity that Philip could turn to his own advantage; but the cardinals, well aware of the troubled situation in Italy and wary of Emperor Frederick, responded by electing Honorius III just two days after Innocent's death. So swiftly had this happened that the name of the new pope must have reached Philip at the same time as the news of the death of the old one, a *fait accompli*.

Honorius, although newly elected, was actually ten years older than Innocent and already in his mid-sixties.* It remained to be seen how he would act in the long term, but for now he conservatively and cautiously followed the policies of his predecessor, at least with regard to France and Louis's campaign in England: Louis remained excommunicated, and Philip still had to watch his step and not be seen to support his son.

There was some excellent family news for Philip Augustus in September 1216, when Blanche gave birth to another son. He was christened Robert, an entirely conventional choice for a third Capetian boy, and he joined young Philip, who turned seven in the same month, and the two-year-old Louis in the royal household. Blanche recovered from her labour without any problems, and the king – with two sons and three grandsons – could bask in the knowledge that the French royal succession was more secure than it had been for a hundred years.

Whether the French royal succession and its English counterpart were to be one and the same thing in future was still in some doubt, as reports from across the Channel were mixed. Responsibility for one aspect of this lay squarely with Philip. Because he had not officially supported the campaign and had refused to put the resources of the crown behind it, Louis had been obliged to recruit privately, with the result that his army was not nearly large enough for the task at hand, and this situation was now being exacerbated by the fact that he had been compelled to split his forces. Louis was himself still at Dover – bogged down in a siege he could not win with such a small host, the trebuchet notwithstanding – which meant that he needed to send other parties elsewhere in order to retain authority over those areas already under his control.

---

* This was much more conventional for a pope – it was Innocent who had been the outlier in being elected at such a young age.

Louis's lack of momentum was enabling John to regroup, and if the situation deteriorated any further it would get to a point where Philip would have to contemplate seriously what would happen if Louis did not succeed. The first question was: how great was his heir's personal danger? Was it within the realms of possibility that he might actually lose his life? And if that were to become a serious prospect, what would Philip do about it?

Philip does not seem to have been unduly worried about this prospect. A cynical interpretation might be that he cared so little about his son that he was callously willing to risk the latter's life in the quest against the Plantagenets, but in fact Philip knew that it was highly unlikely that Louis would be killed. The conventions of war in the early thirteenth century were that noblemen would be captured rather than killed (as had been exemplified at Bouvines), and this held even more true for those of royal rank. The worst that might happen, therefore, was that Philip might be sent a hefty ransom demand, which would put him in something of an awkward position. But he would be able to get round that, and stay in the new pope's good graces, if he played his cards right: it would not be difficult to come up with something plausible along the lines of reiterating that he had never supported the campaign but that he would pay the ransom as long as his son came home like a good boy and did some appropriate penance. In any case, such a scenario might not arise at all if Louis were successful, and Philip was still willing to gamble on that, as he had calculated that the odds remained in their favour. So he was not placing Louis in the sort of mortal danger that might occur at a cursory first glance. Louis might not have been Philip's favourite son, but he *was* his firstborn child, the heir to the French throne, and we should give Philip at least some credit for paternal feelings as well as concern for the future of France.

Louis did not die. But there *was* a death of great significance in England in the autumn of 1216, and it was one that would have profound consequences for the political landscape.

Given the necessary travel time across land and sea, it was probably the end of October before the momentous news reached

Philip. With Louis mired in the siege at Dover, John had taken the opportunity to emerge from the west of England and attempt to strike back; he had blazed a trail of destruction across the southern midlands on his way to East Anglia, burning and ravaging the lands of the barons who were siding with Louis. But he had been taken ill as he did so, stricken by a serious case of dysentery; and, on the night of 18–19 October, he had died.

PART IV

Henry III

1216–23

10

Passing the Torch

Henry II and all four of his sons were dead; Philip had outwitted, outfought and now outlived them all. But the manner in which it had ended was something of an anti-climax, rather than the triumphant finale Philip had probably been dreaming about for years, and this was principally due to the existence of one small boy, a new Henry Plantagenet.

John had been a shockingly bad monarch, but in one aspect of kingship he had outshone his brother Richard, in that he left direct heirs. He fathered five legitimate children, and immediately after his death the eldest of these, Henry, was proclaimed king. Henry had only just turned nine, so there was no question of him ruling in his own name, and a regency council was formed. This was headed by the triumvirate of William Marshal, the earl of Pembroke and Striguil, who would be the regent, ruling in the young king's name; Peter des Roches, the bishop of Winchester, who would be Henry's personal guardian and take charge of his education; and Guala, the papal legate, the representative of their overlord Pope Honorius.* Between them these men had the political wit to realise

---

* It was normal, in cases of minor accession, for the widowed mother to act as regent. However, in this case Isabelle of Angoulême was totally sidelined by the all-male and Church-dominated regency council, and she played no part at all in her son's regime. She returned to France within a year of Henry's coronation, where she married for a second time, to Hugh X de Lusignan, the son of the man to whom she had originally been betrothed. She lived with him in Poitou until her death more than a quarter of a century later, bearing a further nine children and never mentioning John's name again.

the importance of a swift coronation, and Henry was crowned just ten days after John's death. This meant that he took his father's place as the only crowned and anointed king in England, while Louis remained a mere claimant to the throne.

There was worse to come, politically speaking. When Louis had arrived in England, he was already in conflict with the papacy, but on a secular level he could at least position himself as the invited saviour coming to rescue the oppressed barons and people from the tyrant John. Now he was a foreign aggressor trying to steal the crown from the head of an innocent child, which was hardly a good look. And when the regency council re-issued Magna Carta in November 1216, promising that the new king would abide by its terms, they took away the basis on which the discontented English barons had rebelled in the first place. The political ground had shifted so seismically that it was no longer safe to stand on.

Philip Augustus probably saw the long-term implications of this rather earlier than most others, but it was worth persisting, at least for the time being, until he could see more clearly how matters were going to play out. A truce was declared in England over the winter, to last until April 1217, and it was in February, during this cessation of hostilities, that Louis himself returned to France in order to discuss matters with his father and to seek what further aid he could.

Philip's problem was still the same one: Pope Honorius was very much against the idea of the French invasion of England, and his legate Guala had already proclaimed papal support for the young Henry III. Philip, therefore, had to remain cautious. Publicly he refused to engage – 'King Philip, fearing excommunication, gave no aid to his son [...] like the most Christian man he was, he would not speak with him' – but, again, a bit of reading between the lines indicates that he and Louis came to some arrangement in private.[1] When Louis departed for England again in April, he still did not have the official backing of the crown, and Philip had not given him any troops; however, once again, the king had not prevented him from raising more himself. And, perhaps not coincidentally, a letter from the pope, in which Honorius pressed

Philip to forbid Louis outright from returning to England, somehow failed to reach the king until after Louis had already left. Philip could therefore only reply with regret that he had not been able to discuss the matter with his heir.[2]

Philip's lack of real opposition then became clearer when Blanche entered the fray, asking the king for money so that she could support her husband in his endeavour. This was a clever move all round: intercession was a recognised duty of royal women, and of course as a loyal wife it was only to be expected that Blanche would make every possible effort on Louis's behalf. Even the pope would have to accept her duty to her husband, so she was above criticism in the situation and her intervention cannot have taken anyone by surprise. What *was* unexpected – or, at least, unexpected to anyone who had genuinely believed in Philip's opposition to Louis's campaign – was that it worked: Philip opened his amply stocked treasury and provided Blanche with funds.

Other than William the Breton, who dutifully maintains that Philip 'offered no aid to his son', and only makes a vague mention of Louis raising more troops, all the contemporary commentators are clear that it was Blanche who was the driving force behind the provision of these funds to Louis.[3] But the exact degree of Philip's reluctance is open to interpretation, and the chroniclers' depictions of the episode range from the matter-of-fact to the Minstrel of Reims's highly entertaining stand-up row between Blanche and Philip in which she threatens to pawn her three sons – his royal heirs – to the highest bidder in order to raise money if he will not give her any.[4] Roger of Wendover, rather more prosaically, seems to see through the situation: 'The king was afraid to give assistance to his excommunicated son [...] He laid the burden of the business on the wife of Louis, who was not slow in fulfilling the duty imposed on her.'[5] This implies that it was Philip who was supporting and directing Blanche, rather than she making demands of him, and – given that he could easily have refused to help if he had wanted to – we might even go so far as to suspect that they cooked the whole plan up between them. The outcome was that Philip could still (just about) claim that he was not supporting Louis: he had only given money to Blanche, and what she did with it was her own affair.

In another indication of his lack of opposition, Philip then sat back and made no attempt to intervene as Blanche used his money to pay for troops, provisions and a fleet. She was not about to overstep the bounds of conventional behaviour to the extent of leading the new army overseas herself, so when all the preparations were complete she handed command over to Robert of Courtenay, lord of Champignelles, King Philip's first cousin and a man experienced in military matters.[*] But the recruitment process and the assembly of host and fleet had taken some time, and it was late August 1217 before they set sail, which was, alas for Blanche, too late. By then the combined French and English rebel host had been defeated in battle at Lincoln (an engagement at which Louis was not present, as he was again besieging Dover before moving back to London), and the English royalists had been able to regroup and induce a number of defections. When the new French fleet approached England, the royalists were already mustered on the south-east coast, and were able to send their own ships out to intercept it, resulting in their victory in a sea battle off Sandwich on 24 August. Many knights and nobles were captured, including Robert of Courtenay himself, and not one single reinforcement made it through to Louis in London.

Even from his detached viewing position in France, Philip could see that the writing was on the wall for the campaign, insofar as Louis was able to prosecute it by himself. This, then, was the point at which the king had to decide whether or not to throw the might of the French crown into the fray. He could make a major difference either way, but was he prepared to engage in an official war of conquest in England?

---

* Robert was a younger son of Peter I of Courtenay, but was the most senior member of the family still in France, as his elder brother Peter II was by now the Latin emperor of Constantinople. Robert was also, as it happens, a great-uncle of the new English king, Henry III, as his sister Alice of Courtenay was Isabelle of Angoulême's mother.

He was not. Philip made no move to intervene, and we might conjecture several reasons for this, chief among them the pragmatic realism he had always demonstrated when a political situation changed, and also a waning enthusiasm for the project now that John was dead. Henry III was a small child, and it would do Philip's international reputation no good to attack him. He had never met or even seen Henry; his visceral, decades-long conflict with the Plantagenet family had been with Henry II and his sons, all of whom Philip knew well enough to despise. But what was the point in continuing a vendetta against a young boy? How could he justify it, either legally or morally? And, more pointedly, where would be the glory in defeating a child? There was none. Philip's five lifelong opponents were all in their graves and France was safe, so there was no need to engage in what might turn out to be a long, unpopular, legally indefensible and ultimately unsuccessful war.

Louis was therefore left to his own devices, and when the English royalist supporters of Henry III asked for peace talks he had no choice but to agree. He had not exactly lost the war – he was personally undefeated on the field, his side's losses having been incurred under the command of subordinates – but he knew that he could no longer win it. Negotiations of a relatively amicable nature therefore took place, captives and hostages were released, and Louis accepted a large indemnity of 10,000 marks and returned to France.

From Philip's point of view this was not a triumph, but it was not a disaster either: his son was not on the English throne, but John was dead, the Plantagenets almost eradicated, and Capetian honour satisfied and intact. And, of course, Philip was still a king while his son was not, so he had retained his superior position.

The two of them were now able to form an effective partnership. Philip, in his fifties, was physically slowing down a little more with each passing year, while Louis, in his early thirties, was a warrior in his prime. The king was therefore able to deal with the politics while the prince did the fighting, which suited both of them, and it was not long before Louis set off southwards to continue the prosecution of the Albigensian Crusade, in which Philip had never shown much personal interest. Meanwhile, there was certainly no decline in Philip's mental capacities, and he could plan his next moves. He did not intend to relinquish any of his authority just yet, but a prudent king would start planning for what would happen after he was gone, and Philip was nothing if not prudent. It was time to turn his eye to the future.

Unhappily, one of the first things that happened as Philip began to make his plans was a tragedy: in mid-1218 his eldest grandson, young Philip, the heir of Louis and Blanche, died. He was eight years old and thus past the dangers of early infancy, but mortality could strike at any age, and older children also succumbed to illness or accident (we do not know which, in this case) with distressing frequency.

This was a shocking personal blow for the parents and the grandfather, not to mention the bereaved little brothers, but in dynastic terms it was at least not a disaster for the succession — it merely disrupted Philip's plans rather than throwing everything into absolute chaos, as his own or Louis's death at the same age would have done. Louis and Blanche had two other sons — Louis, aged four, and two-year-old Robert — and young Louis was simply promoted to the position of next heir after his father. The elder Louis and Blanche would, in fact, go on to have three more sons in very rapid succession now that they were reunited: John in 1219, Alphonse in 1220 and Philip-Dagobert in 1222,* so there

---

* With their three eldest sons given the very traditional Capetian names of Philip, Louis and Robert, Louis and Blanche might have been expected to follow the pattern with Peter, Henry or Hugh, all of which had been used in recent generations. However — and much to the relief of modern historians trying to disambiguate the many figures of the era who shared the same few names — they widened their scope. Alphonse was clearly named for Blanche's father, Alfonso VIII of Castile. Philip-Dagobert, normally referred to simply as *Dagobertus* in contemporary records, was both a nod to his deceased elder brother and a reminder that Prince Louis's lineage encompassed the Carolingian and Merovingian lines as well as the Capetian one. The reasons behind the name John are more difficult to discern, as it is hardly likely that he was named after the late king of England. We do not know the exact date of birth of this child, but it does appear to have been somewhere in the middle of

could be no question of the continuation of the male line, and by the early 1220s the king's second son, Philip Hurepel, also had two children of his own. Philip Augustus could, therefore, allow himself to feel satisfied with the dynastic position of the royal family, knowing that he had done his duty in that respect and that the line would continue uninterrupted. He did make one significant change to royal tradition, in that he was the first Capetian not to have his designated heir crowned as junior king during his own lifetime. It is not clear whether this was due to Philip's extreme caution and paranoia, or whether it was simply that he considered the ceremony redundant, as the family's position on the throne was by now so secure; in any case, Louis had been recognised as heir since the day of his birth, and nobody could possibly supplant him. King Philip's death, whenever it occurred, would not cause the turmoil of a fight between rival claimants to his throne.

These were the golden years of Philip's reign. His crushing victory at Bouvines meant that he had nothing to fear either at home or abroad, and as he moved further into his fifties he enjoyed a luxury that his long-ago foe Henry II never had: the leisure to retire from active campaigning and plan for a peaceful future. Philip had no need to be constantly in the saddle, criss-crossing his domains and fighting to stamp out rebellions, as Henry had been forced to do right up until his death. Instead he was able to become a benevolent father-figure to his subjects, many of whom could, after forty years, remember no other king. 'The whole kingdom enjoyed peace,' William the Breton wrote, 'which was very agreeable to the people. The king governed his kingdom and his people with a paternal affection, caring for all of them and beloved by all.'[6]

Domestically, developments that Philip had set in motion earlier in his reign were coming to fruition. The walls encircling Paris, begun in 1190, were by now complete, and the capital was thriving and growing. When they were first planned, the walls had been more extensive than was necessary at the time, encompassing

---

1219, so it is not impossible that he was born on the Feast of St John the Baptist (24 June) and named after the saint.

fields and vineyards outside of the contemporary built-up area, but the security and prestige offered by being inside the fortifications meant that many more people wanted to move there. A great deal of building work had therefore taken place in the intervening years, and by 1220 the entire space inside the walls (an area of approximately 1 square mile or 250 hectares) was urban. During Philip's reign as a whole, the population of Paris probably doubled in size.[7] The capital's university attracted students and masters from all over Europe, and it was a hub of trade as well as scholarship, the inhabitants and visitors all appreciating the street paving that Philip had ordered as a young man. Construction of the cathedral of Notre Dame, near the royal palace on the Ile-de-la-Cité, which had been going on for decades, was heading towards completion, the building's towers reaching up into the Parisian sky.

There was a sense of time passing in this autumn of Philip's life, and of the changing of the old guard among the higher nobility. He lost both of the senior Dreux brothers in quick succession, Bishop Philip in 1217 and Count Robert II in 1218, the latter succeeded by his eldest son, who became Robert III.* Odo, the duke of Burgundy, also died in 1218, and was succeeded by his son Hugh IV, who was only five years old. With the count of Champagne and the countess of Flanders still being in their teens, the only major peer older than Philip was Raymond VI, the count of faraway Toulouse (who would himself die in 1222), so it would be no surprise if the king were beginning to feel his age. By the early 1220s he was travelling less, restricting himself to locations and residences within 50 miles or so of Paris.

There was one important respect in which Philip did not forget that time was passing, and that was in his relationship with the remnant of the ruling family of England. As we noted

---

* The Dreux family, while becoming further removed from the direct royal line with every generation, would continue to occupy senior positions in France. Count Robert III would be a staunch supporter of Louis VIII and Louis IX, and his next brother, Peter, was already the duke of Brittany by marriage. The third son, Henry, was a clergyman who would later rise to become archbishop of Reims; and the fourth, John, who had fought at Bouvines as a youngster, would become count of Vienne and Mâcon by marriage as well as being both a poet and a crusader.

earlier in this chapter, Henry III had been just nine years old at the time of his accession and was no threat, so Philip was happy to leave him undisturbed on his throne, unwilling to tarnish his own reputation by attacking a small boy who was under the pope's personal protection. Besides, there was enough in-fighting going on in England to mean that nobody there had much attention to spare for France. Changes in personnel had occurred in the ruling triumvirate, following the retirement as papal legate and departure from England of Guala, in 1218, and the death of William Marshal the following year. The final member of the original group, Peter des Roches, the bishop of Winchester, sought to have himself named sole regent, but as he was already the personal guardian of the child king, it was felt that this would invest too much power in one individual. A new triumvirate was therefore formed, with Guala replaced by a different papal legate, Pandulf, and William Marshal by Hubert de Burgh, who had led the determined defence of Dover castle against Louis's long siege. Unfortunately for them and for England – but happily for Philip Augustus – these men did not get on with each other very well, with particular tension being evident between Peter and Hubert. By the early 1220s the new arrangement had broken down, with Pandulf resigning and Peter being sidelined while Hubert took on more responsibility, leading to unrest and suspicion among the nobility that he was overreaching himself. Henry III was still only thirteen at that point, so Philip could reasonably expect the instability to last for a few more years, to his own benefit.

But Henry would not always be underage, and he was, after all, a Plantagenet, while Philip was ever a player of the long game. The French king's lifelong vendetta against the older generations of Henry's family had drawn to a close with him victorious, but he wanted to stamp down, to make absolutely sure that there would be no future resurgence of Plantagenet authority in France. As prudent as ever, he was prepared to lay the groundwork now so that his successors would be in an advantageous position in whatever dynastic struggle might arise in future.

The latest truce between France and England was due to expire in 1220, and in the spring of 1219 Pope Honorius suggested a renewal. Philip was happy to open negotiations, and eventually terms were agreed that extended the peace until mid-1224, by which time he would be nearly sixty and Henry sixteen. On the surface this might look like a gentle downward canter into retirement, but the tone of the negotiations shows that Philip had not yet entirely lost his contempt for the Plantagenets.

In his correspondence with Honorius, Philip is condescendingly dismissive of Henry. He does not call him by his name at all, nor recognise him as king in his own right; instead, he refers only generally and plurally to 'the children of John, formerly king of England', and notes that they 'have neither so much money nor so much power with which to defend themselves' as John had. In his letter Philip says that he will not ratify the agreement by swearing a solemn oath, because he, 'being of an advanced age', will be bound to stand by his word, whereas they 'are young children, and are not bound to observe the oath, since they have been appointed under the legal age'.[8] The ancient distrust and suspicion had not gone away, and nor would they as long as Philip lived and breathed. However, he did agree to an exchange of hostages and confirmed that he would keep the truce so long as no attack was made on his own lands by Henry or his forces. Louis, as an adult himself (and Philip's 'very dear and loyal eldest son', as the formal truce document refers to him, with an unexpected public display of affection), confirmed separately that he would abide by Philip's agreement.[9]

This new truce meant that neither Philip nor his heir would make any further military attempt on England or on Plantagenet-held lands in France for the time being; but they could, of course, consolidate their hold on what they already had, and use the respite to make future plans. Henry retained the titles 'duke of Normandy', 'count of Anjou' and 'duke of Aquitaine' in his official styles, indicating that he (and his regency advisors) still considered that he had a right to them, which might well lead to a future attempt at regaining those lands. Philip was determined this would not happen, even as he promised peace.

Given that there would be no need for any kind of martial operation for the next four years at least, this truce of 1220 does seem to represent a definitive retirement from active campaigning for Philip, as the military torch was passed to the keen warrior Louis. Indeed, the king even let his heir put one hand on the political torch as well, although he was not yet ready to let go of that one himself. He had, at last, got over his long-standing paranoia that Louis would act as the sons of Henry II had done, belatedly appreciating that his thirty-three-year-old heir had been unquestioningly loyal throughout his life and had never made the slightest attempt to rebel against him. Philip now began to involve Louis more closely in his governance, and his name appears with the king's in some charters in the early 1220s.[10] Philip might still only be in his mid-fifties, but he was always a planner for the long term, and he knew that some regal training for Louis, and a period of transition, would be best for France.

As it turned out, Philip was right to act as he did, because the end came rather more quickly than anyone had expected. In September 1222 he fell ill, seriously enough that he drew up his testament, with Brother Guérin as his first-named executor.* Some of the content of this document is exactly what might be expected: charitable bequests to the Church, the poor, orphans, lepers, and so on, plus a cash sum for his second son, Philip Hurepel. But there are one or two surprises, not least the 10,000 *livres parisis* left to his 'very dear wife, Ingeborg'.† Was Philip finally relenting on his

---

* Philip's drawing up of a testament, and the impending death it implied, was such an ill omen that several chroniclers note that the occasion was marked by the appearance of a 'fiery-tailed comet'. Normally we might take this symbolism with a pinch of salt, as being the writers' imagination running away with them, but in fact one of the appearances of Halley's comet took place in September 1222.

† Exchange rates fluctuated over the years, but in general a *livre parisis*, or Parisian pound, was worth a little less than a pound sterling. Still, this was a considerable sum, and the scale of Philip's bequests shows that he was rather well off at the time of his death.

hardline stance, as he faced the Almighty? There does not seem to be much of an alternative explanation.

A deathbed change of heart towards a long-suffering wronged wife was one thing, but there were some matters on which Philip would never compromise, and two of them were the safety of France and the prevention of a revival of Plantagenet power. The largest bequest in the testament is a specific one to Louis – on top of his general patrimonial inheritance – of 380,000 *livres parisis* for the 'defence of the realm'.* Henry III is not mentioned by name, but with domestic peace reigning and an alliance with the Emperor on France's other side, who else can be meant? The young king of England was in no position to invade just at the moment, but Philip's final vow to himself, to his son and to his people was that Henry III was never to be allowed to accrue the sort of power in France that Henry II had once enjoyed.[11]

The completion of his testament was a great relief, but Philip did not lie back and give himself up to death. In fact, he made something of a recovery and survived the winter, despite ignoring the advice of his doctors to go on a diet and abstain from drinking wine. Life was still for living. He was, however, suffering from a severe fever that would never leave him, and which weakened him further after every exhausting, delirium-filled bout. And yet he continued to rule and to work, unwilling to relinquish his grip on royal power while there was breath left in his body. The fever was 'quartan' in nature, which meant that the worst attacks struck him every four days, and in between those he could still more or less function, if he put his mind to it; he even risked further travel.

Philip continued thus throughout the first half of 1223, but by July he was realistic enough to know that the end was near, and he summoned his two direct heirs, the elder and the younger Louis, to his side. He was at that time at Pacy-sur-Eure, in the

---

* Oddly, the exact figure was later scratched out of the manuscript of the testament, and it was only with modern examination and reconstruction techniques that it could be deciphered (it is omitted and represented only by a line of dots in earlier printed editions of the document). There is unfortunately no way to tell whether the deletion was made during Philip's lifetime, because he changed his mind about the amount, or whether it was done later for another reason.

long-contested region of the Vexin that was now completely under French crown control thanks to his own success; but, instead of remaining there, he made one last Herculean effort to return to Paris, which was the venue for a forthcoming major international council of bishops and abbots, meeting to discuss the possibility of yet another new crusade.

Philip never made it back to his capital. Desperately ill now, he managed only 15 of the 45 miles before he was compelled to stop and take to his bed at Mantes, where he died on 14 July 1223, with his son and grandson at his side.

At the time of his death, Philip Augustus was a month short of his fifty-eighth birthday, and he had ruled France with absolute authority for forty-three years. Such was his power and his hold on the crown that it had probably seemed as though he would go on forever, and his loss was a profound shock to his nobles and his people. But their grief was real: he had been a good king and father to them.

Philip's body was transported with all honour to Paris, his capital and the place of his birth, and he was buried at Saint-Denis in a ceremony more splendid than any ever seen there, thanks to the large number of prelates present in the city for the ecclesiastical council. The requiem Mass was sung by both the papal legate to France, Hugo di Conti (who was later to be Pope Gregory IX), and the archbishop of Reims, and there were a further twenty bishops in attendance as well as two kings: the new Louis VIII and John of Brienne, the king of Jerusalem. Such was the respect in which the monks of Saint-Denis held Philip that he was interred in a prime position next to Dagobert I, their original royal patron and the first king to be buried in the abbey.

Naturally, many epitaphs of Philip were written, with their content tending very much towards the positive. Earlier in Philip's life he had been the subject of some criticism, with Rigord and others hazarding disapproval of his treatment of Ingeborg and of his impetuosity. The poet Giles of Paris, writing around the year 1200, had compared Philip's authoritarian nature unfavourably with the mildness of his father, Louis VII: 'If he had drunk a little more of the sweetness [...] if he had the meekness of his father, controlling himself with circumspect control [...] he would still be allowed to hope for greater and better profits for his kingdom.'[12] But any thoughts of that nature had disappeared as Philip's reign had continued, as he had gone from strength to strength and made France a better and more secure place to live.

A chronicler based at the monastery of Tours noted Philip's death at the time it happened, and inserted a detailed pen-picture of him which manages to be both warts-and-all and positive:

[Philip had] an agreeable appearance, well-formed body, cheerful face, a bald pate, ruddy complexion. [He was] given to drink and food, prone to sexual desire, generous to his friends, miserly to his foes, skilled in stratagems, orthodox in belief, solicitous of counsel, holding to his word, a scrupulous and expeditious judge, fortunate in victory, fearful of his life, easily moved, easily assuaged, putting down the wicked of the realm by sowing discord among them, killing no-one in prison, availing himself of counsel of lesser men, bearing grudges only momentarily, subduing the proud, defending the Church, and providing for the poor.[13]

William the Breton, a long-time member of Philip's household and someone who knew the king well, was understandably a little more emotional in his own tribute:

[Philip] was a man prudent in his address, strong in courage, great in his actions, of illustrious renown, victorious in combat, distinguished by many and great victories, who augmented marvellously the rights and the power of the kingdom of the French and enriched it considerably. He vanquished and tamed by force many illustrious and powerful princes and knights who violently attacked him and his realm [...] Defender and zealous protector of the Church, and a defender of Christianity since his tenderest years; with the sign of the cross on his shoulder, he travelled across the sea and fought courageously and effectively at the siege of Acre [...] A most generous distributor of alms to the poor.[14]

And it is William, the writer who knew Philip best, who shows us what the king's main preoccupation was. He had concluded his *Philippide* with Philip's death, but he took up his pen once more to add a coda, addressed to the new King Louis VIII, in which the family feud with the Plantagenets, both in England and in France, was front and centre:

You will suffer no longer to reign in peace this new king who dares to bear the English sceptre [...] Taking up arms under favourable omens, and marching under the auspices of your father, re-establish your rights in that kingdom [...] When Aquitaine has submitted to you, when the foreigner possesses nothing more in your kingdom [...] Take no rest until the child of England, vanquished by your armies, has resigned into your hands the sceptre to which he has no right, so that you may at last reign over both realms, having rooted out from our gardens the last trace of the venom of the race of the serpent.[15]

Philip Augustus had laid down his sword and schemed his last scheme. He had achieved all of his reign's goals, and could rest in peace at Saint-Denis in the knowledge of a job well done. But his life's work would go on, even as the crown was placed on a new head, and his influence would reverberate through France for many years to come.

Conclusion

Philip was correct to have put in place measures against Henry III and his advisors, because they made a move as soon as they heard of his demise. 'On his [Philip's] death being made public,' wrote Roger of Wendover, 'Henry the English king sent the archbishop of Canterbury with three bishops to Louis his son, as soon as he was crowned, asking him to restore Normandy and the other transmarine provinces to him.' The new Louis VIII might not have resembled his father in every respect, but on this point he was well prepared: 'To this demand Louis replied that he held possession of Normandy and other lands as his right, as he would be prepared to prove in his own court if the king of England would appear to support his claim there.' This had the desired effect, at least in the short term, as 'the archbishop and bishops, on this reply, being unable to obtain any other, returned home and told the king'.[1]

Louis was able to hit the ground running. All of Philip's planning and preparation paid off, as his son was acclaimed and crowned with no trace of dissent and then got down to business straight away. Louis retained the services of Philip's excellent administrators, and indeed named Brother Guérin chancellor, something Philip had never quite got round to despite all the years the ex-Hospitaller had effectively been performing the role without the title. Then the new king set about continuing his father's work. With the full power and resources of the crown now behind him, he attacked English-held lands in Aquitaine, diminishing Plantagenet control in France even further and adding Poitou, Saintonge and Périgord to the royal domain before turning his attention once more to the Albigensian Crusade.

It was during this campaign that Louis VIII unexpectedly died, in November 1226, aged only thirty-nine and after a reign of just three years.* But such was the stability in France after Philip's long tenure that the realm weathered this crisis, and the early accession of the twelve-year-old Louis IX, without too much of a problem. The younger Louis was aided by having one of the most capable regents imaginable in his mother, Blanche of Castile; she was a woman of great intelligence, and she had not wasted the years she had spent at Philip's court, learning the art of governance from one of its masters.†

Unlike his own father, Philip Augustus had been the real king of France right up until the moment of his death. In his final years he might have associated Louis in some of his acts of governance, and employed him as an able lieutenant in the field, but Philip kept the reins of power firmly in his own hands at all times. There was no challenge to his rule – his illness was not an excuse or an opportunity for anyone to attempt to take advantage or to rebel against him. He simply had too much authority, having started off on the right foot in the very earliest days of his reign and having become more and more dominant as time passed. Without ever being flamboyant or ostentatious about it, Philip exuded royal power: 'I am just a man,' one French chronicler depicts him saying, 'but I am a man who is king of France.'² Nobody could doubt that he was still in full possession of that status even as he lay dying.

---

* Louis was on his way back to Paris, and his wife, at the end of the campaigning season when he contracted dysentery, a common malady among soldiers on campaign. He became too ill to travel further, and died at Montpensier in Auvergne. Blanche had apparently set out from the capital to meet him on the road, only to encounter his coffin coming the other way.

† Blanche also, as it happened, had seven small fatherless children to look after, as well as being pregnant with an eighth. This was obviously not something that your average king had to deal with, and only makes her short- and long-term achievements all the greater.

A medieval king had to negotiate a complex web of inter-personal relationships, both with his own family and with his vassals, and Philip's situation here differed from that of many of his contemporaries in that he had very few close male relatives – something which both hindered and aided him in various respects. Unlike Louis VII, he did not benefit from a string of helpful younger brothers at court and in the Church; and, until the very last stages of his reign, he had only one adult son. But that son was an asset, and Philip was also extremely fortunate in his wider family connections, the Capetian cadet branches of Courtenay and particularly Dreux. As his cousins, they were close enough to support him and remain loyal, and royal enough for their word to carry weight, while being too far removed from the main line of succession to be any kind of threat. The course of Philip's reign was made considerably smoother by the backing of all three Count Roberts in turn, plus that of the inimitable bishop of Beauvais. And once he had brought them into line, the other members of France's higher nobility were also firm in their support. Philip's vassals seem to have genuinely admired, respected, and we might even go as far as to say *liked*, him. So he cannot have been quite as personally unpleasant as some English chroniclers (and later historians) made him out to be.

Having said that, in any assessment of Philip's character we should not overlook his less attractive qualities, among them a virulent anti-Semitism, intolerance towards those of other religions or those deviating from his own, an ambition that could border on the ruthless and a significant measure of misogyny. It might perhaps be argued that these traits were no worse in him than in other kings or noblemen of his time, but he did sometimes cross a line in his personal behaviour. This was notable particularly in his failure to protect or to prevent the murder of the young Arthur of Brittany, and in his treatment of Ingeborg, which was considered so reprehensible that it was criticised even by loyal contemporaries.

On the other side of the scale, Philip was ahead of his time in recognising and utilising the talents of men of non-noble birth, and he seemingly had a genuine concern for the welfare of all classes of his people, commoners as well as nobles:

> Doing harm to nobody, burdening nobody, just to all and above all protecting the clergy, his bounty was demonstrated by his favouring the peaceful with a tender heart, but punishing harshly those who did wrong. He was spoken of with respect by all [...] It was difficult to know whether the king loved his people more than they loved their king.[3]

Philip was certainly unscrupulous when he needed to be, making a show of adhering to the letter of the law while he was happy to transgress its spirit, as illustrated by his decision to attack King Richard's lands when the latter had been captured on his way back from the crusade. However, we should be careful to view this behaviour within the context of the nature of medieval kingship. 'Being a jolly nice chap' and 'being an effective medieval king' were in no way synonymous; indeed, they were mutually incompatible, and affable fellows who sought to please everybody were not respected as rulers.

Being a medieval king was a terrifying responsibility. The man who carried that burden had to combine a wide range of often contradictory attributes: he had to be at once a priest (because kingship was a religious vocation as well as a secular one), a judge (as he had to impose and enforce laws) and a knight (because he was his realm's military leader). The only way to do this effectively was to be authoritarian, because any hint of weakness was sure to be exploited, either by ambitious vassals or by rival kings. This is not to say that it was necessary to be a tyrant, which Philip was not: there were several occasions in his reign when he would have been justified, by the customs of the time, in ordering massacres or executions, but he refrained from doing so. He had a better sense than many of his contemporaries of exactly when it was most advantageous to deploy violence or to show mercy, and he found a balance when some of his peers could not. From his very earliest days he exhibited a profound belief in kingship and in the hallowed nature of it: a king was not merely the mightiest among a group of nobles, but rather a sacred figure with God-given power and responsibility who was set apart from and above ordinary mortals. It was his vocation, and even those commentators who are not fans of Philip – whether medieval or modern – admit that he was an effective king.

The history of France would be very different without Philip's contribution to it. At the age of just fourteen he inherited a small kingdom that was in a precarious position, with over-mighty vassals jostling for power and the looming threat of Henry II and his family casting a forbidding shadow. Philip not only survived this, but thrived and improved his position with every year that passed, demonstrating an immense talent for politics as well as no small degree of martial skill. Champagne, Blois, Brittany, Flanders, Normandy – these were all regions that he either conquered directly or brought under his overall control, regions that would cause few problems for his successors. He also cemented the regal position of the Capetian line; the tradition of crowning a junior king would never be revived after his death, because it did not need to be.

We can also say with confidence that the history of *England* would be very different without Philip. How much longer might Henry II have lived, if Philip had not encouraged his sons to rebel against him, forcing the English king to remain in the saddle without rest or respite for years on end? How much more might the Plantagenet sons have achieved, if Philip had not set them all against each other? His constant ploy of knowing exactly which sore spot to press, which aspect of each Plantagenet's psyche to attack, was astonishingly successful. The suspicions of Henry II against his sons and the jealousies of those sons among themselves were all fruitfully exploited, to their detriment. There is even a case to be made that if John had lived a little longer – rather than dying and leaving as his heir an innocent child – the crown of England itself might have fallen into Capetian hands, and the destruction of the house of Plantagenet would have been complete.

In the traditional historical narrative, Philip has suffered in comparison with the glamorous and attention-hogging family of Henry II. He has been characterised partly as a Machiavellian schemer but also as a non-military, almost cowardly man; a mere background antagonist who was lucky that the Plantagenets fought against themselves so often. But few medieval kings were as success-ful as Philip, and this was no accident. His collection of epithets tells us something about how he was perceived and appreciated during and after his lifetime: Philip the God-Given, Philip Augustus, Philip the Magnanimous, Philip the Conqueror. It is right that his political intelligence has been recognised, but he was also a more capable military leader than he has generally been given credit for. We only have to look at a map of 1179 and a map of 1223 to see how much territory he gained, and this did not happen – would never have happened – if Philip had not been prepared to ride, fight and besiege as well as plot and scheme. His greatest victory, that of Bouvines, occurred when he was in the thick of the press, fight-ing in the centre of the front line, and neither Acre nor Château Gaillard would have fallen were it not for his siege expertise.

Siege warfare – involving as it did patience, strategy, planning and logistics, rather than merely charging into combat with a drawn sword – was one of the least prestigious aspects of war. It was thus of less interest to contemporaries seeking to write exciting narra-tives for a knightly audience, and therefore another reason why Philip's martial reputation has suffered over the years. But it was an indispensable skill for anyone wishing to succeed in the military arena of the twelfth and thirteenth centuries, and the excellence in it that Philip demonstrated over years and decades is one of the greatest factors in his success against the Plantagenet dynasty.

Philip's struggle with the Plantagenets can be divided into five major phases. The first was his attempt, very early in his reign, to remove or reduce Henry II's power in France, mainly via the tactic of turning his two eldest sons against him. This did not result in extensive territorial gains at the time, but it did set in motion the destabilisation process that would come to fruition later on.

As part of this initial strategy Philip was allied with Richard, so the second stage of the conflict was a brief period of peace when Henry died and Richard acceded. But this did not last long and soon morphed into dispute and outright war, beginning with their quarrels while on crusade and continuing upon Philip's return to France and then Richard's own reappearance.

This third phase was the only time in his career when Philip took a backward step, due to Richard's ferocity and skill as a warrior, but Richard was a less effective politician and king, and Philip was still in a relatively advantageous position when Richard died. This kicked off the fourth stage, an overwhelmingly successful one which saw Philip making huge gains against John. The result was a French reconquest of many Plantagenet-held lands in France and even a stab at England itself. After John's death, the fifth and final phase was mainly political and planning for the future, rather than military, as Philip had no real interest in waging war against the child Henry III, although he did succeed in guarding against any future resurgence of Plantagenet power in France.

Philip's antagonists from that family fell one by one. Henry II died a broken man, his sons rebelling against him and in alliance with Philip. Henry the Young King perished while in revolt against his father, with Philip's support. Richard was killed during a pointless minor siege, his Poitevin barons defying him and Philip's hand evident in their insurrection. Geoffrey died young, having quarrelled with his father and all his brothers at Philip's instigation, and leaving his wife pregnant with an heir who would cause the family to fall into further murderous conflict later on, again encouraged by Philip. And John breathed his last as a deposed fugitive in his own land, with Philip's son and heir halfway to taking his throne and England in total chaos. Philip himself, meanwhile, died in his bed, his kingdom at peace and greatly enlarged, his vassals compliant, his enemies cold in their graves and his family succession secure in the hands of a trusted son and grandson, who were both at his side.

So there really is only one answer to the simple and essential question. Who won?

Notes

A list of abbreviations and full references to all works cited may be found in the bibliography. Quotations from primary sources have been taken from published English translations where possible; where works are only available in their original language, translations into English are my own except where otherwise stated.

EPIGRAPH

1   GW, pp. 699–701. For clarity, I have split the first paragraph into separate sentences by making minor changes to punctuation.

INTRODUCTION

1   On his use of the epithet, see Rigord, pp. 44–5.
2   GW, pp. 675–7.
3   Philip Augustus is the subject of a number of full-length biographies. They all use his name as the main title, so we will not repeat it multiple times here: see the 'biographies' section of the bibliography for a list of the works in French by Bordonove, Flori, Galland, Luchaire and Sivéry; in German by Cartellieri; and in English by Baldwin and by Bradbury. They are all presented chronologically, so further discussion of any of the incidents and events we discuss here in our book may be easily located. We will not, therefore, make constant reference in these notes to specific page ranges in each separate biography.
4   This episode is related by Rigord, pp. 48–9.

CHAPTER 1: A NEST OF VIPERS

1   Henry II and Eleanor of Aquitaine have been the subjects of numerous studies. As a start, see Warren, *Henry II*; Barber, *Henry Plantagenet*;

Turner, *Eleanor of Aquitaine*. On Henry's military career, see Hosler, *Henry II: A Medieval Soldier at War*.

2 Young Henry is the subject of an academic biography: see Strickland, *Henry the Young King*.

3 Biographies of Richard include Gillingham, *Richard I*; Flori, *Richard Coeur de Lion*, and its English translation *Richard the Lionheart*; Minois, *Richard Coeur de Lion*.

4 Henry II's daughters do not play a great part in this book, but they all led fascinating and adventure-filled lives: for more on their stories, see Andrews, *The Families of Eleanor of Aquitaine*.

5 *Catalogue des actes*, p. lxix.

6 GW, p. 571.

7 The first few acts of Philip's reign are documents in which he confirms rights or grants awarded by Louis VII (*Catalogue des actes*, pp. 1–5). In them he refers warmly to Louis as 'our most Christian father' or 'our dearest father' and refers to his 'divine piety' (*Recueil des Actes*, pp. 4 and 19). The style he later adopted was the straightforward *Philippus, Dei gratia Francorum rex* ('Philip, by the grace of God king of the Franks'; see the full text of the charters in *Catalogue des actes*, pp. 495 onwards). Around the year 1200 he changed *Francorum rex* to *rex Francie* ('king of France'; *Layettes*, p. 217).

8 RH, vol. 1, p. 520.

9 Quote from RH, vol. 1, p. 521. A translation of the full text of the agreement may be found in ibid., pp. 521–3. A letter from Henry II to his justiciar in England giving details of the peace appears in GW, p. 499.

10 Rigord, p. 57.

11 WB, *Philippide*, pp. 19, 25 and 26.

12 GW, p. 483.

13 RH, vol. 2, p. 14; see also GRH, vol. 2, pp. 286–9.

14 RT, p. 146. The war between the Plantagenet brothers and the Young King's death are covered in more depth in Strickland, *Henry the Young King*, pp. 282–313. A rather melodramatic primary-source narration of the scene at Young Henry's deathbed is HWM, vol. 1, pp. 351–7.

15 RH, vol. 2, p. 25, and GW, p. 481, respectively.

16 GM, p. 85.

17 GM, p. 85.

18 GM, p. 86. Isabelle of Hainaut is little-studied, though she is the subject of a chapter in a book about Capetian women: Hornaday, 'A Capetian Queen as Street Demonstrator'.

19 *mandans patri suo, se nunquam concessurum quod aliquis alius haberet Pictaviam quam ipse. Quod multum displicuit domino regi* ('telling his father that he would never allow anyone to have Poitou other than himself. This greatly displeased the lord king' (GRH, vol. 1, p. 308)).

20 Quote from GW, p. 479.

21 RH, vol. 2, p. 14.

22 GW, p. 479. The tournament cause of death is given by RH, vol. 2, p. 56. Gerald of Wales mentions 'a hot fever' (GW, p. 479), while Rigord merely says that Geoffrey 'fell sick upon his arrival in Paris' (Rigord, p. 91).

CHAPTER 2: FROM THE DEVIL HE CAME

1 Constance's life story is a remarkable one: see her chapter in Andrews, *The Families of Eleanor of Aquitaine*, pp. 181–203. She is also the subject of a full-length biography in French: Borgnis Desbordes, *Constance de Bretagne*.

2 The narrative of the engagement and all the quotes pertaining to it that follow are from WB, *Philippide*, pp. 61–2.

3 An interesting article that argues this point is McGlynn, 'Fighting the Image of the Reluctant Warrior'. McGlynn is not generally a fan of Philip Augustus (describing him to me in a personal communication as 'a fat, bald git who nobody liked'), so this recognition of Philip's martial skill is all the more valuable.

4 RH, vol. 2, p. 64.

5 *Reges Anglorum, pater et filius, in Angliam venientes, per dies singulos in eadem mensa sunt refecti, et idem thalamus fomenta quietis eisdem de noctibus ministaravit* ('The kings of England, father and son, arrived in England [in 1176 after one of their reconciliations]; every day they ate at the same table, and they rested in the same chamber at night'). MP, vol. 2, p. 297.

6 HWM, vol. 1, pp. 411–13.

7 Rigord, p. 100. See also GC, pp. 166–7.

8 For a discussion of all the contemporary sources that mention Philip's appearance, see Baldwin, *The Government of Philip Augustus*, pp. 356–9. For a debunking of the myth that Philip was one-eyed, see Bradbury, *Philip Augustus*, p. 45.

9 As described by Rigord, pp. 51–2 and 57–62.

10 Baldwin makes the point that Pope Innocent III complained more than once that his letters to Philip were being 'misinterpreted' by the French royal clerks, which implies that Philip could not read the Latin missives himself (*The Government of Philip Augustus*, p. 359).

11 GW, p. 669.

12 Quotes from Rigord, pp. 65 (markets) and 79 (paving).

13 Rigord, p. 101.

14 RH, vol. 2, pp. 83–4; GRH, vol. 2, p. 36.

15 WB, *Philippide*, pp. 69–72 (quote from p. 72). See also WB, *Vie*, p. 202; Diceto, p. 55.

16 Quotes from Rigord, p. 108; GW, p. 611; RW, p. 72, respectively. See also Gervase, vol. 1, pp. 435–6; GRH, vol. 2, p. 50; *HWM*, vol. 1, pp. 413–17.

17 GW, p. 661; see also *HWM*, vol. 1, pp. 445–7; Diceto, p. 63.

18 GW, p. 545.

19 *HWM*, vol. 1, p. 457.

20 *HWM*, vol. 1, p. 459. See also GW, pp. 665–7.

21 GW, p. 667.

22 For details of the full terms, see RH, vol. 2, pp. 109–10.

23 RW, p. 75.

24 GW, pp. 683 and 701–3.

25 WB, *Philippide*, p. 95, and Rigord, p. 111, respectively.

CHAPTER 3: CRUSADING KINGS AND RIVALS

1 Isabelle of Gloucester was (like Alice of France) a woman whose personal fate was determined by her rank in society and her usefulness to the male members of her family. Her story is told in Andrews, *The Families of Eleanor of Aquitaine*, pp. 205–13.

2 RD, p. 9.

3 Quote from RW, p. 88; see also RH, vol. 2, p. 135; *Catalogue des actes*, p. 63. The full text of the original agreement, written on the spot, is available (in Latin) in *Recueil des Actes*, pp. 348–9, with a slightly later and tidier version in ibid., pp. 350–2.

4 Ambroise, p. 33; see also Diceto, p. 77.

5 IP, p. 148.

6 All quotes from the testament in this section are from Rigord, pp. 113–18. The full text is also available (in Old French) in GC, pp. 187–94, and (in Latin) in *Recueil des Actes*, pp. 416–20.

7 IP, p. 151; see also Ambroise, p. 35.

8 IP, pp. 150–1.

9 IP, p. 151.

10 On the Emperor's death, see *Eracles*, pp. 87–8; GW, pp. 653–5; GM, p. 129. A biography of this remarkable man is Freed, *Frederick Barbarossa*.

11 *Catalogue des actes*, pp. 78–9.

12 Joanna's life story is a fascinating one, and she is the subject of a recent biography: see Hanley, *Lionessheart*.

13 RD, pp. 24–5.

14 RH, vol. 2, p. 165; very similar wording occurs in RW, p. 95, and Diceto (p. 86) is also clear that 'Richard appointed the aforesaid Arthur as his heir, if he should die without issue'.

15 Quote from RH, vol. 2, p. 196. William the Breton puts an extremely magnanimous and gracious speech into Philip's mouth at this point – so gracious, in fact ('I make no complaint, I ask nothing [...] A greater business calls us, so let us put aside our differences, pledging ourselves without reserve to the service of the cross [...]') that we can only assume that William made it up in order to portray Philip in the best light (WB, *Philippide*, p. 103). The charter confirming the agreement is listed (in French) in *Catalogue des actes*, p. 81, and the full text appears (in Latin) in *Recueil des Actes*, pp. 464–6.

16 Rigord, p. 119.

17 There are many published works dealing with the Third Crusade. As a start, see Asbridge, *The Crusades*, pp. 367–516; Tyerman, *God's War*, pp. 341–500; Phillips, *Holy Warriors*, pp. 103–65; Riley-Smith, *The Crusades*, pp. 109–18; Bartlett, *God Wills It!*, pp. 148–95; Bennett, *Elite Participation in the Third Crusade*. The most detailed treatment of the siege itself is Hosler, *The Siege of Acre*.

18 IP, p. 163; IP, p. 165; RD, p. 42; RH, vol. 2, p. 207, respectively. The slightly later Roger of Wendover was nearer the mark when he said that Philip 'was annoyed beyond measure at all the credit of the success of the Christian army being given to king Richard' (RW, p. 106). For a long while modern scholarship seemed to agree with the earlier chroniclers' narrative, and gave Richard most of the credit for the success at Acre, but Philip's contribution has been reassessed more positively in recent years: see Naus, *Constructing Kingship*, pp. 124–6; Hosler, *Siege of Acre*, pp. 162–71; Hanley, *Two Houses, Two Kingdoms*, p. 135.

19 Ralph of Diceto gives a detailed description of the layout of the camp, including who was encamped next to whom (Diceto, pp. 79–81).

20 There is a great deal of information available about siege machinery at this time; see, among others, Fulton, *Artillery in the Age of the Crusades*; DeVries and Smith, *Medieval Military Technology*, pp. 117–36 and 165–81; Bradbury, *Medieval Siege*, pp. 241–95; Hanley, *War and*

Combat, pp. 18–20. On the specific subject of Philip's machines at Acre, see Hosler, *Siege of Acre*, p. 110.

21 Quote about Bishop Philip from IP, p. 76.
22 Quotes from IP, p. 192 and Ambroise, p. 58, respectively.
23 *Eracles*, p. 105.
24 WB, *Vie*, p. 207 (on Philip's condition); MR, p. 30 (on Richard's supposed poisoning of Philip).
25 *Eracles*, p. 109. On Philip receiving news from France about Louis, see also RD, p. 48; and on Louis's illness itself, see Rigord (who was on the spot in Paris), pp. 122–3.
26 IP, pp. 208 (stone-throwing machines) and 210 (cat).
27 MR, p. 29.
28 RH, vol. 2, p. 211.
29 IP, p. 222.
30 The letter is reproduced in RH, vol. 2, p. 221.
31 WB, *Philippide*, p. 110.
32 Diceto, p. 104.
33 Rigord, pp. 129–30; WB, *Vie*, pp. 207–8. On the Assassins, see also GC, pp. 215–16.
34 Emperor Henry's letter is reproduced in RH, vol. 2, pp. 278–9.

CHAPTER 4: A CLEAR FIELD

1 RW, p. 132, and RH, vol. 2, p. 281, respectively.
2 Gervase, vol. 1, p. 515.
3 RH, vol. 2, p. 289.
4 The episode is narrated in RH, vol. 2, p. 289; see also Gervase, vol. 1, pp. 515–16.
5 RD, p. 59.
6 *Recueil des actes*, p. 552.
7 Both quotes from Rigord, p. 133.
8 For more on Ingeborg and her marriage to Philip, see Conklin, 'Ingeborg of Denmark'; Karras, *Unmarriages*, pp. 59–67. Some of Ingeborg's letters to popes Celestine III and Innocent III survive; see Epistolae, at https://epistolae.ctl.columbia.edu/woman/68.html.
9 This letter of Eleanor's, and two more on the same subject, may be found at Epistolae, https://epistolae.ctl.columbia.edu/woman/24.html.
10 *Eracles*, p. 123.
11 The full text of Richard's letter appears in RH, vol. 2, pp. 290–2; see also HWM, vol. 1, pp. 507–9.

12 *Layettes*, vol. 1, pp. 175–6; see also *Catalogue des actes*, p. 98; Rigord, pp. 133–4. A translation of sections of this letter appears in Church, *King John*, pp. 55–6.

13 *HWM*, vol. 2, p. 9.

14 RH, vol. 2, p. 297.

15 Diceto, pp. 114–15.

CHAPTER 5: WAR MOST GRAND AND CRUEL

1 AB, *Rois*, p. 758.

2 Quotes from RH, vol. 2, p. 281, and *HWM*, vol. 2, p. 21, respectively.

3 WB, *Philippide*, pp. 115–16.

4 *HWM*, vol. 2, p. 25.

5 Quote from RH, vol. 2, p. 327.

6 Rigord, p. 135.

7 On the proposed truce and Richard's refusal to agree to it, see RH, vol. 2, p. 327.

8 Diceto, p. 121.

9 For a thorough analysis of the issuing of challenges to single combat at this time, see Strickland, 'Provoking or Avoiding Battle?'.

10 RH, vol. 2, p. 327.

11 Quotes from Rigord, p. 136; RH, vol. 2, pp. 327–8; *HWM*, vol. 2, p. 31, respectively. For modern analysis of the encounter, see Steven Isaac, 'Fréteval, Battle of', *OEMW*, vol. 2, pp. 138–9.

12 WB, *Philippide*, p. 125.

13 As described by *HWM*, vol. 2, p. 27; RH, vol. 2, p. 369.

14 *Catalogue des actes*, p. 110. The full text appears (in Latin) in *Layettes*, pp. 182–4. It is not included in the English translation of Rigord's work, but does appear in the earlier French version: Rigord (ed. Guizot), pp. 124–30.

15 Further technical details about the construction of the castle may be found in Kelly DeVries, 'Château-Gaillard', *OEMW*, vol. 1, pp. 368–9; Salch (ed.), *Dictionnaire des châteaux*, pp. 32–6. There is also a detailed analysis online at the Warfare History Network: see https://warfare historynetwork.com/article/king-richards-chateau-gaillard/.

16 GW, p. 671.

17 For more on Eleanor (in modern works often called Leonor, the name by which she was known in Castile), see her chapter in Andrews, *The Families of Eleanor of Aquitaine*, pp. 69–88.

18 All the quotes in this section on the subject of Nonancourt and Aumale are from Rigord, p. 141.

19 RH, vol. 2, pp. 402–3.
20 Quotes from *HWM*, vol. 2, p. 65 and RW, p. 148, respectively.
21 Rigord, pp. 145–6.
22 Quotes from WB, *Philippide*, p. 142; RH, vol. 2, p. 428; RW, p. 175, respectively.
23 Innocent III, one of the most famous and influential popes of the Middle Ages, is the subject of numerous biographies and studies. See, among others, Sayers, *Innocent III*; Moore, *Pope Innocent III*; Powell (ed.), *Innocent III*. A briefer introductory overview is available at https://popehistory.com/popes/pope-innocent-iii/.
24 Quotes from Rigord, p. 147, and *HWM*, vol. 2, p. 83, respectively.
25 *HWM*, vol. 2, p. 83.
26 WB, *Vie*, p. 219.
27 RC, p. 95 (*nec potuit ferrum* **in corpore nimis obeso** *immersura leviter reperire*), and RH, vol. 2, p. 453, respectively.
28 On Richard's final siege and the circumstances of his death, see RH, vol. 2, pp. 452–5; modern discussion may be found in Gillingham, *Richard I*, pp. 323–8.

CHAPTER 6: THE LAST OF THE PLANTAGENETS

1 *Layettes*, p. 199.
2 RW, p. 182.
3 RH, vol. 2, p. 456.
4 RW, p. 183.
5 On this episode, see RH, vol. 2, p. 464; RW, p. 183.
6 The full text of the treaty is published in its original Latin in *Layettes*, pp. 217–19 (from where all treaty quotes in this section are taken), and in translation in the French edition of Rigord's chronicle: see Rigord (ed. Guizot), pp. 148–53. An approximate English translation may be found in RH, vol. 2, pp. 508–12. The treaty is discussed in detail in Powicke, *Loss of Normandy*, pp. 200–5; Power, *The Norman Frontier*, pp. 416–18.
7 Innocent, p. 24.
8 RH, vol. 2, p. 483.
9 Rigord, p. 149; see also RC, p. 112.
10 Rigord, p. 152.
11 The full letter may be found at Epistolae, https://epistolae.ctl.columbia.edu/letter/24140.html.
12 *Catalogue des actes*, pp. 157 (Philip Hurepel and Matilda de Dammartin) and 166 (Marie and Arthur of Brittany).

13 *Layettes*, p. 236; Rigord (ed. Guizot), p. 156.
14 AB, *Dukes*, pp. 106–8. For further discussion of this important engagement and the sources for it, see McGlynn, *Blood Cries Afar*, pp. 36–40.
15 *HWM*, vol. 2, p. 111.
16 *Catalogue des actes*, pp. 173 (Maurice de Craon) and 177 (if Arthur is still alive).
17 See, for example, RW, pp. 205–6; RC, pp. 139–41 and 145; WB, *Philippide*, pp. 173–4; AB, *Rois*, p. 762. For a detailed analysis of all the contemporary sources for Arthur's death, see Powicke, *Loss of Normandy*, pp. 453–81.

CHAPTER 7: PHILIP THE CONQUEROR

1 What little is known of Brother Guérin's life and career up to this point is summarised in Baldwin, *The Government of Philip Augustus*, pp. 115–18.
2 AB, *Dukes*, p. 109, and RW, p. 207, respectively.
3 This long letter is given in full (in the original Latin and in English translation) in Innocent, pp. 56–9.
4 The pope's full letter to John appears in Innocent, pp. 60–2.
5 See the various entries in *Catalogue des actes*, pp. 174–7; *Layettes*, pp. 242–4.
6 Rigord, p. 158 (including the quote).
7 WB, *Philippide*, pp. 178–9 and 193. William the Breton's eye-witness accounts of the siege of Château Gaillard are the fullest among contemporaries: see WB, *Philippide*, pp. 176–210; WB, *Vie*, pp. 222–34. The engagement also features in less detail in the writings of Rigord (pp. 158–9); Roger of Wendover (RW, pp. 207–8 and 213–14); Ralph of Coggeshall (RC, pp. 143–4); the Anonymous of Béthune (AB, *Dukes*, pp. 109–11); and (in a more dramatic and fictionalised account) the Minstrel of Reims (MR, pp. 112–14). The most detailed modern account and analysis is McGlynn, *Blood Cries Afar*, pp. 42–59; see also Laurence Marvin, 'Château-Gaillard, Siege of', in *OEMW*, vol. 1, pp. 370–1. A pictorial representation, showing the successive phases of combat, may be found in Bennett et al., *Fighting Techniques*, pp. 194–5.
8 MR, p. 112.
9 Quote from RW, p. 213.
10 WB, *Vie*, p. 231.

11 WB, *Philippide*, pp. 197–201; WB, *Vie*, pp. 231–2. Distressing scenes such as this were replicated at sieges across a wide geographical area throughout the Middle Ages, and they cannot all have been fictional. Those with the stomach for it may find further discussion of medieval atrocities in McGlynn, *Blood Cries Afar*, pp. 49–55; McGlynn, *By Sword and Fire*, pp. 164–70.

12 WB, *Philippide*, p. 200.

13 AB, *Dukes*, p. 114.

14 WB, *Philippide*, p. 201.

15 WB, *Vie*, p. 234.

16 AB, *Dukes*, p. 114; see also MR, pp. 113 and 114.

17 RW, pp. 213–14.

18 This embassy is described in several sources: see Gervase, vol. 2, p. 95; RC, pp. 144–5; HWM, vol. 2, pp. 143–5.

19 WB, *Philippide*, p. 213.

20 *Layettes*, p. 250.

21 WB, *Vie*, p. 236, and WB, *Philippide*, p. 219, respectively.

CHAPTER 8: THE BATTLE TO END ALL BATTLES

1 The text of the treaty may be found (in French) in Rigord (ed. Guizot), pp. 174–7.

2 RW, p. 241.

3 Biographies of Louis include (in English) Hanley, *Louis*; (in French) Sivéry, *Louis VIII le Lion*; Gobry, *Louis VIII*.

4 *Catalogue des actes*, p. 307.

5 *Catalogue des actes*, p. 320; see also WB, *Vie*, p. 250; GC, p. 299. Biographies of Frederick include Allshorn, *Stupor Mundi*; Kantorowicz, *Frederick the Second*; David Abulafia, *Frederick II*.

6 RW, p. 259.

7 WB, *Vie*, p. 261.

8 *Catalogue des actes*, pp. 326–7.

9 The letter appears in full in Innocent, pp. 149–51. The text of John's own charter ceding England to the pope appears in English translation in RW, pp. 268–70.

10 AB, *Dukes*, p. 129.

11 Quotes from RW, p. 272, and HWM, vol. 2, p. 233, respectively.

12 MR, p. 120.

13 Accounts of the engagement at La-Roche-aux-Moines may be found in WB, *Vie*, pp. 270–3; WB, *Philippide*, pp. 290–7; GC, pp. 320–4; Nangis,

pp. 112–13; AB, *Dukes*, p. 142. For modern analysis, see McGlynn, *Blood Cries Afar*, pp. 96–100; Hanley, *Louis*, pp. 55–6; Bradbury, *Philip Augustus*, pp. 293–5.

14 Quote from *GC*, p. 349.

15 WB, *Vie*, p. 279. William the Breton's two narratives (WB, *Vie*, pp. 274–92, and WB, *Philippide*, pp. 299–349) are the major primary sources for the battle of Bouvines, and our narrative here is largely based on his accounts, with additional information from RW, pp. 299–302; *GC*, pp. 326–54; AB, *Rois*, pp. 767–70; MR, pp. 119–23; Nangis, pp. 113–15. English translations of various excerpts from these texts may be found online at https://deremilitari.org/2014 /03/the-battle-of-bouvines-1214/. For modern analysis, see (in French) Duby, *Le Dimanche de Bouvines*, and Barthélemy, *La Bataille de Bouvines*; and (in English) John France, 'Bouvines, Battle of', *OEMW*, vol. 1, pp. 163–5; Bradbury, *Philip Augustus*, pp. 295–311; Baldwin, *Government of Philip Augustus*, pp. 215–19; McGlynn, *Blood Cries Afar*, pp. 102–17; Verbruggen, *The Art of Warfare*, pp. 239–60 (including a detailed breakdown of the number of combatants supplied by each French lord). A pictorial representation, showing the deployment of the armies, may be found in Bennett et al., *Fighting Techniques*, pp. 118–19.

16 RW, p. 299.

17 See the calculations in McGlynn, *Blood Cries Afar*, p. 107; Verbruggen, *Art of Warfare*, pp. 242–6. See also the appendix on 'Knight Service at Bouvines' in Baldwin, *Government of Philip Augustus*, pp. 450–3.

18 WB, *Vie*, pp. 278–9.

19 WB, *Philippide*, p. 323.

20 WB, *Vie*, p. 283.

21 WB, *Philippide*, p. 316.

22 WB, *Philippide*, pp. 325 and 327–8.

23 WB, *Vie*, p. 288.

24 WB, *Philippide*, pp. 331–2.

25 WB, *Philippide*, p. 342.

26 WB, *Philippide* p. 349.

CHAPTER 9: THINKING THE UNTHINKABLE

1 WB, *Vie*, p. 292.

2 AB, *Rois*, p. 769.

3 WB, *Vie*, p. 302, and WB, *Philippide*, p. 361, respectively.

4 WB, *Vie*, p. 294.

5 RW, p. 362.

6 WB, *Vie*, pp. 321–2.

7 For Guala's act of excommunication against Louis (but not Philip), dated 29 May 1216 and then renewed November 1216 and May 1217, see Guala, pp. 43–4.

8 AB, *Rois*, p. 770.

9 This is Philip's story, not Louis's, so we will remain in France with the king while his son is in England. For details on what was happening across the Channel, see Hanley, 1217; Hanley, *Louis*, pp. 85–177; McGlynn, *Blood Cries Afar*, pp. 159–241.

10 AB, *Rois*, p. 770.

11 *Catalogue des actes*, pp. 367–79; the letter to the bishop of Beauvais is on p. 376.

12 The deployment, during Louis's siege of Dover, of a trebuchet sent by Philip, and the difference this made to the assault on the castle, is discussed in Hanley, 1217, pp. 80–2.

CHAPTER 10: PASSING THE TORCH

1 WB, *Vie*, p. 326.

2 Honorius's letter to Philip appears (in Latin) in Honorius, pp. 629–31.

3 WB, *Vie*, p. 326.

4 MR, pp. 128–9.

5 RW, pp. 398–9.

6 WB, *Philippide*, pp. 361–2.

7 The best estimate is that the population of Paris was around 25,000 in 1179 and around 50,000 by 1223. For this and the area enclosed by the walls, see Baldwin, *The Government of Philip Augustus*, p. 346; Baldwin, *Paris, 1200*, pp. 30–1.

8 The exchange of letters between Honorius and Philip may be found (in Latin) in Honorius, pp. 680 and 684–5.

9 The full terms of the 1220 truce may be found (in Latin) in *Layettes*, pp. 496–7 and (in French) in WB, *Vie*, pp. 338–41; see also *Catalogue des actes*, p. 432.

10 See, for example, *Catalogue des actes*, pp. 451–2; *Layettes*, p. 514.

11 The full text of the testament may be found (in Latin) in *Layettes*, pp. 549–50 and (in French) in WB, *Vie*, pp. 345–8; see also *Catalogue des actes*, p. 478.

12 GP, pp. 305–6.
13 *Tours*, p. 304; the English translation appears in Baldwin, *Government of Philip Augustus*, p. 356.
14 WB, *Vie*, pp. 348–9. Similar wording may be found in the later GC, pp. 370–1.
15 WB, *Philippide*, pp. 385–7.

CONCLUSION

1 RW, pp. 444–5; the same story is told in RC, p. 197.
2 PM, p. 359.
3 WB, *Philippide*, p. 362.

Bibliography

PRIMARY SOURCES AND ENCYCLOPAEDIAS

AB, Dukes Anonymous of Béthune, *History of the Dukes of Normandy and the Kings of England*, trans. Janet Shirley, with historical notes by Paul Webster (Oxford: Routledge, 2021)

AB, Rois Anonymous of Béthune, *Chronique des rois de France*, ed. L. Delisle, in *Recueil des Historiens des Gaules et de la France*, vol. 24 (Paris: Imprimerie nationale, 1904), pp. 750–75

Ambroise Ambroise, *The History of the Holy War: Ambroise's Estoire de la Guerre Sainte*, trans. Marianne Ailes, introduction and notes by Marianne Ailes and Malcolm Barber (Woodbridge: Boydell, 2011; orig. 2003)

Catalogue des actes *Catalogue des actes de Philippe-Auguste*, ed. Léopold Delisle (Paris: Auguste Durand, 1856)

Diceto Volume 2 of Ralph of Diceto, *Radulphi de Diceto Opera Historica: The Historical Works of Master Ralph de Diceto*, ed. William Stubbs, 2 vols (London: Rolls Series, 1876)

Epistolae Epistolae: Medieval Women's Latin Letters, online, available at https://epistolae.ccnmtl.columbia.edu/

Eracles The Old French continuation of William of Tyre [Lyon Eracles], in *The Conquest of Jerusalem and the Third Crusade: Sources in Translation*, trans. Peter W. Edbury (Aldershot: Ashgate, 1998), pp. 11–145

GC *Les grandes chroniques de France, tome sixième, Louis VII le Jeune et Philippe II Auguste*, ed. Jules Viard (Paris: Honoré Champion, 1930)

Gervase Gervase of Canterbury, *The Historical Works of Gervase of Canterbury*, ed. William Stubbs, 2 vols (London: Rolls Series, 1879–80)

GM Gilbert of Mons, *Chronicle of Hainaut*, trans. Laura Napran (Woodbridge: Boydell, 2005)

GP Giles of Paris, *Karolinus*, ed. Marvin L. Colker, in *Traditio*, 29 (1973), 199–325

GRH *Gesta regis Henrici secundi Benedicti abbatis: The Chronicle of the Reigns of Henry II and Richard I, AD 1169–1192*, ed. William Stubbs, 2 vols (London: Rolls Series, 1867)

Guala *The Letters and Charters of Cardinal Guala Bicchieri, Papal Legate in England 1216–1218*, ed. Nicholas Vincent (Woodbridge: Canterbury and York Society, 1996)

GW Gerald of Wales, *Instruction for a Ruler: De Principis Instructione*, ed. and trans. Robert Bartlett (Oxford: Clarendon, 2018)

Honorius Letters of Pope Honorius III to France during the reigns of Philip II and Louis VIII of France, ed. Michel-Jean-Joseph Brial, in *Recueil des Historiens des Gaules et de la France*, vol. 19 (Paris: Imprimerie royale, 1833), pp. 609–778

HWM *History of William Marshal*, ed. and trans. A.J. Holden, S. Gregory and D. Crouch, 3 vols (London: Anglo-Norman Text Society, 2002–6)

Innocent *Selected Letters of Pope Innocent III Concerning England (1198–1216)*, ed. and trans. C.R. Cheney and W.H. Semple (London: Nelson and Sons, 1953)

IP *The Chronicle of the Third Crusade: The Itinerarium Peregrinorum et Gesta Regis Ricardi*, trans. Helen J. Nicholson (London and New York: Routledge, 2001; orig. 1997)

Layettes Volume 1 of *Layettes du Trésor des Chartes*, ed. A. Teulet, 4 vols (Paris: Henri Plon, 1863–1902)

MP Matthew Paris, *Matthæi Pariensis Chronica Majora*, ed. Henry Richards Luard, 7 vols (London: Rolls Series, 1872–83)

MR Minstrel of Reims, *Tales of a Minstrel of Reims in the Thirteenth Century*, trans. Samuel N. Rosenberg, annotated by Randall Todd Pippenger, with an introduction by William Chester Jordan (Washington DC: Catholic University of America Press, 2022)

Nangis William of Nangis, *Chronique de Guillaume de Nangis*, ed. F. Guizot (Paris: Brière, 1825)

OEMW *Oxford Encyclopaedia of Medieval Warfare and Military Technology*, ed. Clifford J. Rogers, 3 vols (New York: Oxford University Press, 2010)

PM Volume 2 of Philip Mousket, *Chronique rimée de Philippe Mouskes*, ed. le Baron de Reiffenberg, 2 vols (Brussels: M. Hayez, 1836–8)

RC Ralph of Coggeshall, *Radulphi de Coggeshall Chronicon Anglicanum*, ed. J. Stevenson (London: Rolls Series, 1875)

RD Richard of Devizes, *The Chronicle of Richard of Devizes*, ed. and trans. John T. Appleby (London: Nelson and Sons, 1963)

Recueil des actes Volume 1 of *Recueil des actes de Philippe Auguste*, ed. Henri-François Delaborde et al., 5 vols (Paris: Imprimerie nationale, 1916–2005)

RH Roger of Howden, *The Annals of Roger of Hoveden*, trans. Henry T. Riley, 2 vols (London: Henry Bohn, 1853; facsimile repr. Felinfach: Llanerch, 1997)

Rigord Rigord, *The Deeds of Philip Augustus: An English Translation of Rigord's Gesta Philippi Augusti*, trans. Larry F. Field, ed. M. Cecilia Gaposchkin and Sean L. Field (Ithaca and London: Cornell University Press, 2022)

Rigord (ed. Guizot) Rigord, *Vie de Philippe Auguste*, ed. F. Guizot, in *Collection des Mémoires relatifs à l'histoire de France*, vol. 11 (Paris: Brière, 1825), pp. 9–180

RT Robert de Torigni, *The Chronicles of Robert de Monte*, trans. Joseph Stevenson (London: Seeleys, 1856; facsimile repr. Felinfach: Llanerch, 1991)

RW Volume 2 of Roger of Wendover, *Roger of Wendover's Flowers of History*, trans. J.A. Giles, 2 vols (London: Henry G. Bohn, 1849; facsimile repr. Felinfach: Llanerch, 1995–96)

Tours *Ex Chronico Turonensi auctore anonyme S. Martini Turonensis canonico*, ed. Michel-Jean-Joseph Brial, in *Recueil des historiens des Gaules et de la France*, vol. 18 (Paris: Imprimerie royale, 1822), pp. 290–322

WB, Philippide William the Breton, *La Philippide*, ed. F. Guizot, in *Collection des Mémoires relatifs à l'histoire de France*, vol. 12 (Paris: Brière, 1825), pp. 1–390

WB, Vie William the Breton, *Vie de Philippe Auguste*, ed. F. Guizot, in *Collection des Mémoires relatifs à l'histoire de France*, vol. 11 (Paris: Brière, 1825), pp. 181–354

All of the pre-1900 editions cited are freely available for consultation online: see, variously, archive.org and gallica.fr.

BIOGRAPHIES AND STUDIES OF THE REIGN OF PHILIP AUGUSTUS

Baldwin, John W., *The Government of Philip Augustus: Foundations of French Royal Power in the Middle Ages* (Berkeley: University of California Press, 1986)

Bautier, Robert-Henri (ed.), *La France de Philippe Auguste: le temps des mutations* (Paris: Éditions du CNRS, 1982)

Bordonove, Georges, *Philippe Auguste: le conquérant* (Paris: Marabout, 1983)

Bradbury, Jim, *Philip Augustus: King of France, 1180–1223* (London and New York: Longman, 1998)

Cartellieri, Alexander, *Philipp II. August, König von Frankreich*, 4 vols (Leipzig: Dyksche, 1899–1922)

Flori, Jean, *Philippe Auguste: la naissance de l'État monarchique, 1165–1223* (Paris: Tallandier, 2007)

Galland, Bruno, *Philippe Auguste: le bâtisseur du royaume* (Paris: Belin, 2014)

Luchaire, Achille, *Philippe Auguste et son temps* (Paris: Tallandier, 1980; orig. 1902)

Sivéry, Gérard, *Philippe Auguste* (Paris: Perrin, 2003; orig. Librairie Plon, 1993)

OTHER SECONDARY SOURCES

Abalain, Hervé, *Le Français et les langues historiques de la France* (Paris: Éditions Jean-Paul Gisserot, 2007)

Abels, Richard, 'Cultural Representation and the Practice of War in the Middle Ages', *Journal of Medieval Military History*, 6 (2008), 1–31

Abulafia, David, *Frederick II: A Medieval Emperor* (Oxford: Oxford University Press, 1988)

Allmand, Christopher, 'War and the Non-Combatant in the Middle Ages', in *Medieval Warfare: A History*, ed. Maurice Keen (Oxford: Oxford University Press, 1999), pp. 253–72

—— 'The Reporting of War in the Middle Ages', in *War and Society in Medieval and Early Modern Britain*, ed. Diana Dunn (Liverpool: Liverpool University Press, 2000), pp. 17–33

Allshorn, Lionel, *Stupor Mundi: The Life and Times of Frederick II, Emperor of the Romans, King of Sicily and Jerusalem, 1194–1250* (London: M. Secker, 1912)

Andrews, J.F., *Lost Heirs of the Medieval Crown* (Barnsley: Pen & Sword, 2019)

—— *The Families of Eleanor of Aquitaine: A Female Network of Power in the Middle Ages* (Cheltenham: The History Press, 2023)

Asbridge, Thomas, 'Talking to the Enemy: The Role and Purpose of Negotiations Between Saladin and Richard the Lionheart during the Third Crusade', *Journal of Medieval History*, 39 (2013), 275–96

—— *The Greatest Knight: The Remarkable Life of William Marshal, the Power Behind Five English Thrones* (London: Simon and Schuster, 2015)

—— *The Crusades: The War for the Holy Land* (London: Simon and Schuster, 2020; orig. 2010)

Audoin, Edouard, *Essai sur l'armée royale au temps de Philippe Auguste* (Paris: Champion, 1913; facsimile repr. London: Forgotten Books, 2018)

Aurell, Martin, *L'Empire des Plantagenêt* (Paris: Tempus, 2017; orig. 2004)

Ayton, Andrew, *Knights and Warhorses* (Woodbridge: Boydell, 1994)

—— 'Arms, Armour and Horses', in *Medieval Warfare: A History*, ed. Maurice Keen (Oxford: Oxford University Press, 1999), pp. 186–208

Bachrach, Bernard, 'Medieval Siege Warfare: A Reconnaissance', *Journal of Military History*, 58 (1994), 119–33

Bachrach, Bernard and David Bachrach, *Warfare in Medieval Europe c. 400–c. 1453* (London and New York: Routledge, 2017)

Baldwin, John W., 'Qu'est-ce que les Capétiens ont appris les Plantagenêt?', *Cahiers de Civilisation Médiévale*, 29 (1986), 3–8

—— 'Le Sens de Bouvines', *Cahiers de Civilisation Médiévale*, 30 (1987), 119–30

—— *Aristocratic Life in Medieval France* (Baltimore and London: Johns Hopkins University Press, 2000)

—— *Paris, 1200* (Stanford: Stanford University Press, 2010; orig. Paris: Éditions Flammarion, 2006)

Baldwin, John and Walter Simons, 'The Consequences of Bouvines', *French Historical Studies*, 37 (2014), 243–69

Barber, Richard, *The Knight and Chivalry* (London: Longman, 1970)

—— *Henry Plantagenet* (Woodbridge: Boydell, 2001; orig. 1964)

—— *Henry II: A Prince among Princes* (London: Allen Lane, 2015)

Barratt, Nick, 'The Revenues of John and Philip Augustus Revisited', in *King John: New Interpretations*, ed. S.D. Church (Woodbridge: Boydell, 1999), pp. 75–99

Barthélemy, Dominique, *La Bataille de Bouvines* (Paris: Perrin, 2018)

Bartlett, Robert, *England under the Norman and Angevin Kings, 1075–1225* (Oxford: Oxford University Press, 2000)

—— *Gerald of Wales: A Voice of the Middle Ages* (Stroud: The History Press, 2006)

—— *Blood Royal: Dynastic Politics in Medieval Europe* (Cambridge: Cambridge University Press, 2020)

Bartlett, W.B., *God Wills It! An Illustrated History of the Crusades* (Stroud: Sutton, 1999)

Bassett, Hayley, 'An Instrument of Diplomacy? The Curious Case of Princess Alice of France', in *Queens in Waiting: Potential and Prospective Queens*, ed. Sarah Betts and Chloe McKenzie (Basingstoke: Palgrave Macmillan, forthcoming)

Bates, David and Anne Curry (eds), *England and Normandy in the Middle Ages* (London: Hambledon, 1994)

Beaune, Colette, *Naissance de la nation France* (Paris: Gallimard, 1985)

Beem, Charles (ed.), *The Royal Minorities of Medieval and Early Modern England* (New York: Palgrave Macmillan, 2008)

Benham, Jenny, *Peacemaking in the Middle Ages: Principles and Practice* (Manchester: Manchester University Press, 2007)

Bennett, Matthew, 'The Myth of the Military Supremacy of Knightly Cavalry', in *Medieval Warfare 1000–1300*, ed. John France (Abingdon: Ashgate, 2006), pp. 171–84

—— 'Three Conquests of Normandy, c. 1099–c. 1204', in *La guerre en Normandie (XIe–XVe siècle)*, ed. Anne Curry and Véronique Gazeau (Caen: Presses Universitaires de Caen, 2018), pp. 25–35

Bennett, Matthew and Katherine Weikert (eds), *Medieval Hostageship c.700–c.1500: Hostage, Captive, Prisoner of War, Guarantee, Peacemaker* (Oxford and New York: Routledge, 2016)

Bennett, Matthew, Jim Bradbury, Kelly DeVries, Ian Dickie and Phyllis G. Jestice, *Fighting Techniques of the Medieval World, AD 500–AD 1500* (Staplehurst: Spellmount, 2005)

Bennett, Stephen, *Elite Participation in the Third Crusade* (Woodbridge: Boydell, 2021)

Berend, Nora, Przemysław Urbańczyk and Przemysław Wiszewski, *Central Europe in the High Middle Ages: Bohemia, Hungary and Poland, c. 900–c. 1300* (Cambridge: Cambridge University Press, 2013)

Bliese, John, 'The Just War as Concept and Motive in the Central Middle Ages', *Medievalia et Humanistica*, 17 (1991), 1–26

Borgnis Desbordes, Eric, *Constance de Bretagne (1161–1201), une duchesse face à Richard Coeur de Lion et Jean sans Terre* (Fouesnant, Brittany: Yoran Embanner, 2018)

Bowie, Colette, *The Daughters of Henry II and Eleanor of Aquitaine* (Turnhout: Brepols, 2014)

Bradbury, Jim, *The Medieval Siege* (Woodbridge: Boydell, 1992)

—— 'Philip Augustus and King John: Personality and History', in *King John: New Interpretations*, ed. S.D. Church (Woodbridge: Boydell, 1999), pp. 347–61

—— *The Routledge Companion to Medieval Warfare* (London: Routledge, 2004)

—— *The Capetians: Kings of France 987–1328* (London: Continuum, 2007)

Cannon, Henry, 'The Battle of Sandwich and Eustace the Monk', *English Historical Review*, 27 (1912), 649–70

Carpenter, David, *The Minority of Henry III* (London: Methuen, 1990)

—— 'Abbot Ralph of Coggeshall's Account of the Last Years of King Richard and the First Years of King John', *English Historical Review*, 113 (1998), 1210–30

—— *The Struggle for Mastery: Britain 1066–1284* (London: Penguin, 2004)

—— *Magna Carta* (London: Penguin Classics, 2015)

—— *Henry III: The Rise to Power and Personal Rule, 1207–1258* (New Haven and London: Yale University Press, 2020)

Cassard, Jean-Christophe, *1180–1328: l'âge d'or capétien* (Paris: Bellin, 2011)

Chamberlin, E.R., *Life in Medieval France* (London: Batsford, 1967)

Cheney, Christopher, 'The Alleged Deposition of King John', in *Studies in Medieval History Presented to Frederick Maurice Powicke*, ed. R.W. Hunt, W.A. Pantin and R.W. Southern (Oxford: Clarendon, 1948), pp. 100–16

—— 'King John's Reaction to the Papal Interdict in England', *Transactions of the Royal Historical Society*, 4th series, 21 (1949), 129–50

—— *Pope Innocent III and England* (Stuttgart: Hiersemann, 1976)

Church, Stephen, *King John: England, Magna Carta and the Making of a Tyrant* (Basingstoke: Macmillan, 2015)

Clanchy, M.T., *England and Its Rulers, 1066–1272* (London: Wiley-Blackwell, 1983)

—— *From Memory to Written Record: England 1066–1307*, 2nd ed. (Oxford: Blackwell, 1993; orig. 1979)

Clarke, Peter D., *The Interdict in the Thirteenth Century: A Question of Collective Guilt* (Oxford: Oxford University Press, 2007)

Conklin, George, 'Ingeborg of Denmark, Queen of France, 1193–1223', in *Queens and Queenship in Medieval Europe*, ed. Anne J. Duggan (Woodbridge: Boydell, 1997), pp. 39–52

Contamine, Philippe, '"Le Royaume de France ne peut tomber en fille." Fondement, formulation et implication d'une théorie politique à la fin du Moyen Âge', *Perspectives médiévales*, 13 (1987), 67–81

—— *La Guerre au moyen âge* (Paris: Presses Universitaires de France, 1992)

—— *War in the Middle Ages*, trans. Michael Jones (Oxford: Blackwell, 1992)

—— *Histoire militaire de la France, tome 1: Des origines à 1715*, 2nd ed. (Paris: Presses Universitaires de France, 1997; orig. 1992)

Coulson, Charles, *Castles in Medieval Society: Fortresses in England, France and Ireland in the Central Middle Ages* (Oxford: Oxford University Press, 2003)

Crouch, David, *William Marshal: Court, Career and Chivalry in the Angevin Empire 1147–1219* (Harlow: Longman, 1990)

—— 'Baronial Paranoia in King John's Reign', in *Magna Carta and the England of King John*, ed. Janet S. Loengard (Woodbridge: Boydell, 2010), pp. 45–62

—— *The English Aristocracy 1070–1272: A Social Transformation* (New Haven and London: Yale University Press, 2011)

Danziger, Danny and John Gillingham, *1215: The Year of Magna Carta* (London: Hodder, 2003)

Delorme, Philippe, *Aliénor d'Aquitaine* (Paris: Pygmalion, 2001)

—— *Blanche de Castille* (Paris: Pygmalion, 2002)

DeVries, Kelly, 'God and Defeat in Medieval Warfare: Some Preliminary Thoughts', in *The Circle of War in the Middle Ages: Essays on Medieval Military and Naval History*, ed. Donald J. Kagay and L.J. Andrew Villalon (Woodbridge: Boydell, 1999), pp. 87–97

DeVries, Kelly and Robert Douglas Smith, *Medieval Military Technology*, 2nd ed. (Toronto: University of Toronto Press, 2012; orig. Peterborough, Ontario: Broadview, 1992)

DeVries, Kelly, Martin J. Dougherty, Iain Dickie, Phyllis G. Jestice and Christer Jorgensen, *Battles of the Medieval World, 1000–1500: From Hastings to Constantinople* (New York: Barnes and Noble, 2006)

Duby, Georges, *The Chivalrous Society*, trans. Cynthia Postan (London: Arnold, 1977)

—— *Le Dimanche de Bouvines* (Paris: Gallimard, 1985; orig. 1973)

—— *The Legend of Bouvines: War, Religion and Culture in the Middle Ages*, trans. Catherine Tihanyi (Cambridge: Polity Press, 1990)

—— *France in the Middle Ages 987–1460*, trans. Juliet Vale (Oxford: Blackwell, 1994)

Dufresne, Eugène, *Mémoires pour servir à l'histoire du chancelier Guérin* (Paris, 1888)

Dunbabin, Jean, *France in the Making, 843–1180*, 2nd ed. (Oxford: Oxford University Press, 2000; orig. 1985)

Erler, Mary and Maryanne Kowaleski (eds), *Women and Power in the Middle Ages* (Athens, GA: University of Georgia Press, 1988)

Everard, Judith, *Brittany and the Angevins: Province and Empire, 1158–1203* (Cambridge: Cambridge University Press, 2000)

Evergates, Theodore, *The Aristocracy in the County of Champagne, 1100–1300* (Philadelphia: University of Pennsylvania Press, 2007)

—— *Marie of France: Countess of Champagne, 1145–1198* (Philadelphia: University of Pennsylvania Press, 2019)

Eyton, R.W., *Court, Household, and Itinerary of King Henry II* (London: Taylor & Co., 1878; facsimile repr. Ann Arbor: UMI, 1992)

Facinger, Marion, 'A Study of Medieval Queenship: Capetian France 987–1237', *Studies in Medieval and Renaissance History*, 5 (1968), 1–48

Favier, Jean, *Les Plantagenêts: origines et destin d'un empire XIe–XIVe siècles* (Paris: Fayard, 2015; orig. 2004)

Fawtier, R., *The Capetian Kings of France: Monarchy and Nation 987–1328* (Basingstoke: Macmillan, 1960)

Flori, Jean, *La Chevalerie en France au Moyen Age* (Paris: Presses Universitaires de France, 1995)

—— *Chevaliers et chevalerie au Moyen Age* (Paris: Hachette, 1998)

—— *Richard Coeur de Lion: le roi-chevalier* (Paris: Payot et Rivage, 1999)

—— *Richard the Lionheart: King and Knight*, trans. Jean Birrell (Edinburgh: Edinburgh University Press, 2006)

Forde, Simon, Lesley Johnson and Alan V. Murray, *Concepts of National Identity in the Middle Ages* (Leeds: Leeds Studies in English, 1995)

Foundation for Medieval Genealogy, online, available at http://fmg.ac/

France, John, *Western Warfare in the Age of the Crusades 1000–1300* (London: University College London Press, 1999)

Freed, John B., *Frederick Barbarossa: The Prince and the Myth* (New Haven and London: Yale University Press, 2016)

Fuhrmann, Horst, *Germany in the High Middle Ages c. 1050–1200*, trans. Timothy Reuter (Cambridge: Cambridge University Press, 1986)

Fulton, Michael, *Artillery in the Age of the Crusades* (Leiden: Brill, 2018)

Gillingham, John, 'Richard I and the Science of War in the Middle Ages', in *War and Government in the Middle Ages*, ed. John Gillingham and J.C. Holt (Woodbridge: Boydell, 1984), pp. 78–91

—— 'War and Chivalry in the *History of William the Marshal*', in *Thirteenth-Century England II: Proceedings of the Newcastle-upon-Tyne Conference 1987*, ed. P.R. Coss and S.D. Lloyd (Woodbridge: Boydell, 1988), pp. 1–13

—— 'Love, Marriage and Politics in the Twelfth Century', *Forum for Modern Language Studies*, 25 (1989), 292–303

—— *Richard I* (New Haven and London: Yale University Press, 1999)

—— *The English in the Twelfth Century: Imperialism, National Identity and Political Values* (Woodbridge: Boydell, 2000)

—— *The Angevin Empire*, 2nd ed. (London: Bloomsbury, 2001; orig. 1984)

—— 'The Meetings of the Kings of France and England, 1066–1204', in *Normandy and Its Neighbours, 900–1250: Essays for David Bates*, ed. David Crouch and Kathleen Thompson (Turnhout: Brepols, 2011), pp. 17–42

Given-Wilson, Chris, *Chronicles: The Writing of History in Medieval England* (London and New York: Hambledon and London, 2004)

Given-Wilson, Chris and Alice Curteis, *The Royal Bastards of Medieval England* (London: Routledge and Kegan Paul, 1984)

Gobry, Ivan, *Louis VIII, fils de Philippe II, 1223–1226* (Paris: Pygmalion, 2009)

Goodall, John, 'Dover Castle and the Great Siege of 1216', *Château Gaillard*, 19 (2000), 91–102

—— *The English Castle* (New Haven and London: Yale University Press, 2011)

Gransden, Antonia, *Historical Writing in England*, vol. I: *c. 550–c. 1307* (London: Routledge and Kegan Paul, 1974)

Grant, Lindy, *Blanche of Castile: Queen of France* (New Haven and London: Yale University Press, 2016)

Hajdu, Robert, 'Castles, Castellans and the Structure of Politics in Poitou, 1152–1271', *Journal of Medieval History*, 4 (1978), 27–53

Hallam, Elizabeth M. and Judith Everard, *Capetian France 987–1328*, 2nd ed. (Harlow: Pearson, 2001; orig. London: Longman, 1980)

Hamilton, Bernard, 'Women in the Crusader States: The Queens of Jerusalem, 1100–1190', in *Medieval Women*, ed. Derek Baker (Oxford: Studies in Church History, Subsidia I, 1978), pp. 143–74

—— *The Leper King and His Heirs: Baldwin IV and the Crusader Kingdom of Jerusalem* (Cambridge: Cambridge University Press, 2000)

Hanley, Catherine, *War and Combat 1150–1270: The Evidence from Old French Literature* (Woodbridge: D.S. Brewer, 2003)

—— *Louis: The French Prince Who Invaded England* (New Haven and London: Yale University Press, 2016)

—— *Matilda: Empress, Queen, Warrior* (New Haven and London: Yale University Press, 2019)

—— *Two Houses, Two Kingdoms: A History of France and England, 1100–1300* (New Haven and London: Yale University Press, 2022)

—— *1217: The Battles That Saved England* (Oxford: Osprey, 2024)

—— *Lionessheart: The Life and Times of Joanna Plantagenet* (Cheltenham: The History Press, 2025)

Hattendorf, J. and R. Unger (eds), *War at Sea in the Middle Ages and Renaissance* (Woodbridge: Boydell, 2003)

Héliot, Pierre, 'Le Château-Gaillard et les fortresses des XIIe et XIIIe siècles', *Château Gaillard*, 1 (1962), 53–75

Heuser, Beatrice, *The Evolution of Strategy: Thinking War from Antiquity to the Present* (Cambridge: Cambridge University Press, 2010)

Hibbard-Loomis, Laura, 'L'Oriflamme et le cri "Munjoie" au XIIe siècle', *Le Moyen Âge*, 65 (1959), 469–99

Holt, J.C., *The Northerners: A Study in the Reign of King John* (Westport: Greenwood Press, 1981; orig. Oxford: Oxford University Press, 1961)

—— *Magna Carta*, 2nd ed. (Cambridge: Cambridge University Press, 1992; orig. 1965)

—— 'King John and Arthur of Brittany', *Nottingham Medieval Studies*, 44 (2000), 82–103

Hornaday, Aline, 'A Capetian Queen as Street Demonstrator: Isabelle of Hainaut', in *Capetian Women*, ed. Kathleen Nolan (New York and Basingstoke: Palgrave Macmillan, 2003), pp. 77–97

Hosler, John D., *Henry II: A Medieval Soldier at War, 1147–1189* (Leiden: Brill, 2007)

—— *The Siege of Acre, 1189–1191: Saladin, Richard the Lionheart, and the Battle That Decided the Third Crusade* (New Haven and London: Yale University Press, 2018)

—— 'Embedded Reporters? Ambroise, Richard de Templo, and Roger of Howden on the Third Crusade', in *Military Cultures and Martial Enterprises in the Middle Ages: Essays in Honour of Richard P. Abels*, ed. John D. Hosler and Steven Isaac (Woodbridge: Boydell, 2020), pp. 177–91

—— 'Countermeasures: The Destruction of Siege Equipment at Acre, 1189–1191', in *The Art of Siege Warfare and Military Architecture from the Classical World to the Middle Ages*, ed. Michael Eisenberg and Rabei Khamisy (Oxford: Oxbow Books, 2021), pp. 163–71

Housley, Norman, 'European Warfare, c. 1200–1320', in *Medieval Warfare: A History*, ed. Maurice Keen (Oxford: Oxford University Press, 1999), pp. 113–35

Howard, Michael, *War in European History* (Oxford: Oxford University Press, 1977)

Isaac, Stephen, 'The Problem with Mercenaries', in *The Circle of War in the Middle Ages: Essays on Medieval Military and Naval History*, ed. Donald J. Kagay and L.J. Andrew Villalon (Woodbridge: Boydell, 1999), pp. 101–10

Jeep, John M., *Medieval Germany: An Encyclopedia* (New York: Garland, 2001)

Jones, Michael, 'The Capetians and Brittany', *Historical Research*, 63 (1990), 1–16

Jones, Richard, 'Fortifications and Sieges in Western Europe, c. 800–1450', in *Medieval Warfare: A History*, ed. Maurice Keen (Oxford: Oxford University Press, 1999), pp. 163–85

Jones, Robert W., *Bloodied Banners: Martial Display on the Medieval Battlefield* (Woodbridge: Boydell, 2010)

Jones, Robert W. and Peter Coss (eds), *A Companion to Chivalry* (Woodbridge: Boydell, 2019)

Kaeuper, Richard, *Chivalry and Violence in Medieval Europe* (Oxford: Oxford University Press, 1999)

Kantorowicz, Ernst, *Frederick the Second, 1194–1250*, trans. E.O. Lorimer (New York: Frederick Ungar, 1957; orig. 1931)

Karras, Ruth Mazo, *Unmarriages: Women, Men, and Sexual Unions in the Middle Ages* (Philadelphia: University of Pennsylvania Press, 2012)

Kosto, Adam J., *Hostages in the Middle Ages* (Oxford: Oxford University Press, 2012)

Krynen, Jacques, 'Rex Christianissimus: A Medieval Theme at the Roots of French Absolutism', *History and Anthropology*, 4 (1989), 76–96

Lachaud, Frédérique, *Jean sans Terre* (Paris: Perrin, 2018)

Lalou, Élisabeth, 'La Flotte normande à la fin du XIIIe siècle', in *La Guerre en Normandie (XIe–XVe siècle)*, ed. Anne Curry and Véronique Gazeau (Caen: Presses Universitaires de Caen, 2018), pp. 73–82

Legge, M. Dominica, *Anglo-Norman Literature and Its Background* (Oxford: Clarendon, 1963)

Lewis, Andrew, 'The Capetian Apanages and the Nature of the French Kingdom', *Journal of Medieval History*, 11 (1976), 119–34

—— 'Anticipatory Association of the Heir in Early Capetian France', *American Historical Review*, 83 (1979), 906–27

—— *Royal Succession in Capetian France: Studies on Familial Order and the State* (Cambridge, MA: Harvard University Press, 1981)

—— *Le Sang royal: la famille capétienne et l'état, France X–XIV siècles* (Paris: Gallimard, 1986)

Leyser, Karl, *Medieval Germany and Its Neighbours, 900–1250* (London: Hambledon, 1982)

Loengard, Janet S. (ed.), *Magna Carta and the England of King John* (Woodbridge: Boydell, 2010)

Luchaire, Achille, 'La Condamnation de Jean Sans-Terre par la cour de France', *Revue Historique*, 27 (1900), 285–90

—— *Social France at the Time of Philip Augustus*, trans. Edward Krehbiel (London: John Murray, 1912)

Martindale, Jane, 'Eleanor of Aquitaine: The Last Years', in *King John: New Interpretations*, ed. S.D. Church (Woodbridge: Boydell, 1999), pp. 137–64

Marvin, Laurence W., 'Philip II's "Eye of Command" and the Battle of Bouvines', *Journal of Medieval Military History*, 21 (2023), 129–45

McDougall, Sara, *Royal Bastards: The Birth of Illegitimacy, 800–1230* (Oxford: Oxford University Press, 2017)

McGlynn, Sean, 'Roger of Wendover and the Wars of Henry III, 1216–1234', in *England and Europe in the Reign of Henry III, 1216–1272*, ed. Björn K.U. Weiler and Ifor W. Rowlands (Aldershot: Ashgate, 2002), pp. 183–206

—— *By Sword and Fire: Cruelty and Atrocity in Medieval Warfare* (London: Weidenfeld & Nicolson, 2008)

—— *Blood Cries Afar: The Forgotten Invasion of England 1216* (Stroud: Spellmount, 2011)

—— 'Fighting the Image of the Reluctant Warrior: Philip Augustus as Rex-Not-Quite-So-Bellicosus', in *The Image and Perception of Monarchy in*

Medieval and Early Modern Europe, ed. Sean McGlynn and Elena Woodacre (Newcastle: Cambridge Scholars Publishing, 2014), pp. 148–67
—— *Kill Them All: Cathars and Carnage in the Albigensian Crusade* (Stroud: The History Press, 2015)
—— '"Pro patria": National Identity and War in Early Medieval England', in *Nationalism, Patriotism, Ancient and Modern: An Interdisciplinary Approach*, ed. Alexander Peck, forthcoming
Menant, François, Hervé Martin, Bernard Merdrignac and Monique Chauvin, *Les Capetiens, 987–1326* (Paris: Tempus, 2018; orig. 2008)
Meuleau, Maurice, *Histoire de la chevalerie* (Rennes: Ouest-France, 2014)
Minois, Georges, *Richard Coeur de Lion* (Paris: Perrin, 2017)
Monaque, Rémi, *Une histoire de la marine de guerre française* (Paris: Perrin, 2016)
Moore, John C., *Pope Innocent III (1160/61–1216): To Root Up and to Plant* (Leiden and Boston: Brill, 2003)
Morby, John, 'The Soubriquets of Medieval European Princes', *Canadian Journal of History*, 13 (1978), 1–16
Morris, Marc, *King John: Treachery, Tyranny and the Road to Magna Carta* (London: Hutchinson, 2015)
Naus, James, *Constructing Kingship: The Capetian Monarchs of France and the Early Crusades* (Manchester: Manchester University Press, 2016)
Nicolle, David, *French Medieval Armies 1000–1300* (London: Osprey, 1991)
—— 'Warfare and Technology', *Medieval World*, 6 (1992), 49–54
—— *Medieval Warfare Source Book*, 2 vols (London: Brockhampton Press, 1998)
—— *Arms and Armour of the Crusading Era, 1050–1350* (London: Greenhill, 1999; orig. 1988)
—— (ed.), *A Companion to Medieval Arms and Armour* (Woodbridge: Boydell, 2002)
Painter, Sidney, *French Chivalry: Chivalric Ideals and Practice in Medieval France* (Baltimore: Johns Hopkins University Press, 1940)
—— *Medieval Society* (Ithaca: Cornell University Press, 1951)
Papin, Yves D., *Chronologie du moyen âge* (Paris: Éditions Jean-Paul Gisserot, 2001)
Pegg, Mark Gregory, *A Most Holy War: The Albigensian Crusade and the Battle for Christendom* (Oxford: Oxford University Press, 2008)
Phillips, Jonathan, *Holy Warriors: A Modern History of the Crusades* (London: Vintage Books, 2010)
—— *The Life and Legend of the Sultan Saladin* (New Haven and London: Yale University Press, 2019)

Poulet, André, 'Capetian Women and the Regency: The Genesis of a Vocation', in *Medieval Queenship*, ed. John Carmi Parsons (Stroud: Sutton, 1998; orig. 1994), pp. 93–116

Powell, James M. (ed.), *Innocent III: Vicar of Christ or Lord of the World?*, 2nd ed. (Washington DC: Catholic University of America Press, 1994; orig. 1963)

Power, Daniel, 'King John and the Norman Aristocracy', in *King John: New Interpretations*, ed. S.D. Church (Woodbridge: Boydell, 1999), pp. 117–36

—— *The Norman Frontier in the Twelfth and Early Thirteenth Centuries* (Cambridge: Cambridge University Press, 2004)

—— 'Les Dernières années du régime angevin en Normandie', in *Plantagenêts et Capétiens: confrontations et héritages*, ed. Martin Aurell and Yves Tonnerre (Turnhout: Brepols, 2006), pp. 163–92

—— 'La Chute de la Normandie ducale (1202–1204): un réexamen', in *La Guerre en Normandie (XIe–XVe siècle)*, ed. Anne Curry and Véronique Gazeau (Caen: Presses Universitaires de Caen, 2018), pp. 37–62

Powicke, F.M., *The Loss of Normandy (1189–1204): Studies in the History of the Angevin Empire* (Manchester: Manchester University Press, 1913)

—— *The Thirteenth Century*, 2nd ed. (Oxford: Oxford University Press, 1962; orig. 1953)

Pryor, John H. (ed.), *The Logistics of Warfare in the Age of the Crusades* (Aldershot: Ashgate, 2006)

Purton, Peter, *A History of the Early Medieval Siege, c. 450–1200* (Woodbridge: Boydell, 2009)

—— *A History of the Late Medieval Siege, 1200–1500* (Woodbridge: Boydell, 2010)

—— *The Medieval Military Engineer: From the Roman Empire to the Sixteenth Century* (Woodbridge: Boydell, 2018)

Riley-Smith, Jonathan, *The Crusades: A Short History* (London: Athlone Press, 2001; orig. 1987)

Rose, Susan, *England's Medieval Navy, 1066–1509* (Barnsley: Seaforth Publishing, 2013)

Russell, Frederick, *The Just War in the Middle Ages* (Cambridge: Cambridge University Press, 1975)

Salch, Charles-Laurent (ed.), *Dictionnaire des châteaux et des fortifications du moyen âge en France* (Strasbourg: Éditions Publitotal, 1987)

Sassier, Yves, *Louis VII* (Paris: Fayard, 1991)

Sayers, Jane E., *Innocent III: Leader of Europe, 1198–1216* (London: Longman, 1994)

Seabourne, Gwen, 'Eleanor of Brittany and Her Treatment by King John and Henry III', *Nottingham Medieval Studies*, 51 (2007), 73–111
—— *Imprisoning Medieval Women: The Non-Judicial Confinement and Abduction of Women in England, c. 1170–1509* (Farnham: Ashgate, 2011)
Sivéry, Gérard, *Blanche de Castille* (Paris: Fayard, 1990)
—— *Louis VIII le Lion* (Paris: Fayard, 1995)
Spencer, Stephen J., '"Like a Raging Lion": Richard the Lionheart's Anger during the Third Crusade in Medieval and Modern Historiography', *English Historical Review*, 132 (2017), 495–532
Spiegel, Gabrielle, 'The Cult of Saint Denis and Capetian Kingship', *Journal of Medieval History*, 1 (1975), 43–69
Stanton, Charles D., *Medieval Maritime Warfare* (Barnsley: Pen & Sword, 2015)
Staunton, Michael, *The Historians of Angevin England* (Oxford: Oxford University Press, 2017)
Strickland, Matthew, 'Provoking or Avoiding Battle? Challenge, Duel and Single Combat in Warfare of the High Middle Ages', in *Armies, Chivalry and Warfare in Medieval Britain and France*, ed. Matthew Strickland (Stamford: Paul Watkins, 1998), pp. 317–43
—— *Henry the Young King, 1155–1183* (New Haven and London: Yale University Press, 2016)
Thompson, Kathleen, *Power and Border Lordship in Medieval France: The County of the Perche, 1000–1226* (Woodbridge: Boydell, 2002)
Turner, Ralph V., *Eleanor of Aquitaine: Queen of France, Queen of England* (New Haven and London: Yale University Press, 2009)
Tyerman, Christopher, *Who's Who in Early Medieval England* (London: Shepheard-Walwyn, 1996)
—— *God's War: A New History of the Crusades* (London: Penguin, 2006)
Unger, Richard, *The Ship in the Medieval Economy, 600–1600* (Montreal: McGill-Queen's University Press, 1980)
Vale, Malcolm, *War and Chivalry* (London: Duckworth, 1981)
—— *The Ancient Enemy: England, France and Europe from the Angevins to the Tudors* (London: Bloomsbury Academic, 2009)
Van den Broucke, Serge, 'Château-Gaillard: The Mighty Lock of Normandy's Gate', *Medieval History Magazine*, 1 (2003), 1–25
Verbruggen, J.F., *The Art of Warfare in Western Europe during the Middle Ages*, trans. Sumner Willard and Mrs R.W. Southern (Woodbridge: Boydell, 1997; orig. Brussels: Koninklijke Academie voor Wetenschappen, Letteren en Schone Kunsten van België, 1954)
Volkmann, Jean-Charles, *Généalogies complètes des rois de France* (Paris: Éditions Jean-Paul Gisserot, 1999)

Wagner, Thomas Gregor and Piers D. Mitchell, 'The Illnesses of King Richard and King Philippe on the Third Crusade: An Understanding of *arnoldia* and *leonardie*', *Crusades*, 10 (2011), 23–44.

Warner, Philip, *Sieges of the Middle Ages* (London: Bell and Sons, 1968)

Warren, W.L., *The Governance of Anglo-Norman and Angevin England, 1086–1272* (Stanford: Stanford University Press, 1987)

—— *King John*, 2nd ed. (New Haven and London: Yale University Press, 1997; orig. 1961)

—— *Henry II*, 3rd ed. (New Haven and London: Yale University Press, 2000; orig. 1973)

Wickham, Chris, *Medieval Europe* (New Haven and London: Yale University Press, 2016)

Wilson, Peter H., *The Holy Roman Empire: A Thousand Years of Europe's History* (London: Allen Lane, 2016)

Woodacre, Elena and Carey Fleiner (eds), *Royal Mothers and Their Ruling Children: Wielding Political Authority from Antiquity to the Early Modern Era* (New York: Palgrave Macmillan, 2015)

Index